Not For Profit
... Not For Charity
... But For Service.

CREDIT UNION MOTTO

BUT FOR SERVICE

A History of the Credit Union Movement in Pennsylvania

Mark H. Dorfman

Pacul Services, Inc.
Harrisburg, PA

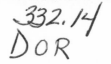

Published 1984 by Pacul Services, Inc.
4309 North Front Street, Harrisburg, Pennsylvania 17110

Manufactured in the United States of America by Members of
Haddon Craftsman Employees Federal Credit Union

Book Design by Bright Eyes Graphic Design

First Edition

*This book is dedicated
to the thousands of credit union volunteers
whose names do not appear in its pages—
the selfless men and women
who traditionally have been the real strength
of the credit union movement.*

M.H.D.

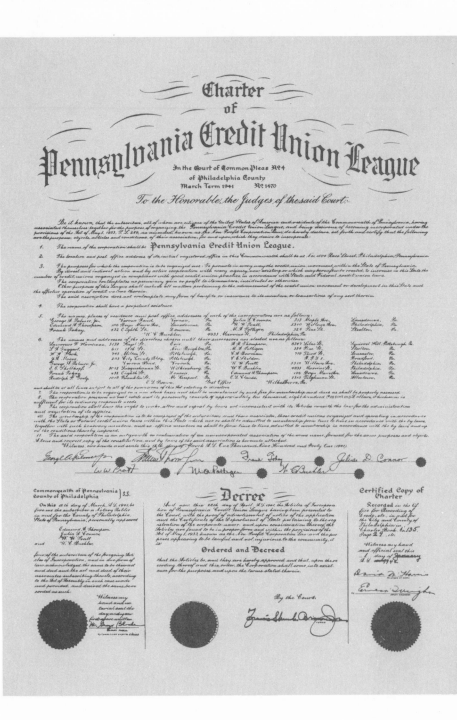

Charter
of
Pennsylvania Credit Union League

In the Court of Common Pleas No 4
of Philadelphia County
March Term 1941   No 1470

To the Honorable, the Judges of the said Court:

Be it known, that the subscribers, all of whom are citizens of the United States of America and residents of the Commonwealth of Pennsylvania, having associated themselves together for the purpose of organizing this Pennsylvania Credit Union League, and being desirous of becoming incorporated under the provisions of the Act of May 5, 1933, P.L. 289, as amended, known as the Non Profit Corporation Law, do hereby declare, set forth and certify that the following are the purposes, objects, articles and conditions of their association, for and upon which they desire to incorporate.

1. The name of the corporation shall be **Pennsylvania Credit Union League.**

2. The location and post office address of its initial registered office in this Commonwealth shall be at No 1500 Race Street, Philadelphia, Pennsylvania.

3. The purposes for which the corporation is to be organized are: To promote in every way the credit union movement within the State of Pennsylvania. By closed and indirect action and by active cooperation with every agency now existing or which may hereafter be created, to increase in this State the number of credit unions organized in compliance with good credit union practice in accordance with State and Federal credit union laws.
The corporation contemplates no pecuniary gain or profit to its members, incidental or otherwise.
Other purposes of this League shall include all matters pertaining to the advancement of the credit union movement or development in this State and the effective operation of credit unions therein.
The said association does not contemplate any form of benefits or insurance to its members, or transactions of any sort therein.

4. The corporation shall have a perpetual existence.

5. The names, places of residence and post office addresses of each of the incorporators are as follows:

George A. Palmer, Jr.	Terrace Road	Vernon,	Pa	Julia D. Connor	313 Maple Ave.	Lansdowne, Pa.
Edward A. Thompson	106 Bryn Mawr Ave.	Lansdowne,	Pa	W. W. Pratt	1310 Hellings Ave.	Philadelphia, Pa.
Frank Tokay	432 E Eighth St.	Lenoiva,	Pa	W. E. Pottigen	329 Pine St.	Stealton, Pa.
		"W" E. Buehler,		1935 Marion St.	Philadelphia, Pa.	

6. The names and addresses of the directors chosen with their successors are elected are as follows:

Laurence F. Henneman	3132 Hazel St.	Erie	Pa	E. A. Thompson	6347 Silas St.	Squirrel Hill Pittsburgh, Pa.
J. A. Tsappell	611 13th St.	New Brighton, Pa.		W. A. Pottigen	329 Pine St.	Steelton, Pa.
W. A. Slack	743 Milton St.	Pittsburgh, Pa.		E. A. Bowman	719 Trout St.	Lancaster, Pa.
G. A. Story	203 City County Bldg.	Pittsburgh, Pa.		E. E. Sheldon	N. F. S. L.	Brockford, Pa.
George A. Palmer Jr.	Terrace Road	Vernon, Pa.		W. W. Pratt	1310 Hellings Ave.	Philadelphia, Pa.
F. E. Dellakapp	1012 Susquehanna St.	Wilkinsburg, Pa.		Edmund A. Thompson	106 Bryn Mawr Ave.	Lansdowne, Pa.
Frank Tokay	432 Eighth St.	Lenova, Pa.		E. L. Claiss	1310 Telphman St.	Allentown, Pa.
Rudolph J. Fordy	1018 Franklin P.L. Row,	Post Office				Wilkesbarre, Pa.

and shall be at all times subject to all of the provisions of this Act relating to directors

7. The corporation is to be organized on a non stock basis and shall be sustained by such fees for membership and dues as shall be properly assessed.

8. The corporation possesses no real estate and is personality, consists of approximately five thousand, eight hundred ($5801.01) dollars, which sum is sufficient for the ordinary corporate needs.
The corporation shall have the right to make, alter and repeal by laws not inconsistent with its Articles would the law for the administration and regulation of its affairs.

10. The membership of the corporation is to be composed of the subscribers and their associates, those credit unions organized and operating in accordance with the State or Federal credit union laws within this State which are or shall be admitted to membership from time to time in accordance with the by laws, together with such honorary members, such as officers members as shall be from time to time admitted to membership in accordance with the by laws and up on the conditions thereby imposed.

11. The said corporation is an outgrowth or continuation of an unincorporated association of the same name, formed for the same purposes and objects. A true and correct copy of the constitution and by laws of the said association is herewith attached.

Witness our hands and seals this 11th day of March A.D. One thousand nine hundred and forty two (1941).

George A. Palmer Jr.   William Thompson   Frank Tokay   Julia D. Connor

W. W. Pratt   W. A. Pottigen   W. E. Buehler

Commonwealth of Pennsylvania ss.
County of Philadelphia

On this 11th day of March, A.D. 1941, before me the subscriber a Notary Public in and for the County of Philadelphia, State of Pennsylvania, personally appeared

Edward A. Thompson
Julia D. Connor
W. W. Pratt
and   W. E. Buehler

four of the subscribers to the foregoing Act of Incorporation, and in their form of law acknowledged the same to be the and deed and the act and deed of their associates subscribing thereto, according to the Act of Assembly in such case made and provided, and desired the same, be recorded as such.

Witness my hand and official seal the day and year first above written.
Wm. Geo. Blake
Notary Public

Decree

And now this 20th day of April A.D. 1941 the Articles of Incorporation of Pennsylvania Credit Union League having been presented to the Court, with the proof of advertisement of notice of the application and the Certificate of the Department of State pertaining to the registration of the corporate name, and upon consideration thereof, the Articles are found to be in proper form and within the provisions of the Act of May 5, 1933 known as the Non Profit Corporation Law and the purposes appearing to be lawful and not injurious to the community, it

Ordered and Decreed

that the Articles be, and they are hereby approved and that, upon the recording thereof and this order, the Corporation shall come into existence for the purposes and upon the terms stated therein.

By the Court:

Francis Shunk Brown Jr.

Certified Copy of Charter

Recorded in the Office for Recording of Deeds, etc., in and for the City and County of Philadelphia in Charter Book No 135, Page 2 & C.

Witness my hand and official seal this day of January A.D. 1942.

David M. Harris

Edward Dwight

Table of Contents

Foreword

> "You cannot build character and courage by taking away man's initiative and independence. You cannot help men permanently by doing for them what they could and should do for themselves."
>
> *Abraham Lincoln*

MARK DORFMAN HAS COMPILED a brilliant history of a great cooperative movement, which he researched over a period of seven years. He originally began his study of the Pennsylvania credit union movement as a basis for his doctoral dissertation and found the evolution of this people movement so fascinating that he continued the research that has resulted in this distinguished work.

The author is a respected scholar and historian. He is a noted financial journalist and a former assistant professor of history and American studies at The Pennsylvania State University. His work has been thoroughly researched and well documented. As a person who lived through much of what he recounts, I can attest to his accuracy of detail.

And yet, as I read his work, I feel that something is missing. It may be that only someone who lived through those dramatic years could know that it is missing. Perhaps you had to be there, to see it and live it in order to understand the tremedeous love that poured into the credit union movement. This exciting avenue for helping everday working people to build a better life inspired those credit union pioneers with a missionary fervor. A burning zeal drove ordinary men and women in an almost superhuman effort to build a better world.

"Those who cannot remember the past are condemned to repeat it," said American poet-philosopher George Santayana. I believe that those who can remember the 1930s would never want to see them repeated. They were difficult years, with unemployment running to 25% and higher in some areas of Pennsylvania. There was no unemployment insurance, no union benefits, no social security, no welfare, and no jobs. There was much suffering, even among those fortunate enough to be regularly employed.

Ordinary people had little in the way of financial services available to them. Commercial banks got their name because they were in business to serve business. They did not want to be bothered with the ordinary person's small savings. And they certainly were not needed to pay doctor bills or buy a ton of coal. That is why credit unions came into existence. It was a cooperative, self-help, "boot-strap" effort by which people could provide desperately needed financial services for themselves.

Credit unions in those days were operated almost entirely by volunteers, and the volunteers worked long and hard to build their new credit unions. Credit committees held emergency meetings at all hours of the day and night to approve loans for members in need. Boards of directors met until late night, often with heated arguments over what would be best for the members.

We were imbued with the cooperative spirit. We attended League meetings at our own personal expense. Even when our credit unions grew large enough to pick up the tab, we still worried about the expense. It wasn't unusual to bunk four or more to a room on overnight trips, and many a credit union volunteer slept on the floor to keep costs down.

And it was all done for love of humankind, out of a sincere desire to help others. Love is what seems to be missing from the pages of this book, but as I say, maybe yoy had to be there.

Today's world is a far cry from the world we knew in 1934.

In some respects, today's credit unions are different from those early credit unions. Many credit unions have experinced a growth never imagined in the beginning. Credit unions are offering their members services that nobody had heard of in 1934: share drafts, automated teller machines, IRA accounts, credit cards and much more.

Todya's credit unions, however, are more similar to their early cousins than they are dissimilar. They offer services in tune with their member's needs of today, just as their as their offerings in 1934 met the needs of members in the Depression era.

The Pennsylvania credit union movement emerged in the midst of the Great Depression of the 1930s. The problems, in retrospect, might well have seemed insoluble. Nevertheless, we obtained the necessary legislation, built, a movement, formed a League and continued to serve our members by relying on the credit union philosophy. And that, in turn, is built on love.

I consider myself priviledged to have been around to see the Pennsylvania Credit Union Act passed in 1933 and the Federal Credit Union Act signed in 1934, and the Pennsylvania Credit Union League formed in 1934 . . . and to have had a share in celebrating the golden anniversary of the League in 1984. It has been a gratifying experience to have been involved in those years of hope and struggle and early development.

Fifty years in the credit union movement have been personally rewarding to me. I have known and worked with people who cared about people. I know that as long as there are such people in the world, there will be credit unions. And the world will be a better place for it.

Robert F. Neubaum
Pennsylvania Credit Union League
Chairman of the Board, 1982–84

Overture

"The credit union...is the expression in the field of economics of a great social ideal."

Alphonse Desjardins

"A credit union is a legally chartered nonprofit corporation run by amateurs."

Charles M. Wilson

ALPHONSE DESJARDINS, the great North American credit union pioneer and Charles M. Wilson, author of *Common Sense Credit* had remarkably different perspectives as they sought to identify the essential nature of credit unions. Yet each in his own way was saying the same thing. The world of economics is no place for idealists. The world of finance is no place for amateurism.

Credit unions, by existing, defy this cynical complacency of conventional wisdom, for the credit union movement was created by amateurs as an idealistic response to the pragmatic and professional institutions of bankers. That it has survived is a tribute to the perversity of human nature. That it has thrived is a triumph of the human spirit.

Credit union movement founder and financier Edward Filene valued this practical idealism of credit unions and cooperative capitalism: "The cooperative movement...is more than economic. It is charged with aspiration and with idealism. It is warmly, humanly passionate; and it is demonstrating day by day that there is more real satisfaction and more business success in working together for the common good than there ever could be in a free-for-all struggle on the part of everybody to get ahead of everybody else."

That such different men as Filene and Desjardins should both be crucially involved in credit unions has fascinated many who explore their history. Thirty years ago Richard Giles looked with puzzlement at the two pioneers:

> "Desjardins and Filene stand in sharp contrast. Desjardins had little experience with twentieth-century economic problems and presumably little insight into them. His credit union philosophy reflected the moral virtues not, precisely, of the nineteenth century, but of the ancient Christian tradition. Filene's religion, on the other hand, amounted to little more than an occasional kind word for the Golden Rule; his main interest was in making money serve man."

As Roy Bergengren would later phrase the same common ground, "You are obliged...to have some notion of the principle of brotherhood of man if you would operate a successful credit union."

Other hard-nosed business people found similar special ground for supporting the credit union movement. David Lubin was a successful businessman and credit union pioneer from California, yet he looked to the credit union movement for solutions to complex financial problems which had long plagued farmers. To Italian credit union pioneer Luigi Luzzatti he wrote, "There is a median between speculation and losing money; but one must always remember that it is not here a concern of financial institutions, but of institutions which will redeem agriculture."

In their different ways, all were saying the same thing. For Desjardins, Filene, Bergengren, and Lubin the credit union movement was founded on dreams of a better world but rooted in reality. Their credit union ideals were wondrous visions, but they were always critically aware that individual credit unions are made of real people, balance sheets and passbooks.

As cooperatives, credit unions have traditionally been exempt from most taxation, but they hold no exemption from the laws of economics. They were created as an expression of the finest aspects of the human spirit, but they are just as subject to the foibles of human nature.

This history of the Pennsylvania credit union movement tells the story of that continuous conflict between idealism and practicality. It is played out in a state remarkable for its ethnic, economic, social and demographic diversity. It is the story of simultaneous conflict and cooperation.

This is a story of people who did not know how to run financial institutions or manage a statewide political-economic movement—but who built both, anyway. It is a story of amateurism, ignorance, inconsistency, and arrogant ambition. Despite which, it is the story of a mission completed, of a vision fulfilled.

At times, it seems that the pioneers of the Pennsylvania credit union movement acted like clumsy neophytes, stumbling in the dark, building without tools or blueprints. Yet they muddled through, and they learned, and became highly skilled at their craft. In the full light of day, friends and enemies alike now recognize that Pennsylvania's credit unions work and work well.

The first two chapters of this book define the dimensions of the dream as it first emerged long ago and far away. They tell of the credit union movement in Europe and of its early days in Canada and the United States. They tell of issues and concerns endemic to the credit union concept, of conflicts which are as much a part of the movement as its philosophical credo, "Not for Profit. Not for Charity. But for Service."

Chapters three and four tell of the Pennsylvania credit union movement before it became organized. They discuss credit unions founded before there were credit union laws, and credit union laws passed before anyone really understood credit unions. Finally, they tell of the ten-year fight and the broad-based coalition that created the legal foundation for the credit union movement in the Commonwealth.

The balance of the work is devoted to the organized credit union movement in the state. It tells of the leaders and battles and of the conflicts that eventually built consensus. It tells of disputes over the membership fee or the distribution of seats on the board of directors. It tells of debates over many issues important to the credit union movement and of the constantly changing relationships that have gradually determined the form and substance of the Pennsylvania credit union movement.

I would like to express my gratitude to the board of directors and the staff of the Pennsylvania Credit Union League for their belief in, commitment to, and cooperation with this project. Especially, I must thank League chairman Robert Neubaum and past chairman Joseph Finn without whose support this project could never have proceeded.

President Michael Judge and his staff provided continual encouragement and guidance as well as the benefit of their extensive knowledge of the credit union movement. They helped me contact and work with the many individuals whose memories and insights enriched my research and this effort. Special thanks are here due to Doris Ellis who coordinated the production of this book and to Roger Kelley who prepared the index.

I am especially grateful to Jerry Burns, historical librarian at the Information Resource Center of the Credit Union National Association. His cheerful manner and knowledgeable guidance through the collections of CUNA and CUNA Mutual helped me to discover and present the national context for the Pennsylvania movement. Without his help, the record of the interaction of the work of many Pennsylvania credit union leaders with the national scene would have gone undocumented. Judith Sayers of the CUNA Information Resource Center also provided much valuable assistance.

This work benefits from materials housed at the Library of Congress, and in the Archives of the Pennsylvania Historical and Museum Commission. Access to and assistance with those records were provided by a group of talented and dedicated public servants. For their assistance in tracing obscure and sketchy references through tortuous paper trails, and for their perseverance which occasionally outlasted my own, I thank them. I also thank the members of the board of the National Credit Union Administration for access to the records of NCUA.

Many more people helped create this work by contributing their papers and their memories of years spent with the credit union movement. For their time and cooperation, I would like to thank Mike Judge, Bob Neubaum, Dorothy Pratt, Art Thompson, Louise Herring, Lucy Smith, John McCullough, Frank Wielga, and the many other credit union volunteers and professionals who gave their time, energy, and insights to this project.

This book has benefitted from the assistance of a great many people, but I remain individually responsible for the materials and views—and all errors—contained herein.

Mark H. Dorfman
Harrisburg, Pennsylvania

Proud of Our Past . . .
Prepared for the Future
1934–1984

The Pennsylvania Credit Union League looks proudly at 50 years of unparalleled growth and success. Our League has made tremendous strides, and will continue to move forward because we believe credit unions are the best financial idea in the nation. But, the real strenght of the Pennsylvania Credit Union League is the people, both volunteers and professionals, who make it work, who give of their time and energy. It has truly been a cooperative effort—a partnership of caring and dedication.

As we look to tomorrow . . . we remember the past . . . because the best times are the times we spend together.

Michael J. Judge
President, Pennsylvania Credit Union League
1984 Annual meeting

I

Prelude and Fugue

"Cooperation of all types ... can be looked upon as an attempt by agrarians, craftsmen, and other small producers to improve their position in a nonfeudal, modern capitalistic society. They were ... concerned with restoring a spirit of community."

J. Carroll Moody
Gilbert C. Fite

THE FEUD BETWEEN BORROWERS and lenders is as old as western culture. Biblical injunctions against usury stand as testimony to the ancient roots of the dispute; legislation such as the Truth-in-Lending Act gives evidence of the modern form. The credit union idea—merging the interests of borrowers and lenders by combining the interests in a single cooperative institution—tries to bridge this ancient gap.

By confining themselves to activity within a field of membership defined by the "common bond," credit unions have sought to make their services available to members by knowing them as individuals, rather than by relying on abstract rules and standards of credit-worthiness. In brief, the credit union movement is an attempt to construct humanized credit institutions, making financial tools and knowledge available on a widespread, mass-movement scale. If members were both borrower and lender their interests would be combined. The traditional confrontation of the two groups would be broken.

"The basic idea of the credit union is that a group of people can organize cooperatively, pool their individual savings and, from the pool, take care of their own credit problems without usury," wrote Bergengren.

To understand the course of the credit union movement in Pennsylvania, it is necessary to explore fully the intellectual and institutional background of the international credit union movement. We will discover that many aspects of Pennsylvania credit union history are not unique, but mirrors of issues and challenges inherent in credit union history. While the Pennsylvania Credit Union Act was passed as recently as 1933, the international credit union movement itself has more than 130 years of history.

The Pennsylvania movement is part of that long international development. The credit union idea started in Germany and was nourished throughout Europe and parts of Asia. It migrated to North America by way of Canada, and came to Pennsylvania by way of Massachusetts. Its roots, like those of Pennsylvania's population, are multi-national and multi-ethnic. Its philosophy is a similarly complex multi-faceted blend of pragmatism, idealism and capitalism.

The basic credit union concept, cooperative credit, is but one form of the cooperative movement which gained attention and popularity throughout Europe and America in the 1830s and 1840s. These were hard, turbulent times. The old rules were no longer working. Too many things were happening too quickly. The American Revolution had redefined political power. The industrial revolution was redefining economic power. And the availability of open lands in America was redefining the entire social order.

The middle of the nineteenth century was a remarkably unstable era throughout Europe. It was a time of revolution, of challenge to established authority. Economic, political, and social philosophers envisioned the advent of a new order in which many ancient, established ills could finally be ended.

The commercial cooperative movement was part of a wide-ranging search for a new social and economic order. It is held by most scholars to have originated with a group of weavers who opened their own store in Rochdale, England, in December, 1844. The weavers had just lost a strike. They had no money and no jobs. They did have some strong philosophic ideals along with their professional skills. These they set down in their "Rochdale Principles," a basic set of rules established by the weavers' cooperative. These "Rochdale Principles" became the basic tenets of cooperative capitalism.

- Membership would be open to all who wished to join;
- Interest on capital invested in the cooperative would be

strictly limited;
- Each member would have one vote, regardless of investment;
- No proxies would be accepted at any time;
- Members would receive refunds (rebates) on purchases of goods or services from the cooperative;
- Surplus income would be used to benefit the cooperative, to publicize the movement, and to help create a new economic order.

"A cooperative is an organization of people, not of money," wrote Bergengren when describing the Rochdale principles. "It is not a charity; its sole reason for existence is the service it can render to its member patrons. By applying the principles of democracy to economics, it is the declaration of freedom for enterprise and recognizes that there is no freedom of enterprise in monopoly."

New entrepreneurs such as the Rochdale weavers were well aware of the importance of credit in financing new business ventures. These infant industries had no access to traditional sources of credit, and no traditional collateral. The need for a new source of credit was pressing. Cooperative credit soon suggested itself as a new solution to the needs of new entrepreneurs and industrialists.

At the same time, the agricultural economy was encountering severe stresses. Farming is traditionally a credit-dependent business. The farmer borrows for seed and supplies, anticipating repayment after the harvest. The feudal farmer or serf had been able to rely on his lord; the free farmer had to rely on banks or other sources of financing.

Into this rapidly overheating atmosphere of social, political, and economic unrest came the poor harvests of 1844-1847. Combinations of flood, drought, brutal weather, and crop epidemics resulted in widespread famine. Throughout the British Isles (especially Ireland) and the European continent, physical distress and emigration stimulated political revolutions. The entrenched power structure survived the era; the traditional relationships between social classes did not.

As the relationship between the landed aristocracy and the working farmer changed, existing economic institutions failed to recognize that changes were taking place, that some system of credit to support the new rural economy and maintain the traditional rural values was vitally needed. Here too, cooperative credit would emerge as a likely and attractive solution.

Both the agricultural and urban sectors experienced this revolutionary change simultaneously. It brought a collapse of the old restrictions imposed by aristocracy, offered a range of new opportunities, and presented a whole series of new threats to farmers, artisans and laborers. Cooperative credit emerged as a way to respond, to take advantage of the new opportunities while gaining shelter and protection from the new threats of economic disaster.

Cooperative credit was quickly welcomed as part of the general cooperative movement. In France, Pierre Joseph Proudhon, Frances Bouchez, and Louis Blanc all proposed forms of popular, cooperative banking. In Belgium, M. Francois Haeck developed a unique credit cooperative composed exclusively of wealthy investors. While it was designed primarily as a profit-making institution formed to benefit its select group of investors (and to close off the development of a new banker class), Haeck's organization still reflects the popularity of the cooperative concept.

In Germany Hermann Schulze of Delitzsch (Schulze-Delitzsch), Friedrich Wilhelm Raiffeisen, and Victor Aime Huber all espoused cooperative credit systems intended to benefit the "common man." Schulze-Delitzsch and Raiffeisen are today credited with creating the modern credit union. Huber is now regarded as a publicist, not an innovator. But all should be viewed as part of the cooperative intellectual approach then current. The credit union concept has no single source, and the idea should be seen as an evolutionary concept.

Friedrich Raiffeisen is often spoken of as the "Father of the

*Hermann Schulze-Delitzsch
pioneered the Peoples Banks
system of urban cooperative
credit in Germany.*

Credit Union Movement." Raiffeisen was the first to popular-
ize the term credit union, and it was he who adapted cooperative credit to rural applications. But most modern American
credit unions are urban institutions. And most elements of
the contemporary credit union movement are actually based
on the work of Schulze-Deliztsch, founder of the German
system of People's Banks.

Schulze-Delitzsch was a bureaucrat, social activist and political reformer. He came to power as a liberal member of
the German parliament, elected following the famine of
1846-1847, and the revolutions of 1848. In the conservative re-
surgence of 1850 he was tried and acquitted of high treason,
but lost his seat in parliament and was reassigned to a less
attractive post.

Schulze-Delitzsch was an early convert to the cooperative
concept. By 1850 he had founded a cooperative association for
crafts people that provided mutual insurance against sickness
and death. He had also founded a cooperative for master
shoemakers to enable them to buy leather at wholesale prices.
He founded his first cooperative credit association in 1850.

27

Schulze-Delitzsch's first cooperative credit society collapsed while he was absent on government business. As one result, he resigned government service to pursue his cooperative ideals more closely. As a second, he gave more careful thought to the infrastructures of his new financial institutions.

Studying more successful societies founded by friends following his early lead, he learned that it would be a good idea to exclude wealthy patrons and force the society to be responsible for its own affairs. Henceforth, all members would have to contribute capital (buy shares) if they wished to borrow. To further capitalize his society, the group as a whole would borrow additional funds (accept deposits) from nonmembers on the basis of unlimited liability.[1]

The unlimited liability principle made it possible for Schulze-Delitzsch to put his restructured association into financial good health. But he had learned another lesson from the collapse of his first association. Loans made by the society would be available only for 'productive' purposes. No loans were to be made as charity or as gifts. All loans would be secured by the good character of the borrower.

The new society was called a "People's Bank." Membership was open to anyone who wished to participate. It was not limited by occupation or social class, but available to all seekers of credit who were of worthy character. Reflecting the values of its urban world, the society was designed to serve the needs of artisans and small shopkeepers.

Schulze-Delitzsch's organization followed the best cooperative principles. Total authority was vested in monthly meetings of the full membership. Each member had one vote, regardless of shareholdings or deposits. All members were

1. That is to say that each member of the society became fully responsible for all debts of the group, even beyond the limits of individual shareholdings. Each member of Schulze-Delitzsch's association would be wholly responsible for all of its debts. Within the context of the German economy of the day, this was the only way in which the society would be able to attract deposits.

28

eligible to sign passbooks or promisory notes, thus every member had the right to incur the obligation of the entire membership of the society.

Elected committees took care of administrative matters. One smaller group, the Vorstand or executive committee, had supervisory responsibility. Inevitably, this group gradually assumed the authority to conduct most of the routine business of the society. Thus the systems created by Schulze-Delitzsch's society clearly established many of the precedents that would become keystones of the modern credit union movement.[2]

Schulze-Delitzsch remained active in the German credit union movement throughout his life. An accomplished writer, he became its leading public relations practitioner; a tireless traveler throughout Germany, he became its leading missionary.

Schulze-Delitzsch was also a leader of the comprehensive German cooperative movement. While he is popularly regarded by contemporary credit union experts primarily as a founder of the credit cooperatives, Schulze-Delitzsch saw himself as a pioneer not only of cooperative credit, but of the wide-ranging and rapidly expanding collection of German cooperatives. He was instrumental in organizing the cooperative *Nationalverein*, an association of cooperative societies, and its broader based successor, the Universal Federation of German Cooperative Societies. When Schulze-Delitzsch died in 1883 he left behind an extensive and growing network of People's Banks. By the time World War I broke out there were more than 1000 of them, with a total membership well over 600,000.

Schulze-Delitzsch and many of his followers were somewhat troubled by another group of cooperative credit organizations which were gaining popularity throughout Germany.

---

2. One other precedent that he set was that of establishing cooperative credit associations before gaining legal permission for them to function. Despite his membership in the German legislature, it was not until 1867 that he was able to secure enabling legislation for his credit societies.

They regarded this growing network as rivals, and found many of their practices distasteful and unsafe. They were the rural credit societies based on a model originally created by Raiffeisen.

Raiffeisen, mayor of rural Flammersfeld, was also troubled by the crises of the late 1840s; like Schulze-Delitzsch, Raiffeisen thought cooperative effort the answer and he too began to organize societies. His first was an association designed to provide bread for his community at low prices. Its mission was the cooperative purchase of flour and cooperative construction of baking facilities. A second group formed by Raiffeisen borrowed money to purchase seed, and then purchased crops for redistribution at below-market prices. A later group was formed to buy cattle for resale to farmers on a long-term credit basis.

None of these were true cooperatives. They were good-hearted charitable associations, supported largely by patrons who were anxious to relieve the distresses of farmers and other rural citizens. Even when the latter association began making loans to area farmers (for productive purposes only, especially improvement of their farms), it was not a credit union. The affairs of the association were controlled by its wealthy patrons. Members who were admitted so that they could take loans had no voice in the affairs of the association. Control rested with patrons, wealthy "investors" with a social conscience (or fears of revolution), not the farmers themselves.

In 1854, Raiffeisen moved from Flammersfeld to Heddesdorf and organized a second social welfare society. While it too was financed by patrons, this group had several new elements. Designed to become self-sufficient and not to require additional capitalization from its sponsors, it provided for creation and maintenance of a reserve fund. Interested in and helping to finance the care of destitute children, it was doubtless seen by the wealthy burghers and aristocrats of Heddesdorf as an efficient and uplifting solution to the welfare problem. It was only one of many different social welfare experiments being tried throughout Germany during this exceptionally stressful period.

30

The charitable approach left much to be desired. These early Raiffeisen societies were widely observed but rarely imitated. The patrons lost interest in the affairs of the society; the farmer/borrowers had no voice in association activities and the two societies were allowed to drift with no direction or guidance. Like Schulze-Delitzsch before him, Raiffeisen decided to reorganize. He took as his model the growing network of People's Banks.

In his seminal work on the agrarian economy, *Rural Credits,* politician-statesman-economist Myron Herrick quotes a letter from Raiffeisen marking his gradually changing attitude towards the best way to provide credit to farmers.

> "I was loath to give up the idea that cooperative societies should be based on charity without thought of self or pelf.... But experience compels me frankly to admit that such societies must consist only of the persons who personally need their help and thus have an interest in keeping them going.
>
> "I have resolved to allow the society here at Heddesdorf to be dissolved, and then to organize another society at an early date upon the new principles mentioned above. Already I have made most satisfactory progress, practically upon the model of the Schulze-Delitzsch associations. However, since the latter are formed mainly for cities and towns, I have made certain changes in the by-laws to adapt them to local conditions."[3]

Raiffeisen organized his Heddesdorf Credit Union in 1864, but he remained the charitable Christian, insisting that brotherly love was the guiding principle of credit unions. Schulze-Delitzsch relied instead on the idea that people desired to gain their own economic self-sufficiency.

3. Quoted in J. Carroll Moody and Gilbert C. Fite, *The Credit Union Movement: Origins and Develpment, 1850-1927* (Lincoln, University of Nebraska Press, 1971), p. 11. This work is the outstanding history of the American credit union movement and of the Credit Union National Association. A later edition is *Origins and Development 1850-1980* (Dubuque, Kendall/Hunt, 1984).

Friedrich Raiffeisen created the rural credit union movement in Germany.

Raiffeisen required that members possess some assets: land, farming implements, livestock, or other potential collateral. Schulze-Delitzsch did not require that members possess substantial tangible assets, but his people's banks on occasion did demand appropriate security for loans.

Raiffeisen confined membership to local communities and found the parish the best-suited unit; Schulze-Delitzsch continued to draw membership from the widest possible area.

Raiffeisen, like Schulze-Delitzsch, retained the principle of unlimited liability: each of the members was individually liable for all of the debts of the association. But there was one more critical and often overlooked distinction. Raiffeisen's credit unions were not capitalized by the members themselves. Their funds were obtained by borrowing from commercial or community sources.

Raiffeisen's credit union was paternalistic. It was intended to provide help to farmers; Schulze-Delitzsch's People's Banks were true cooperatives designed to help mechanics and artisans help themselves. Political concepts were shared; Raiffeisen took his principles of governance directly from the model provided by the people's banks. All members participated in the general meeting and each had one vote. Most administrative responsibilities were retained by the committees.

The new elements introduced by Raiffeisen are important. He stressed the moral character of members, the provident nature of loans, and the importance of human interaction in all activities of the credit union. He introduced the concept that would become known as the "common bond," a link tying members of the credit union together, reinforcing their economic inter-dependence.

The "common bond" concept, so vital to the modern credit union movement, may well have had its origins in Raiffeisen's class consciousness. Schulze-Delitzsch's People's Banks, while urban-based and, in theory, potentially available to a large cross section of the population, in reality appealed almost exclusively to a narrow social sector. Members were crafts people, artisans and independent merchants.

The rural credit societies were designed to appeal to a broader range of the community. Only the wealthier merchants (burghers) and artistocrats (landlords) were likely to be excluded. Even they participated in the first Raiffeisen societies as patrons, and in the later organizations as depositors. In claiming that members had a "common bond" of residence, Raiffeisen was crossing otherwise rigid local class barriers.[4]

---

4. Credit Union National Association historical librarian Jerry Burns has done extensive research on the origins and development of the "common bond," the ideal considered so important a part of the credit union philosophy. He has found that the actual term "common bond" can be traced only as far back as a pamphlet, *Credit Union Primer*, written by Arthur Harold Ham in 1914. "The basis of membership in a Credit Union must be some *common bond* or community of interest," says Ham. "It may be common occupation, employment by the same establishment or membership in the same church, club, lodge, labor union or other organization. In rural communities the church, parish, school district or local grange furnish a satisfactory foundation for membership." While this specific language and rigid concept did not emerge until 1914, Raiffeisen began working with the concept almost at the begining of the movement.

Both the Schulze-Delitzsch and Raiffeisen types of cooperative credit institutions underwent substantial modifications in subsequent years as their founders traveled throughout Germany, organizing new societies and expanding their systems, but they remained rivals. Raiffeisen's credit union model started later and spread more slowly, but eventually proved the more popular. By 1913 there were almost 17,000 rural credit societies modeled on Raiffeisen's Heddesdorf Credit Union.

Elsewhere in Europe, the idea found imitators and modifiers. Luigi Luzzatti encountered a People's Bank in Germany and brought the concept (but not its unlimited liability) back to Lodi, Milan, Cremona and Bologna. Leone Wollemborg imitated the Raiffeisen model in Loreggia, Italy. Henry H. Wolff brought the concept to England and, more successfully, to the colonies of the Empire. The Irish agricultural cooperative movement under the leadership of Sir Horace Plunkett brought the rural credit cooperative extensive attention and support throughout Ireland.

Even in the early formative days of credit unions, we can see the birth of many controversies which continue to generate debate and internal dissent in the closing years of the twentieth century. These leaders shared the basic concept of credit unions but their plans often differed on many specifics.

Controversial issues included: the necessity for a common bond to unite members; the need for unlimited liability; the acceptability of deposits from nonmembers; distinctions between shares and deposits or between interest and dividends; and the need for statutory limits on interest. These and many other philosophic distinctions separated the early international pioneers as much as their shared basic concept of cooperative credit united them.

The credit union idea was based on European needs, social structures, and economic realities. Without modification, it would not become acceptable in the United States. Indeed, the concept was not particularly popular in England— at least not for home consumption. Wolff was never successful in organizing credit unions in Britain, but from his

34

position in the Colonial Office, he was able to disseminate the idea, often in sharply modified form, throughout the Empire.

It was through the Colonial Office that Wolff became an advisor to Plunkett and Alphonse Desjardins, thus eventually exporting credit unions first to Ireland and Canada, and ultimately to the United States. Wolff encouraged Plunkett to include organizing credit unions in Ireland among his other cooperative agricultural activities. And it was through the Colonial Office that Wolff established credit unions in India, where Edward Filene first encountered them. Filene would later become responsible for bringing credit unions to the United States and building the American credit union movement.

Raiffeisen and Schulze-Delitzsch in Germany, Proudhon, Bouchez and Blanc in France, Haeck in Belgium, Wolff in England, Plunkett in Ireland, Wollemborg and Luzzatti in Italy—all contributed ideas which would be synthesized by Desjardins and his colleagues as the credit union concept gained a North American beachhead in Quebec. Credit unions were truly an international movement—not just a German social experiment.

Desjardins was the critical link between the European background of the credit union movement and its American future. Too little attention is paid to the work of this remarkable Jesuit-trained French Canadian journalist. It was he who understood the European traditions that had produced the credit union movement as well as the values and needs of the new world that would welcome the concept to this side of the Atlantic. It was Desjardins who was able to translate the European traditions into a North American idiom. It was Desjardins who, almost single-handedly, transplanted the European credit union movement to North America. That the roots of the credit union movement were available on this continent was the work of Desjardins. That the roots took hold and spread in the fertile soil of the new world would be the work of many people.

Alfonse Desjardins, Canadian credit union pioneer, helped found the first credit unions in the United States.

Desjardins was a journalist and a Canadian nationalist. He learned about usury while a reporter at the 1897 session of the Canadian Parliament where legislation to outlaw it was under discussion. Greatly troubled by the horror stories that emerged as part of the testimony, he soon contacted Wolff and Charles Rayneri, a director of a French cooperative credit institution. Soon he was corresponding with Luzzatti and others throughout the continent. His intention was clear; he wanted to establish a cooperative credit organization to serve his community at Lévis, Quebec.

La Caisse Populaire de Lévis was founded by a committee of citizens in December 1900. It opened for business in January 1901. In creating it, Desjardins had made several fundamental alterations in the European credit union structure. These changes themselves became fundamental parts of the North American credit union movement.

Desjardins merged the rural ideals of Raiffeisen with the

urban concepts of Schulze-Delitzsch. The distinctions between the rural credit association and the people's banks had been maintained throughout Europe where the varied needs and values of rural and urban communities mandated different institutional structures. Desjardins realized that Canada was too young to have developed disparate histories and traditions.

His decision to unify the rural and urban structures thus came from two opposing directions. One was ideological; he understood the essential community of interests of the rural and urban communities. The second was purely practical; he realized that a sparse population mandated cooperation if anything worthwhile was to be accomplished. He wanted a uniform system.

Desjardins' second modification of the traditional European credit union structure similarly came from two different directions. Like Luzzatti in Italy, Desjardins rejected the principle of unlimited liability, the legal structure which had made each member of the credit union responsible for all the debts (deposits) of the association.

The issue of limited liability *vs.* unlimited liability was a controversial one in the European credit union community. The same controversy—in different guise—would later emerge in the United States and in Pennsylvania as the debate over share insurance came to a head. Luzzatti in Italy was an early advocate of limited liability. He thought it a necessary modification if the credit union movement were to attract widespread popular support and an active membership, and Desjardins took many of his ideas from Luzzatti. The Canadian recognized that, philosophically, the nature of the Canadian population and its economic situation were markedly different from those encountered by Schulze-Delitzsch and Raiffeisen. North America was a speculative world of wide-open economic opportunity. There was no place in North America for mid-Europe's rigid financial conservatism. The credit policies of the staid, big-city banks of the new world, standards that seemed excessively cautious to many Canadians and Americans, seemed imprudent and irresponsible by traditional European standards.

Desjardins realized that a Canadian credit union movement need not be governed by traditions and principles sacred to European authorities. Potential depositors would not expect the cooperatives to offer unlimited liability; potential members would not accept the financial exposure demanded. Different, perhaps better, ways to keep lending policies from becoming irresponsible would have to be found.

In practical terms, Desjardins recognized that the Canadian population simply would not tolerate unlimited liability—would not join an institution that presented such a potential threat.In Europe the concept of limited liability was still the exception; in North America, limited liability was the rule.

These two new developments were critical to the future of the American credit union movement: combining the rural and urban traditions into a single institution and adopting limited liability. Without them, it would have been impossible for the movement to have spread to the United States. With these adaptations, credit unions would become attractive institutions, needing only the right combination of people to bring them here. It is not coincidence that earlier attempts to bring credit unions to the United States had failed. Credit unions could not and did not develop in the United States until after Desjardins had introduced his North American modifications.

Desjardins did more with his changes than simply customizing the concept to the North American environment. His decisive actions resolved controversies that had divided the movement. This accomplishment should not be underrated. Many issues would split the American credit union movement in the future, but the principle of one unified credit union movement with room for all special interests—labor, agriculture, industry, commerce—stands as an unquestioned keystone of the credit union philosophy.

Desjardins worked with several other European credit union controversies. One long-running debate concerned

38

participation in credit union affairs by nonmembers. Another divisive issue involved payments to investors from credit union income. Should credit unions pay dividends to shareholders, or was that too commercial and contrary to the cooperative spirit? Should credit unions pay interest to depositors, and how should the size of such payments be determined? Should credit unions maintain reserves, or should all credit union funds be available for loan to members? These issues had been raised throughout the credit union movement's history.

Desjardins retained the traditional distinction between shares and deposits. People joined the credit union by purchasing shares. Thus all members of the Levis cooperative credit association were shareholders. But others could place deposits in the new credit union. And members could either purchase additional shares or make deposits.

A letter written to Thomas Fry of the New Hampshire legislature during the drafting of the New Hampshire Credit Union Act illustrates Desjardins' ethic. He advises legislating a 3% interest rate on deposits, but leaving the dividend on shares to be determined by the general membership. The dividend, he advised New Hampshire, should not be declared by the officers of the credit union, as would be the case in other corporations, but "by the shareholders themselves . . . because it is a matter of principle. They are the sole masters and their officers should exercise only rights and duties that cannot be conveniently discharged by the general meeting."

Desjardins was insistent that his cooperative credit association maintain a high level of reserves (20%). He was willing to reject the unlimited liability requirements, but he would not compromise on the reserves issue. These concepts are complementary. Both involve the financial security of the association. Desjardins felt that without unlimited liability, rigidly maintained high reserve levels were critical to association safety and member security.

There can be no question of the success of this pioneer

North American credit union. Not only did it thrive, it attracted imitators. One formed at the neighboring Saint Joseph de Lévis Parish and a second at Saint Malo near Quebec City. Within several years there were more than 100 popular credit associations serving both laborers and farmers. And Desjardins himself was following the footsteps of Raiffeisen, Schulze-Delitzsch, Wolff, Luzzatti, and the others. He had become not just the founder of a credit union, but the creator of a credit union system and a pioneering missionary of the movement.

Desjardins is one of the leading figures in the intellectual history of the credit union movement. His credit union philosophy reflected his moral precepts. "A credit union is not an ordinary financial concern, seeking to enrich its members at the expense of the general public," he wrote. "Neither is it a loan company, seeking to make profit at the expense of unfortunates. . . . The credit union is nothing of the kind; *it is the expression in the field of economics of a high social ideal.*"

Desjardins' main principles of credit unionism are, in their own way, as important to the history of the credit union movement as the original Rochdale principles which preceded them. They would become an essential part of the credit union movement. The objectives of this first North American credit union were:

- To encourage economy and financial responsibility among members;
- To promote Christian and humane values;
- To combat usury;
- To provide capital for local individual enterprises;
- To help borrowers achieve economic independence through self-help.

Just to the South of Canada, a diverse group of people was gradually becoming aware of credit unions and curious about their possibilities. They included Massachusetts banking commissioner Pierre Jay, Monsignor Pierre Hevey, Catholic priest of Saint Mary's parish in New Hampshire, and a Jewish merchant in Boston named Edward Filene. These people would become leading players in the next chapter. With help from their friends and neighbors, they would play pivotal roles in introducing credit unions to the United States.

II

The New World Symphony

"Everybody in the world has the right to buy things."

Edward A. Filene

TO EUROPEAN CREDIT UNION ACTIVISTS, the United States must have seemed to be the promised land for expansion of the credit union movement. Here was a world where every opportunity awaited anyone who could start any kind of business. Here was the country where cheap or free land could be had by anyone who could obtain the little money needed to start homesteading.

During the second half of the nineteenth century, here too was a land of need. Especially in the port cities of the East Coast, cities like Boston, New York, Charleston and Philadelphia, poverty was creating a whole set of new and unwelcomed problems. Irish refugees of the famine and other immigrants came seeking the opportunities of the new world but found only unemployment.

Many social institutions developed to help cope with these problems. The new organizations were not restricted to the settlement houses and similar charitable institutions but included self-help organizations created in response to distressed communities. Immigrant aid societies, ethnic insurance companies, and numerous savings and loan associations trace their origins to the self-help efforts of this era.

During the 1840s when Europe was concerning itself with financial and political reform, the United States was starting to tear itself apart over the issue of slavery. Not until after the Civil War would America again turn its attention to problems of banking and monetary policy. The years between the Civil War and World War I witnessed an unprecedented popular American fascination with economics and money.

Yet throughout that period all attempts to bring credit unions to the United States failed. Samuel M. Quincy and his nephew Josiah Quincy, both Boston lawyers and Massachusetts politicians, attempted to import the Schulze-Delitzsch model to the United States. The Massachusetts General Court Committee on Banks and Banking rejected the necessary enabling legislation in 1871.

In the era following the Civil War, the nation experienced many economic distresses. Some politicians made currency reform a leading populist issue. Others, including some leading progressives, became interested in reforming the banking and credit industry. Through reform of the credit establishment, they hoped to ease the plight of farmers and other rural Americans.

The Irish credit union advocate Sir Horace Plunkett's general interest in rural life and values made him part of an important network of friends who were exploring ways to make rural life more attractive. Their main interest was in retaining and spreading the social and intellectual values that they saw as based in rural civilization and threatened by urbanism. This progressive network included Charles McCarthy, legislative librarian of Wisconsin, and Pennsylvanian Gifford Pinchot.

Pinchot later served on the advisory committee of the Credit Union National Extension Bureau during his first term as governor of Pennsylvania. During his second term as governor in the early 1930s, he signed the Pennsylvania Credit Union Act into law. His early friendship with Plunkett is a direct tie from the European phase of the credit union movement to the development and eventual success of the movement in Pennsylvania.

Pennsylvania was not totally inactive on the credit union front, even in these early years. There was an attempt to institute rural cooperative credit institutions in Pennsylvania in 1893. While it passed the legislature, the idea never gained widespread popularity. Only a few of these rural cooperative institutions were ever actually established. Of them, only one actually survived. It later transformed itself into a savings and loan association. This 1893 law does however give Pennsylvania the right to claim precedence as the first state to pass a credit union law. Unfortunately, that is probably its only historical significance.[1]

Justice William A. Potter of the Pennsylvania Supreme Court was deeply interested in the "cooperative bank" concept. In 1913 Potter wrote to Desjardins in Quebec asking information "describing in ... detail the work and purposes of these banks." Potter never became an active participant in the growing American credit union movement, and Pennsylvania would have to wait until 1933 before it would see an effective credit union law.

To many economic philosophers of the day, credit unions lacked appeal because they were not radical enough. Many of the solutions being offered to post-Civil War economic ills were far more radical and gained far more acceptance than credit unions. Many of the monetary reforms of the populists and progressives were broader in their implications and immediate effect, yet they gained many followers. The birth of an infant labor movement, especially as it took form through the Knights of Labor and the International Workers of the World, was far more threatening to the established order. Credit unions were successfully resisted while the labor movement persisted against all opposition.

In comparison with the leading socialists and other radical economic thinkers of their day, Huber, Schulze, Raiffeisen and other credit union pioneers were all extraordinarily conservative. In a day when other liberal thinkers were quick to reject traditional theology along with traditional social and economic institutions, credit union leaders typically retained a strong religious element in their philosophy.

Although this religious commitment was clearly non-sectarian, it was, through Schulze's and Raiffeisen's influence,

1. Credit union historian J. Carroll Moody does not even give the Pennsylvania law that much importance. He claims the institutions were not very much like credit unions.

Protestant in origin.[2] Opponents of the credit union movement argued that it was too radical to find a home in the
United States. That argument was part of the debate that
retarded the movement for ten years in Pennsylvania. Yet
such a position had no basis in theory, in fact, in philosophy,
or in practice.

The basic concept created by the originators of the credit
union idea was to extend the benefits of concentrated capital
to new classes—not to abolish, hinder, or otherwise restrict
or disrupt the activities of bankers or other capitalists. There
was nothing radical about this philosophy, either by contemporary definitions, or by the contemporary standards of the
era.

To that extent, credit cooperatives departed from the Rochdale model. The weavers fully intended that their store be
able to compete with the extant marketing structure. While
the Rochdale experiment relied on traditional methods and
forms, it did constitute a radical new part of the economic
system. It was a threat to the established order. Later cooperatives were, to various degrees, competitive threats to established business practice. The credit cooperatives were
intended to fill a void—to extend the benefits of banking to
classes of people who would otherwise be denied them.

All too often, leaders of the established business community were too frightened to make such subtle distinctions.
There was a strong inclination to reject anything new as
radical and disruptive. To a minor extent, such overreaction
is understandable. These were turbulent times, and far more
radical solutions to widespread social ills were gaining popularity throughout western societies. The ideas of Karl Marx
—the philosophical perspective that would eventually grow

2. As the famous economic sociologist Max Weber demonstrated in his
Protestantism and Capitalism, such a commitment entails a devotion to a
capitalist economic structure. It forced credit union advocates away from
more radical political-economic philosophies. It should also have made the
credit union movement particularly appealing to those whose religious
convictions kept them from adopting the more radical utopian programs.

into communism—were proving attractive in some quarters of the United States and Europe. Marx and Friedrich Engels published *The Communist Manifesto* at the same time that Raiffeisen and Schulze were beginning their work.

Radical competition for the credit union idea also came from the increasingly popular Socialist movement. In England the Fabian Socialism of George Bernard Shaw and Beatrice and Sidney Webb, along with the increasingly powerful Labor party, were much more popular than moderate arguments of credit union reformers.

Yet many contemporary opponents of the credit union movement succeeded in painting it as a radical development. In part this was due to the use of the term "union." The widespread opinion that the credit union was a radical concept could come only from uninformed commentators or from a deliberate attempt to misinform the public.

The radicalism charge would later be a prime tool of those opposing credit union legislation in the states. It would prove successful in delaying the adoption of credit union laws in many states—including Pennsylvania. In Pennsylvania, credit unions were linked to trade unions, inviting the disastrous opposition of the Pennsylvania Railroad power brokers. The technique was also used just as effectively in such other politically conservative states as Connecticut.

Since the days of the Continental Congress, even before the American Revolution, the Keystone State has been moderate and conservative in its politics. The misleading appearance of credit unions as part of a more radical political-economic structure would work against the early development of credit unions in the state. From the time that the first modern credit union act was originally submitted to the Pennsylvania legislature in 1923 through its eventual passage ten years later, the conservative power structure of the commonwealth continued its powerful opposition.

To a Europe in the final stages of the great industrial revolution, the credit union movement had been attractive in the 1850s. In the United States our attention had been subsumed by

Civil War issues. We had little time for the credit union dream. By the turn of the century that situation was changing.

Credit unions came to the North American continent through the work of Alphonse Desjardins, the dedicated credit union pioneer and French-Canadian journalist who, like Raiffeisen before him, was outraged by the depredations of usurers.

Desjardins formed the first credit union in North America at Levis, Quebec, Canada in 1900. The idea crossed the border into the United States nine years later when Desjardins formed a credit union in Manchester, New Hampshire. Pierre Jay, the first banking commissioner of Massachusetts (and later banking commissioner of New York), quickly sought counsel with Desjardins and the two cooperated in attempts to generate appropriate enabling legislation for the Bay State.

The Saint Mary's Cooperative Credit Association of Manchester, New Hampshire thus became the first credit union in the United States. It was organized with extensive help from Desjardins. And like its Quebec predecessors, it was created without legal sanction. New Hampshire recognized and approved its existence in a special law chartering it, passed on April 6, 1909. It continues in existence, and in 1984 celebrated its 75th anniversary.

The Massachusetts credit Union Act became law on April 15, 1909. This Massachusetts law was the first general statute providing for the incorporation of credit unions in the United States.

The Massachusetts Credit Union Act clearly reflected the Rochdale principles, the Levis objectives and the experiences of Schulze-Delitzsch and Raiffeisen. It defined a credit union as "a cooperative association formed for the purpose of promoting thrift among its members." The law required that at least seven persons apply for a charter to organize a credit union. Once incorporated, a credit union could receive the savings of members in the form of shares or deposits and could make loans.

Massachusetts credit unions were to be governed democratically, with each member entitled to only one vote regardless of the number of shares owned or the extent of his or her deposits. The members would elect a board of directors which in turn would choose a president and other officers. Members would elect a credit committee and a supervisory committee. The credit committee had to approve all loans, which must be for useful and beneficial purposes. Neither the directors nor members of the committees could receive compensation. Theirs was to be a volunteer effort, for the good of the community—not for individual gain.

To Edward A. Filene, Bostonian, merchant prince, progressive political activist and cooperative capitalist, such zealous voluntarism was appealing and intriguing. Filene was fascinated by mass production and recognized that extending the availability of credit held the potential of ushering in a new economic order. He also recognized that without mass distribution, mass production was less than useless.

"Business cannot sell more than all the people can buy," Filene would later write in *Speaking of Change*. "A million people each with a thousand dollars to spare can and will buy more than a thousand people with a million dollars each.... We must increase the purchasing power of the masses."

In Filene's Department Store, a Boston landmark, Filene had created the bargain basement and had introduced a whole new approach to sales. He had also become an advocate of cooperative capitalism and had given his employees a new role and power in running the store. Filene was an innovative, imaginative, evangelical spirit in continuous quest of a just, well-ordered society. In him, the American credit union movement would find its most crucial supporter.

Filene's first encounter with the credit union idea came in 1907 during a trip which had taken him to India. His "Trip Book" records his discovery. "All over India the natives are deeply in debt to native money lenders and are working their land under debts on which they are paying 25% a year.... If a crop fails, there is usually famine." Filene was deeply impressed with the work of William Robert Gourlay who was

51

Edward Filene, Boston merchant, led efforts to found the United States credit union movement.

establishing cooperative credit institutions in an attempt to break the vicious usury cycle and restore economic self-sufficiency to the rural communities.

Filene's biographer, Gerald Johnson, claims that Filene was just as concerned with the moneylenders as he was with the other villagers. "He was bound to be.... The moneylenders' problem may have been less urgent, but it was no less threatening than that of the villagers on whom they preyed."

Filene recognized the economic interrelationships in ways that escaped most of his contemporaries. The moneylenders' real wealth, Filene believed, was not their own money but the prosperity of the village from which they drew their incomes. Similarly, he recognized that his own wealth was based on the prosperity of his customers, and that the financial health of any community was based on the total of the wealth and fiscal skills of all its members.

When he returned to the United States, Filene wrote President Theodore Roosevelt suggesting that the United States establish cooperative credit institutions in the Philippines as Britain had been doing in India. He also turned his attention to the home front and to credit union activity is his own state.

Filene watched with close attention as Desjardins and Pierre Jay began work to bring the credit union movement to the Bay State. Jay had become interested in credit unions through Wolff's *People's Banks*, and had contacted Desjardins, inviting him to visit Boston. On November 24, 1908, Desjardins met with Jay and a group of "public spirited citizens," including Filene.

Filene, impressed by what Desjardins had to say, later testified in support of credit unions during the legislative hearings which ultimately produced Massachusetts' Credit Union Act. Filene was not yet an active partcipant. He liked the concept of cooperative credit, but saw credit unions only as a possible supplement to the credit establishment. Filene also still envisioned credit unions as having primarily rural applications.

By mid 1909. both New Hampshire and Massachusetts had credit union laws. Both St. Mary's Parish Credit Union in New Hampshire and *La Caisse Populaire* Saint Jean Baptiste in Massachusetts owed their existence to the work of Desjardins. While Filene, Jay[3], and other public spirited citizens of Boston were interested in the credit union concept, they were less interested in the daily effort and follow-up required to organize credit unions and prepare them to conduct business. And without continuing active local leadership, the credit union movement in the United States appeared likely to collapse.

For a while leadership was supplied by the Boston Chamber of Commerce. Originally founded by Filene, the Chamber continued its support of the credit union movement largely at his instigation.

---

3. While Jay is an important figure in credit union history, credit unions were not particularly important to him. CUNA historical librarian Jerry Burns points out that Jay's interest in credit unions stopped when he resumed banking.

At this time, the Russell Sage Foundation indicated some interest in extending the credit union movement to New York, where the Jewish Agricultural and Industrial Aid Society also provided support to the idea. A young member of the New York senate, Franklin D. Roosevelt, was among the active supporters of credit union legislation in Albany.

The New York bill passed in May 1913, but the credit union movement was already encountering major problems which threatened its existence. Most notably, while the concept and structure of credit unions had been imported with the help of Desjardins, the credit union philosophy had apparently been left behind.

In Massachusetts the law did not specify any limit on loan interest rates, merely stipulating that charge should be "reasonable." For a brief period, there were Massachusetts credit unions charging as much as 52% per year. Similarly, there was no limit on dividends, and some of the New York credit unions paid their shareowners 24% per year on the investment. These credit unions had simply become new forms of banks with little concept of "common bond," community service, or meaningful cooperation. Some even discounted loans, a commercial practice of no value to the membership. It is not surprising that credit union development soon began to languish in both states.

Filene and his fellow public-spirited citizens were not about to give up. In 1914, they formed the Massachusetts Credit Union. Its mission, in addition to serving as a credit union, would be to educate, publicize and organize new credit unions (while serving as a credit union itself). It accepted both individual members and other credit unions as members. It was, in short, an experimental prototype for a credit union league.

Despite their best efforts, these community leaders were unable to organize a viable movement. Most members of the board of the Massachusetts Credit Union did organize credit unions among their own employees, and several influenced friends to do likewise. With the outbreak of World War I in

Europe, it appeared that there would be little time, energy, or interest left for the credit union movement.

That spectre was laid to rest at a statewide meeting of credit unions in Massachusetts held at the Boston City Club in April 1915. The meeting was marked by testimonials from Jewish, Irish, French, Italian, and other ethnic groups about the importance of credit unions in their communities. Desjardins, hearing about the enthusiasm at the Boston meeting, wrote to Arthur Ham of the Russell Sage foundation, urging him to remember that "the social and educating aspect of Credit Unions" was at least as important as the "dry business" function.[4]

The future looked promising but the credit union movement still lacked vital internal leadership. Its vitality had all come from without—from public spirited citizens seeking to bring the benefits of credit unions to other, less fortunate citizens who needed this new institution. The American credit union movement still had no domestic counterpart to Desjardins, no one willing to undertake responsibity for the movement on a continuing basis. As a result, by 1912 the national movement was dying out. There was little interest in the three states with credit union laws—New Hampshire, Massachusetts and New York—for organizing new credit unions. President Theodore Roosevelt's Country Life Commission had noted the critical problem of rural credit and had advocated cooperative credit societies as a likely solution in 1908, but even the flurry of interest sparked by the Commission's work seemed to have dissipated. Neither the Populist Party nor the Progressive Party appeared interested in making an issue out of the credit system.

David Lubin, a California merchant and American delegate to the International Institute of Agriculture in Rome

4. Desjardins was the first to recognize that the social function of credit unions would be critical to the history of the movement. In Canada, and especially in the United States, associated social functions would become critical to the vitality of the movement. In Pennsylvania eventual development of social activities at the chapter meetings provided the movement a vitality it otherwise lacked.

(1910) made some effort to stimulate a national credit union movement, and actively solicited the support of President Roosevelt. Lubin also mailed thousands of pamphlets about credit unions to agricultural societies, farm leaders, and key business persons throughout the country. It was Lubin who impressed Myron T. Herrick, a prominent Republican politician, former governor of Ohio and ambassador to France with the importance of rural credit issues. Herrick in turn interested President William Howard Taft. Questions involving rural life and credit became politically important in 1912, a presidential election year. The Democrats, Republicans, and Progressives all had "rural credit" planks in their national platforms. The Southern Commercial Congress, responding to a suggestion from Lubin, established the "American Commission on Rural Credit and Cooperation" to investigate European solutions to rural credit problems.

Lubin, Taft, Herrick, and others succeeded in creating a special "United States Commission" charged with cooperating with the American commission "to investigate and study in European countries, cooperative land-mortgage banks, cooperative rural credit unions, and similar organizations and institutions devoting their attention to the promotion of agriculture and the betterment of rural conditions." Taft signed the law creating the commission but his successor Woodrow Wilson appointed the commissioners. This was to be a legitimately powerful, cooperative, nonpartisan effort. Pennsylvanians participating in the commission activities included James G. McSparran who would become a leading champion of credit unions in the commonwealth and later, as secretary of agriculture, sponsored the Pennsylvania Credit Union Act. Other Pennsylvanians included Robert L. Munce, secretary of agriculture N. B. Critchfield, deputy secretary of agriculture A. L. Martin, and George G. Hutchison.[5]

5. The tour of the joint American / United States Commission was not overly successful. It stimulated controversy and dissent within the cooperative movement. Lubin's leadership antagonized many European authorities

56

The activities of the American / United States Commission took on special importance when, in the spotlight of attention created by commission activities, the German credit union association led by Jacob de Haas collapsed. The de Haas system was just one of several functioning in Germany, but its failure shook international confidence in the entire credit union concept.[6]

Typically, Wolff blamed government intervention for the Haas system's failure. Other credit union leaders joined with competing explanations. Most simply held that it was a matter of individual failure, not systemic. The directors of the central bank were tried and convicted of malpractice, but the episode did shadow the otherwise brilliant publicity success of commission activities.

The *Report of the American Commission* is a major document in the history of cooperative credit. It did much to spread the word about credit unions throughout agricultural America. As a result, it kindled a new excitement even though it contained virtually nothing that was new. The commissioners had met with bankers, politicians, and credit union leaders throughout Europe. Their report praised the Raiffeisen type cooperative banks. Like Desjardins before, they rejected unlimited liability as unacceptable to the American farmer. They recommended that states consider enacting credit union laws. The report of the commissions influenced the American credit

---

including Luzzatti and Plunkett. But the Joint Commission did succeed in generating considerable national interest in credit unions. Even Plunkett conceded Lubin's promotional genius in a letter to Pennsylvania progressive Gifford Pinchot and Wisconsin agricultural cooperation expert Charles McCarthy. Plunkett described Lubin as "a perfect genius at this kind of promotion, but he is more of the journalist than the student."

6. "What happened," wrote United States Commission member Lionel Smith-Gordon to McCarthy "was that the central bank (at Darmstadt) of the whole union went smash and carried with it four big neighboring banks which were apparently being run on the same capital by a system of book transfers.... At the same time several small banks in Dr. Haas' own province of Hesse collapsed. Owing to the system of decentralization in the Haas union the collapse does not in itself involve all branches...but confidence has been seriously shaken."

union movement in several ways. The most critical is that the federal credit unions would not become deeply involved in long-term mortgage lending until the 1980s.[7]

The final report recommended the creation of a federally subsidized rural mortgage system structured along lines of either the *landschaft* or the *credit foncier*. This system, the report urged, should remain separate and distinct from any credit cooperatives intended to provide short-term loans.

The Federal Farm Loan Act of 1916 dealt with long-term farm mortgages in ways recommended by the commission. This answered the most crying need, and relieved much of the political pressure that had led to creation of the commission.

For short-term credit, the commission advocated adoption of Raiffeisen-type cooperative credit societies (with the elimination of unlimited liability). The report acknowledged the possibility that conventional private banking might meet the needs of rural borrowers, but also suggested that the states enact laws providing for the establishment of cooperative credit societies.

Texas and Wisconsin did pass such laws, although neither was widely used. Oregon, South Carolina, and Utah also passed credit union laws, but these too proved impractical. In North Carolina, John Sprunt Hill succeeded in pushing the legislature to create a credit union bill that became a model for the form and was widely successful.

Hill was a gentleman farmer, banker, merchant and philanthropist. As a member of the American Commission, he had been deeply impressed by what he learned of credit union operations in Europe. He would become a leading American credit union advocate and would later become an active adviser to the national credit union movement.

---

7. The commission had investigated two systems of cooperative mortgages popular throughout Europe, the joint-stock *credit foncier* system (a Schulze/-People's Bank descendant) and the more purely cooperative *landschaft* system (more closely related to Raiffeisen's rural associations). Herrick's support of the *credit foncier* and Lubin's advocacy of *landschaft* had almost destroyed the commission at its inception and troubled the group throughout their tour.

Jacob de Haas, now in the United States and working actively with the Massachusetts Credit Union also helped to spread the good news. De Haas, like Hill, was especially concerned with the potential of credit unions to aid poor blacks and other depressed groups. In addressing the Massachusetts Credit Union, de Haas concisely summed up the experience of the American credit union movement:

> "It is evident that the Credit Union is a new idea for the United States, that it appeals to people with business understanding rather than to social workers, and if a National Committee for the fostering of the Credit Union were started and capitalized, I feel that this movement could be made to cross from Massachusetts to California in two years."

That suggestion coincided with ideas already being explored by Filene and his associates. Filene, typically, was working on a grand scale. He saw an international credit union movement. Once again the future looked bright as Hill, Filene, de Haas, and other philanthropists prepared to give their world the credit union.

There is no doubt that many Americans recognized the need to find new sources of rural credits. Debt-ridden farmers were willing to investigate whatever new schemes were offered. In 1914, *The Pennsylvania Farmer*, official publication of the State Grange, published an article on "Practical Rural Credits" which discussed an experiment with rural credit union type organizations in New Jersey:

> "Since ... last year five cooperative credit unions have been organized by Jewish farmers in New Jersey alone, for the purpose of loaning small sums of money at reasonable rates to such of their own number as may need it.[8]
>
> "Cooperative credit unions have been organized somewhat on the Raiffeisen Bank plan of Europe, for the purpose of

---

8. The experimental credit cooperatives were located at Carmel, Cumberland County (30 members); Flemington, Hunterdon County (22 members); Hightstown, Mercer County (32 members); Perrineville, Monmouth County (29 members); and Woodbine, Cape May County (28 members).

making small loans for a short time, at reasonable interest, to buy stock, seed, fertilizer or farm implements. A number of Jewish farmers get together and form a union.... Any member of the union may then borrow from the union to the extent of $100, for not longer than six months, at 6 per cent upon giving his personal note with two other members as security.

"It is claimed that the cooperative credit associations established in New Jersey and 30 other states, to aid Jewish farmers, are the pioneers of such organizations in this country, and that their successful operation, without the aid of special legislation, proves the adaptability and benefits of the credit system in general use in Europe to the farmers and agricultural interests of the United States."

In 1915 most of the American public remained unaware that they needed credit unions, however, and were not willing to work for establishing such new and untried institutions. No one questioned that problems with both rural credit and credit for the wage-earner and the small merchant were severe. Other solutions just seemed more in line with traditional approaches, or more readily implemented with less effort.

Conversely, more radical solutions were attracting wide audience support. The demands of the socialists went well beyond resolving creditor/debtor relationships. Many potential supporters of credit union style reform were attracted instead to the broad-brush approach of the socialists and other more radical groups. Part of the appeal of the credit union movement for such wealthy philanthropists as Filene, Hill, Pinchot, and other public-spirited citizens was in the fact that they hoped resolving credit difficulties might do much to defuse more general social discontent.

Filene had read the works of Marx and accepted several of his concepts including the description of class. But he rejected the Marxian dialectic arguing that the evolution of modern science had left Marxism functionally outdated even before *Das Kapital* had been published. Filene also recognized the attractiveness of socialism, especially for the oppressed. "I

60

have never been a Socialist, but there were times in my life when I earnestly wanted to be," he wrote in *Speaking of Change.* "Socialism was a beautiful ideal."

This idealism of Filene's was tempered by a powerful pragmatism; his goal was maximization of wealth: individual wealth, community wealth, the Filene family's wealth. As one close associate described the phenomenon, "Filene's devotion to the credit union is easily understood when we evaluate his other primary interests. The credit union was to enable people to mobilize their savings in such fashion that they could greatly increase their power of mass consumption. He hated usury because it was uneconomic.... He saw the credit union as one tangible thing which worked in with his idealism."

Filene's interest in the credit union movement is thus easily understood. If successful, it would enable people to mobilize their savings and greatly increase their purchase power. Usury was uneconomic; it robbed the masses of their purchase and consumption capabilities. He saw the credit union as one means for achieving both idealism and materialism in harmonious concert with his idealism.

Filene knew that he had neither the time nor the single-minded devotion needed to build a national credit union movement. As he had done with his other activities, he sought an associate who would provide the needed drive and administrative attention. William Stanton and George W. Elwell of the Massachusetts Credit Union as well as John Clark Bills, W. F. McCaleb and Charles W. Birtwell of its successor, the Massacusetts Credit Union Association (MCUA), all held executive responsibility for the early credit union movement under the sponsorship of Filene and his associates. None, however, was able to create a viable and effective credit union movement.

A dedicated and impressive group of American intellectuals continued to provide their names and some financial support to the movement. Led by Filene, the group included such outstanding leaders in their own fields as historian Charles A. Beard, labor economist John R. Commons, U.S. Senator Albert J. Beveridge, *Review of Reviews* editor Albert Shaw, banker and Texas bank commissioner W. W. Collier and others. Even their combined support seemed insufficient.

In 1920, Filene hired Roy F. Bergengren to head MCUA. The new man knew virtually nothing about credit unions. He was a graduate of Dartmouth College and Harvard University Law School, had been active in civic affairs, and was a World War I veteran. At this point in his life, he was a failed businessman and in need of a job.

Bergengren was the son of a Swedish immigrant physician. He was married, had two children (a third had died in an accident in 1919) and was 41 years old when he started his credit union career. In the credit union movement, Bergengren found his ideal calling—his life's mission—his crusade. And the credit union movement had found a leader who would steer it into the mainstream of American economic life. Although Bergengren knew nothing of credit unions when he started, he quickly acquired both a firm knowledge of and a strong dedication to the ideals of the movement. He would become its most zealous missionary and its most dedicated disciple. As he later wrote in *Crusade*,

> 'You cannot operate a typical credit union without spiritual purpose. You are obliged, whether you know it or not, to have some notion of the principle of brotherhood of man if you would operate a successful credit union. If you have served on a credit committee, you have, not once but a thousand times and more, played the role of the Good Samaritan. These were Raiffeisen's concepts, and it was our purpose to inculcate these principles in the credit union movement of North America."

During his first ten years, Bergengren would attend over 55 legislative sessions in over 30 states. He would attend countless meetings organizing credit unions and leagues. There were not quite 200 credit unions in the United States when Bergengren assumed leadership of MCUA; ten years later there were more than 1,500.

Filene may have conceived of economics in global terms;

Bergengren's concept was much more personal. At the end of his formal association with the credit union movement, in forced retirement and reviewing his career, he took note of this pragmatic perspective.

"When I speak of 'economics' I am thinking of bread and butter—of the rent I pay or the interest on my mortgage—of the family car—of my pay envelope and what's in it—of good times and plenty—of bad times and soup kitchens—of dwindling bank balances and insurance premiums and of doctors and hospitals and undertakers and union dues and the battle most of us fight to make income balance outgo, with a little left over for the inevitable day when our ability to work has ceased."

Like Filene, Bergengren's pragmatism was part of a larger idealism. Throughout his career, Bergengren saw the credit union as the embodiment of applied brotherhood. "I like to believe that one thing which I have said will be remembered after I am gone, and that is that the primary purpose of the credit union is to prove the practicality of the brotherhood of man," he wrote at the end of his formal association with the organized movement. He and other credit union publicists have long rejoiced in noting, "The credit union as we know it owes its development primarily to three men—a Protestant [Raiffeisen] a Catholic [Desjardins] and a Jew [Filene]."

Bergengren's immediate concerns upon assuming leadership of MCUA were pressing and precise. MCUA lacked adequate funding, effective structure and active community support. In fact, Bergengren actually assumed responsibility for liquidating MCUA rather than expanding it. The activities of MCUA would be taken over by a new organization, the Massachusettes Credit Union League, headed by Frederick Cox as president and Frances B. Habern as *de facto* league manager.

Bergengren was offered a job in the personnel department of a large manufacturing department, but Filene was not about to lose him. Instead, the financier decided to make one more commitment to the credit union movement. Despite the

Roy Bergengren, executive director of the Credit Union National Extension Bureau, helped organize the Pennsylvania Credit Union League in 1934.

failures of the Filene-financed Massachusetts Credit Union, MCUA, and the short-lived National Committee on People's Banks, Filene was willing to try again. He would finance a new organization that would be headed by Bergengren. It would be called the Credit Union National Extension Bureau [CUNEB].

The Massachusetts Credit Union League [MCUL] continued to be the official credit union association. CUNEB was little more than an informal partnership that Filene and Bergengren had formed to promote credit union organization throughout the country. Habern worked for both MCUL and CUNEB, and the two organizations also shared an office and a typewriter.

The contemporary American credit union movement was created by Bergengren, Filene, and CUNEB. Without Filene's vision and financial support, there would have been little more than a handful of isolated credit unions scattered throughout New England. Without Bergengren's work, there would have been only a series of abortive efforts to generate national interest. Within its first year, however, CUNEB organized credit unions in South Carolina where the law created through the efforts of John Sprunt Hill had lain unused; obtained a general law in New Hampshire; achieved a special charter in Rhode Island, passed credit union laws in Kentucky and Virginia, and established preliminary contacts in numerous other states including Pennsylvania.

Most state legislatures met only in odd-numbered years at the time, and 1923 was the first full legislative year for CUNEB. On the surface, it was not overly successful. There were only three important legislative victories: Tennessee and Indiana passed general laws and Wisconsin passed a new credit union act. Credit union associations were forming in other states; people throughout the nation were learning about credit unions; and new credit union leaders were joining the movement.

The progress was sufficient to keep Filene's interest alive. The financier kept purse-strings tight and Bergengren's sal-

Agnes Gartland, an associate of Roy Bergengren, played a critical role in the administration of the early credit union movement in the United States.

ary lower than the latter thought he merited. Filene did make enough money available to keep the effort going. Financing the credit union movement in a style to which he would like to become accustomed remained Bergengren's most elusive goal.

Obtaining credit union laws in state after state would prove to be Bergengren's most successful achievement. By the end of 1925, CUNEB had won legislative campaigns in Illinois, Iowa, Minnesota, Michigan, Georgia and West Virginia in addition to previous victories.

CUNEB experienced defeats, too. Bergengren was bitterly disappointed by the rejection in Ohio; he was somewhat more understanding of the refusal in Pennsylvania. He did not know it at the time, but Ohio and Pennsylvania would become two of the most difficult, and, eventually, two of the largest credit union states in the nation. Ohio finally passed a law in 1931 due in large part to support by such Buckeye leaders as L. B. Palmer (president of the Ohio Farm Bureau

66

Federation) along with other influential state citizens. The Pennsylvania state law would not come until 1933, and then only after a bitter and long legislative battle.[9]

By 1925, Filene and Bergengren had succeeded in establishing the credit union movement as a vital part of the thrift industry in the United States. There was continuing opposition in many states and at the national level, and the crtedit union concept still lacked sharp definition; their work was far from done. But the foundations were solid and the basic mission had been completed.

By then the credit union movement had been stirring in Pennsylvania for some time. And while the Keystone State as yet had no credit union law, several proposals had been submitted to the legislature. Furthermore, despite the lack of enabling legislation, a few hardy groups were already providing their members with credit union service.

9. There was a different problem in the state of Washington, where the legislature consistently passed credit union acts, and the governor equally consistently vetoed them. Finally, the governor was defeated at the polls, and in 1933 Washington, too, joined the credit union family.

III

The Pennsylvania Prelude

"There is an excellent credit union in Reading, Pennsylvania, despite the fact that there is no law governing its operations."

Roy F. Bergengren, 1922

I T IS DIFFICULT TO SPEAK of a single, unified Pennsylvania credit union movement. The credit union movement in the Keystone State, while always operating with unified dedication and single purpose, is more of a collective than a precise unit. Each section of the state reacted differently to the idea of credit unions; each region has continued to function in its own way. A remarkable virtue of the credit union movement is that it could tolerate such internal friction without flying apart.

If we are to appreciate the complex reception that the credit union philosophy received in Pennsylvania, it is critical to understand the Commonwealth's European antecedents and the ways they vary in its different regions. Just as the credit union movement itself is European in origin, so too are most of Pennsylvania's population groups, all of whom draw their intellectual heritage from diverse backgrounds. Recognition of that diversity is critical to an understanding of the unique history of the Pennsylvania credit union movement.

Philadelphia and the eastern counties drew their original settlers primarily from the British Isles. Quakers, Anglicans, Scotch-Irish, and other white, Anglo-Saxon, primarily Protestant groups provided the first effective settlement. Later Philadelphia became home to Irish Catholic immigrants, refugees of the great potato famine that struck Ireland in the mid-1840s. In the late 19th and early 20th centuries, the city attracted immigrants from Italy, Greece, Poland, Hungary, and other nations of Eastern Europe.

Central Pennsylvania was originally settled somewhat later than the East, and in a series of entangled patterns. Central Pennsylvania has no single dominant city such as Philadelphia in the East or Pittsburgh in the West. Rather it is a collection of sub-regions, each centering on its own city. Some of the more important Central Pennsylvania cities include Allentown, Reading, Harrisburg (the state capital), Lancaster, Scranton/Wilkes-Barre, and York.

Central Pennsylvania is not truly a single region of its own, but a cluster of regions. Harrisburg, Lancaster, and York provide urban centers for the rich agricultural districts of the region. They were originally populated by English, Scotch-Irish, and eighteenth-century German immigrants. The Protestant religious sects are the most numerous.

The North-Central section (Scranton/Wilkes-Barre) experienced its most rapid growth with the development of the mining industry in the latter nineteenth century. Its people are primarily Irish or the later German immigrants. Many are also descendants of still later Eastern European immigrants. The Catholic church is the most important religious influence in the region.

The industrial centers of Reading, Allentown and York present the most intricate population picture. Continually evolving and shifting industries attracting labor pools at different times have created remarkably diverse populations. These cities have a powerful trade union presence and are the most politically radical areas of the state. Their populations are drawn from diverse ethnic groups and nations of origin. In addition, many residents have come to these areas from other parts of the United States.

Northwest Pennsylvania focuses on Erie. The region has a long and distinguised history. It is a major inland port that attracted diverse population largely because of its location as a terminus of the Erie Canal. Its population, originally French, defies generalization or categorization. There is a strong Catholic presence dating back to the city's origins as a French port, but other religious groups are also influential. The economy of the region is dominated by shipping and industry.

Western Pennsylvania is dominated by Pittsburgh and Allegheny County. The Fort Pitt frontier region was settled early by westward-moving Protestant pioneers. Later migrations produced a new, primarily Catholic population. As Western Pennsylvania's coal mines opened, they became magnets for a new labor force from Eastern Europe. Then, as steel furnaces and other heavy industries developed around the region's wealth of vital raw materials, Pittsburgh became a popular destination for laborers and others seeking economic opportunity.

They came from many other states and included Blacks, Italians, Irish and Eastern Europeans. Each group added its own particular cultural influence to the turbulence of a city and region experiencing massive industrial development. Western Pennsylvania would have none of the bucolic idealism that had marked William Penn's original dream. It was settled by people who came not in search of streets paved with gold, but by people seeking jobs paving the streets, digging the mines, and stoking the furnaces.

Thus, the main divisions of the Keystone State hold distinct populations. The credit union movement, to succeed in Pennsylvania, had to appeal to all of them. The diversity presented a major challenge of turning natural internal rivalry into cooperation. That challenge was never fully met. Regional, religious, and socio-economic rivalries have played a significant role in Pennsylvania credit union history.

This demographic/historical diversity plays a major role in virtually all Pennsylvania political affairs. The state is divided into the spheres of influence of its two major cities and the unfocused center zone. It is split into industrial factions and agricultural interests. It divides into small municipalities and rural populations which see themselves opposed to the domination of the big cities. And it presents the constant threat of unspoken but omnipresent religious and ethnic fragmentation. One wonders not why Pennsylvania proved a difficult state to organize, but how it was possible to organize the Keystone State at all.

In another respect it is remarkable that the effort to orga-

73

nize a credit union movement in Pennsylvania proved so difficult, for in some ways the state and some of its leaders were well ahead of themselves. In 1893 Pennsylvania passed a law which many historians regard as the first credit union act in America. This effort pre-dated the work of Desjardins. It did not even draw on the collective experience of the European credit union movement, but seems to have been inspired by other cooperatives. The organizations it enabled and created were similar to credit unions primarily because they were cooperative credit associations.

The 1893 Pennsylvania law was "An Act to encourage and authorize the formation of cooperative banking associations where the profits derived from the business, after paying all legitimate expenses, shall accrue to the depositors and borrowers of the association in proportion to their deposits or loans. Act No. 50, Session of 1893." Thus it created organizations that were somewhere between mutual savings associations and credit unions as we know them. These "cooperative banking associations" were denied the use of the names "society" or "company" by the law, distinguishing them from other, more traditional, business firms. Their main functions and operations were only vaguely defined.[1]

The existence of the 1893 cooperative banking society law provides some significant indications. It tells us first that there was early interest in cooperative credit in the Commonwealth. And it tells us that in 1893, little effort was required to pass the law. The Pennsylvania Credit Union Act would take ten years of lobbying and the powerful, concerted efforts of many people before it would receive legislative approval.

The "cooperative banking associations" operated with lim-

---

1. CUNA historical librarian Burns has done extensive work on this law, presenting his findings in the December, 1973 *Credit Union Magazine*. The law was introduced by Rep. Robert C. McMaster and Sen. Samuel James Logan, both of Crawford County in Northwest Pennsylvania. Neither had any clear knowledge of the principles and philosophy of the credit union movement, and there is nothing to indicate that either knew of the European precedents for their plan.

ited liability (as Desjardins would later insist on), but only to *twice* the value of shares held. This was rapidly becoming the popular European practice. Nowhere else in credit union history, tradition, or folklore is there a more apparent compromise between the demands of the traditionalist's insistence on unlimited liability and the revisionist's support of limited liability. A similar compromise is apparent in the law's outline of the association's governing procedures. Control was democratic and left to the owner/members, but voting power was determined by the number of shares held, a distinct violation of traditional cooperative practice.

The first association to be formed under the law, the Farmers' Cooperative Banking Association, was incorporated in 1895. While it was incorporated, however, no bylaws were ever filed and it probably never opened for business. The second association was the First Northern Colored Cooperative Banking Association of Philadelphia, chartered in 1901. It was dissolved by court decree six years later. Next came the Business Men's Cooperative Banking Association of Philadelphia, chartered in 1905 only to disappear from the Banking Commissioner's Annual Report and presumably from existance. The fourth and last association chartered under the 1893 law was the Italian Cooperative Banking Association of Philadelphia, formed in December of 1907. Of the four, it was the only successful association. But in 1916 it abandoned its roots and converted its charter to become a bank of discount and deposit.

Small though this group of associations was, it portended one development significant to later Pennsylvania credit union history. There were four groups—one rural/agricultural, one Black, one Italian, and one a commercial venture. Here were Desjardins' yet-to-be philosophical compromises already in practical application. Designed by its rural sponsors primarily for use by farmers, the law was being adopted by urban ethnic groups. Here, too, was a group of ambitious businessmen seeking ways to alter the cooperative concept to produce a profit-making financial institution while avoiding the restrictions of Pennsylvania banking law.

Most significant, early interest in credit unions by Pennsylvanians came from ethnic minority groups. This was never a focus of the European credit union movement, for European populations were more homogeneous. Spontaneously and apparently without extensive, external direction, these minority communities in Pennsylvania perceived that cooperative credit offered a chance for financial security to those denied service by traditional banking institutions.

In later years, when the credit union movement was frustrated in its attempts to move into Pennsylvania, the quasi-cooperative "mutual" savings and loan associations would prove attractive alternatives for Pennsylvania's ethnic minorities. As early as 1893 these prototype credit unions were available to provide important financial opportunities to Blacks, Orientals, Italians, Germans, Jews, or other minority groups denied service by established financial powers.

New York banking commissioner Pierre Jay, the man who played so large a role in early United States credit union history, knew of the Pennsylvania experiment and disapproved of it. He thought the law ill considered and ill drawn. He questioned "the wisdom of getting people who do not know much about the subject and without any state regulation or supervision to guide them." In this evaluation, Jay clearly recognized the greatest weakness of the 1893 act. In retrospect, it is likely that he identified the primary reason that the act proved to be a failure.

That is not sufficient reason to discard this early Pennsylvania experience as irrelevant to subsequent credit union history. We would do well to remember that New Hampshire, while chartering St. Mary's credit union in 1909, refused to pass a general law, that the Massachusetts and New York laws were full of major problems, and that the pioneering South Carolina law was not actually functional for many years after its adoption. In this respect, the Pennsylvania experience was no less credible than that of other states.

Pennsylvania and its legislative pioneers, McMaster and

Logan, deserve a prominent place in the early history of the American credit union movement.

Pennsylvania also played an important role in early credit union history through the work of Gifford Pinchot. Pinchot was an early agricultural cooperative activist who led important early 20th century efforts to organize national and international agricultural cooperatives. His friends and associates included Presidents William Howard Taft and Theodore Roosevelt. A leading Progressive, pioneering conservationist, former chief forester of the United States and twice governor of Pennsylvania, Pinchot was a powerful and popular figure in the state.

David Lubin, the California merchant, credit union publicist, and United States delegate to the International Institute of Agriculture in Rome, may have provided Pinchot's first knowledge of the credit union movement. In October 1910, Lubin wrote to Pinchot suggesting strongly that Pinchot interest himself in the activities of the "Raiffeisen banks."

Pinchot was also guided towards the credit union idea by Dr. Charles McCarthy, the progressive librarian of the Legislative Reference Bureau in Wisconsin. McCarthy's friends and correspondents included U.S. Secretary of Agriculture James Wilson, attorney and later Supreme Court Justice Louis D. Brandeis, Senator George W. Norris, and Ohio Governor, banker, and statesman Myron T. Herrick. McCarthy was introduced to Pinchot by University of Wisconsin President C. R. Van Hise. In 1910, McCarthy introduced Pinchot to Sir Horace Plunkett, leader of the Irish agricultural cooperative movement.

McCarthy admired Henry Wolff and his book, *People's Banks*. He distributed copies to any of his friends he thought might be interested, doubtless including Gifford Pinchot. Thus the ideas of Wolff, already so influential with Desjardins, now found their way directly to Pennsylvania through the still growing career of Pinchot.

In 1912, McCarthy organized a meeting of Pinchot with William Draper Lewis, dean of the law school at the Univer-

77

sity of Pennsylvania, and the University of Wisconsin's famed labor historian John R. Commons.[2] The meeting was called to work on the 1912 Progressive Party platform for the coming national elections, yet ironically its importance to the credit union movement was probably far greater than its effect on the Progressive Party.

The meeting thus served the special purpose of introducing influential new members to the growing network of progressive credit union supporters. Yet this same network was partially responsible for the political caution with which Pinchot, whose political aspirations were dominated by his ambition to occupy the the White House, approached all issues involving cooperation.

In late 1913, McCarthy cautioned Pinchot that:

> "the word 'cooperation' has a black eye in America.... If I begin to talk about cooperation, immediately they [business persons and professionals] think of something which is a jumble of politics and unscientific quasi-organizations which are always blended with failure. Of course the only way the thing can be worked out is through cooperation, but I really must use the term very sparingly [in Wisconsin]."

This warning may account for Pinchot's later wariness when dealing with the credit union movement.

It is clear from his correspondence that Pinchot advocated cooperatives as a way to strengthen the rural economy and improve the rural lifestyle, an issue dear to his heart. He supported the rural electric cooperative movement, and not only was he knowledgeable about credit unions, he was a close friend of some of the credit union movement's staunchest advocates. Yet Pinchot's career shows little evidence of active, direct support of the credit union movement.

2. Commons would later play an important role in credit union development when he succeeded in persuading the Wisconsin legislature to provide for the state's hiring a fulltime organizer as part of its credit union law. Bergengren later awarded Commons the highest praise. Commons was, wrote Bergengren in *Crusade*, "a *practical* economist."

Pinchot's pro-credit union sympathies were known to Roy Bergengren when he approached Pinchot in 1924 with a request that the then first-term governor of Pennsylvania accept appointment to the national advisory board of the Credit Union National Extension Bureau [CUNEB]:

'We are very anxious to give the movement a greater national significance and are forming a National Advisory Council primarily for that purpose. We also feel from time to time the need of the right sort of direction in connection with work in various states, and we are therefore asking the prospective members of the Council to do nothing more than to give the movement national significance by their association with it, and to assure us the right sort of help in your state, for example, when a credit union law is pending.

"Members of the Council will not be asked to contribute money but from time to time will be asked to advise with us as to the best way and manner of making progress within their respective states, and to permit the use of their names as members of the Council on our stationery."

Other Pennsylvanians contacted by Bergengren at the same time included: Royal Meeker, commissioner of labor; William Disston, Philadelphia industrialist; and Herbert J. Tilly, general manager of Strawbridge & Clothier in Philadelphia. Pinchot accepted Bergengren's invitation, "on the conditions suggested in your letter." So too did Meeker and Disston.[3]

Pinchot allowed his name to be listed on the CUNEB letter-

3. The letter went to 130 prominent Americans. A few later became deeply involved in credit union work. Some of those who received this letter included: Lubin and Leo Shapiro in California; Louis Brehm of the Postmaster General's office in Washington, D.C.; Joseph Defrees in Illinois and Leo Kaminsky in Indiana; William J. Hutchins, president of Kentucky's Berea College; Progressive journalist and Woodrow Wilson biographer Ray Stannard Baker in Massachusetts; Pierre Jay at the Federal Reserve Bank in New York and John Sprunt Hill, president of the Durham Loan & Trust Company of Durham, N.C.; Newton D. Baker of Cleveland and Murray D. Lincoln at the Ohio State Farm Bureau Federation among many national friends of the movement.

head. He began receiving copies of *The Bridge* on a regular basis, each accompanied by a brief note from Roy Bergengren or Bergengren's associate, Agnes C. Gartland. These mailings started with the first issue of *The Bridge*, published in June 1924. It was his first public support of the credit union movement. Ten years later it would be Gifford Pinchot, then in his second term as governor, who signed the Pennsylvania Credit Union Act into Law.

In the meantime, and in the finest traditions of the credit union movement—following the lead of Schulze-Delitzsch, Raiffeisen, Desjardins, and others—Pennsylvania credit union pioneers did not bother to wait for enabling legislation before beginning to create credit unions. The idea was taking root throughout the United States. Labor leaders, cooperative associations, the Grange, the Farm Bureau, and other organizations were already interested in possible applications of the credit union idea in Pennsylvania well before even the first attempt to pass a state law in 1923.

The first known modern Pennsylvania credit union-like organizations in Pennsylvania were both already operating in 1921. One was a part of the general cooperative activities of an organization called the Berks County, Pennsylvania Cooperators. According to the journal *Cooperation*, that group held assets of $22,000. The other was the Workers' Credit Union of Berks County, based in Reading. The same journal reports that this credit union—the first true credit union in Pennsylvania, "started with $70.00 capital and by the end of the first six weeks had $1,050 capital paid in. It had out loans amounting to $860, used to pay off loan sharks, save an increase in the price of land to a member by prompt payment on it, buy 50 barrels of flour for a co-operative bakery at a substantial saving, etc."

Word of that credit union and its activities spread to the CUNEB offices in Boston. In *Cooperative Banking*, a book written by Bergengren in 1922, Bergengren refers to "an excellent credit union operating in Reading, Pennsylvania, despite the fact that there is no law governing its operations." As a lawyer, Bergengren saw his major task as securing credit union laws. It is quite in character that he would have been both impressed by the activities of the Workers' Credit Union of Berks County and upset by the absence of enabling legislation.

The subsequent fate of this pioneer Pennsylvania credit union is lost in history. A 1926 publication, *Monthly Labor Review*, discussing loans for small borrowers, identifies a Pennsylvania credit union with 325 members and $89,800 in assets. This may have been the Workers' Credit Union or a newcomer. A 1930 edition of the same journal published an article on the "Credit Union Movement in the United States" which makes note of two credit unions in Pennsylvania, but does not identify them further. Even more troubling is their disappearance from the following year's report. By then, Reading, Erie, Bradford, and McKeesport all had postal credit unions in operation, yet the journal mentions no Pennsylvania credit unions. Workers' Credit Union may have ceased operations or simply stopped filling out forms and refused to report their activities to the journal.

By now Pennsylvania was deep in the Great Depression. The industrial areas of the Keystone State, and especially Reading, Allentown, York, and Pittsburgh, were among the nation's most severely affected. By 1931, Pennsylvania unemployment was nearing 25%. By 1933, almost one-third of the state's labor force was out of work. Ironically, it was in the midst of this financial disaster that the Pennsylvania credit union movement first began to show real strength.

Florence Parker, a leading chronicler of the American cooperative movement, has identified several early Pennsylvania credit unions. Writing on the "Operations of Cooperative Credit Societies in 1933" for the *Monthly Labor Review*, Parker enumerated several early credit unions, unfortunately without specific identification.

Her charts indicate knowledge of one Pennsylvania credit union in 1925 [Reading Workers' Credit Union], two in 1929 [probably Reading Workers' and Reading Postal Employees], five in 1932 [possibly all postal employees credit unions], and 23 functioning in 1933.[4] Another mention notes that "of the nine Pennsylvania credit unions reporting in 1933, there were a total of 914 members with average deposits of $26 per member."

During 1928, Bergengren had broadcast a series of radio talks about credit unions throughout the United States. He carefully noted responses received as indications of interest and potential support. A map charting responses showed extensive interest from the Commonwealth. One letter came from Erdenheim, Pennsylvania. "I had the pleasure of listening last night over the radio to your wonderful talk on credit unions," wrote the listener. To Bergengren, this letter was a welcome sign that his efforts were bearing fruit in the Keystone State.

The early, pre-law era of Pennsylvania credit unionism attracted substantial attention from Bergengren, who recognized that organizing Pennsylvania could well be the key to constructing a viable national movement. A 1930 issue of *The Bridge* noted the organization of the McKeesport Postal Employees Credit Union under the presidency of John R. Hamlin.

Bergengren took the occasion to comment on the activities in Pennsylvania. "While there is no credit union law as yet in Pennsylvania it is a fact that we have more credit union inquiries from that state than from any other, and the few credit unions unofficially organized in the postal service in Pennsylvania prove the need for the credit union and the potential service which the credit union has to render in that state."

On a national level, creation of the postal employees credit

4. By 1933 the Pennsylvania law was in effect, accounting ro this sudden increase in credit union organization. Parker identifies 495 borrowers in 1933, with a total of $22,141 in loans outstanding at the end of the year. She reports that report that one cooperative credit society had a loss through bad debts of $13.00. It was the first recorded bad loan ever reported by a Pennsylvania credit union.

unions began early. The first was organized in Brockton, Massachusetts in 1923 and, by mid 1925, there were more than 30. By October 1927, the 83 postal employees credit unions in operation had combined assets of more than $1 million. At the end of 1928 there were almost 200 postal employees credit unions in states which had credit union laws, none in Pennsylvania. The Reading, Erie, and McKeesport postal employees credit unions were the first to be set up in a state which had not passed a credit union law.

Organization of postal employees credit unions was primarily the work of the Post Office's Department of Service Relations, directed first by Henry Dennison, later by Louis Brehm. That federal officials would accept responsibility for organizing credit unions in a state without enabling legislation was a courageous act. Brehm deserves a special place in Pennsylvania credit union history for bureaucratic bravery above and beyond the call of duty. He helped create the Pennsylvania credit union movement even as its legislature was actively resisting attempts to work along traditional and legal lines.

Perhaps to further the Pennsylvania campaign, *The Bridge*, in its Christmas 1930 issue, published a picture of the entire board of directors of the new McKeesport Postal Employees Credit Union. It provides us with an important list of early Pennsylvania credit union leaders. The board included Hamlin, Otto Herklotz, A. L. Jackel, William Kniecamp, Edgar Thomas, C. M. Blend, and Rudy Goetz. Herklotz and Goetz would go on to have distinguished careers as members of the board of the directors of the Pennsylvania Credit Union League. They, along with Lawrence Hardman of Erie, are among the few identified leaders of pre-law credit unions whose volunteer efforts continued to include extensive involvement with League activities.

The McKeesport Postal Employees Credit Union does not, however, have legitimate claim to being the first of its type in the state. The Erie Postal Employees organized their credit union in May 1930, two months before their colleagues in

McKeesport. And they were both preceded by the Reading Postal Employees Credit Union which was functioning by August 1929, and may have been organized even earlier.

One list of credit unions organized either by Roy Bergengren personally or by his Credit Union National Extension Bureau—all prior to the Pennsylvania Credit Union Law —includes the following:

1929   Reading Postal Employees Credit Union
1930   Allentown Teachers Credit Union
        Bradford Postal Employees Credit Union
        Pennsylvania State Employees Credit Union
        Philadelphia Post Office Employees Credit Union
        McKeesport Postal Employees Credit Union
1931   None
1932   Teachers Credit Union of Greater Philadelphia
1933   Lancaster Postal Employees Credit Union

In addition, the following credit unions, all well on their way to organizing without benefit of law, when the Pennsylvania law was finally passed, were organized by Bergengren in 1933. They were the first to take advantage of the state law.

Armour Philadelphia Employees Credit Union
Armour Pittsburgh Employees Credit Union
Armour Wilkes-Barre Employees Credit Union
Building & Needle Trade Workers Credit Union
Carbon County Teachers Credit Union
Dill and Collins Employees Credit Union
Ingram Employees Credit Union

To Building & Needle Trade Workers Credit Union goes the distinction of being the first legally organized credit union in the state. It holds Pennsylvania Charter No. 1.

Bergengren would eventually forget the early, ill-fated attempts to pass a credit union law in Pennsylvania. Actually, he and CUNEB had little to do with them, other than providing information, encouragement and a model law. Formal attempts to pass a Pennsylvania credit union law had begun in

Credit unions were formed by postal employees in several Pennsylvania communities even before the state passed a credit union act. This group is from McKeesport Postal Credit Union shown here in the mid-1950s.

1922, even before Bergengren began publishing *The Bridge*. In a March 1922 memorandum concerning proposed "ENLARGEMENT OF FUNCTIONS OF THE CREDIT UNION NATIONAL EXTENSION BUREAU," Bergengren wrote that "the big job really starts with the 1923 session [of state legislatures]. Preliminary work has been done already in the following states, leading to action in the legislatures of next year." The appended list included Pennsylvania, along with 16 other states.

An April 1923 report on CUNEB activities mentions that "we are cooperating with credit union bills pending in Michigan and Pennsylvania." CUNEB published a model law that year, and most of its features were incorporated verbatim in the bill submitted to the 1923 legislature on behalf of a group of industrial union leaders. It was introduced in the House by Repre-

85

sentative Dunn on March 7, was referred to the Committee on Banks and Banking on March 12, and was never seen again.

This first proposed Pennsylvania credit union law would have enabled incorporation of "credit union association instituted and organized for the purpose of accumulating and investing the savings of . . . members and making loans to members for provident purposes." It required that the name of the association include the words "credit union," limited the par value of shares to $10.00, and placed the new associations under the supervision of the Department of Banking. It allowed for two classes of member investment: deposits and shares. It provided for deposits by nonmembers. It also allowed credit unions to purchase shares in each other and other thrift institutions, but mandated that "the funds of the credit union shall be used first...for loans to members and preference shall be given to the smaller loan in the event the available funds do not permit all loans which have passed the credit committee to be made."

Other provisions included the legislation's definition of "members," which included associations, partnerships, and corporations as well as persons. It placed no restrictions on membership, made no provision for a common bond. It gave the credit union an automatic lien against all shares held by a member and all dividends due a member to the extent of any outstanding loans. Following the lead of Wisconsin, the bill attempted to make the state itself responsible for organizing credit unions and for maintaining "an educational campaign in the State looking to the promotion and organization of credit unions." It even mandated that the state supply all forms needed for information, organization, and incorporation.

Other elements of this initial Pennsylvania credit union bill were more familiar. It placed credit union governance in the hands of an elected board of directors (who could not be paid for their services) and provided for the traditional officers, a credit committee, and a supervisory and audit committee. Interest was limited to 1% per month as an absolute maximum. The bill mandated that 20% of annual income be set aside in a reserve fund until that fund contain an amount equal to 100% of "paid in capital" of the credit union. This would have required that shareholdings (as distinct from deposits) be secured in full by the reserve fund!

In some ways, this was an unfortunate start and reflects the disarray of the Pennsylvania credit union forces. While financially conservative, the bill was clearly excessive in other directions. The powerful banking interests of the Commonwealth were not about to permit the state to take responsibility for organizing credit unions. And a membership policy that neither required a common bond nor limited membership to natural persons was bound to offend not only the opponents of the credit union movement, but many supporters as well.

This bill conformed to most of the legislative directives produced by CUNEB. Bergengren produced extensive materials for the benefit of people drafting proposed credit union laws. They promulgated a series of guidelines which provide useful insight into his expectations and priorities:

> "1. The expense of organization must be small.... Keep the initial expense down!
>
> "2. No appreciable paid-up capital stock should be required in advance of organization. Credit unions start with a few dollars.
>
> "3. If possible the law should contain a provision fixing the responsibility on some State official to see to it that those who need the law know of its existence.
>
> "Successful credit union laws are based on the credit union laws now in operation in Massachusetts and North Carolina. The Massachusetts credit unions are urban credit unions of wage-workers; the North Carolina credit unions are composed of small farmers. The draft of a proposed law attached is designed to make possible credit unions of both types."

The 1923 Pennsylvania bill was submitted without the kind of close coordination by CUNEB that would typify later legislative campaigns, but its provisions and language were based on Bergengren's model. While they accepted guidance at least to that extent, the bill's sponsors refused further advice and counsel from CUNEB.

The CUNEB report of April 14, 1923 noted that "we are cooperating with credit union bills pending in Michigan and Pennsylvania. Unfortunately, the Pennsylvania bill originated with a radical group and has aroused violent opposition from the banks and the bank commissioner [Peter Cameron]."

Bergengren expanded on this in his October 18, 1923 report: "In Pennsylvania the American Federation of Labor made an ill-advised attempt to secure legislation which was defeated by the active opposition of the bank commissioner, Mr. Cameron. When appealed to, we did what we could to help."

The active sponsorship and support of the bill by Pennsylvania's trade union movement attracted virtually automatic opposition from the Pennsylvania Railroad and from the steel and coal industries. It is doubtful that any bill could have passed the Pennsylvania legislature during the 1920s over the concerted efforts of that extraordinarily influential group.

The 1923 attempt to pass a Pennsylvania credit union law was doomed from the start. Bergengren's CUNEB report of April 4, 1924, noted that Pennsylvania's Governor Pinchot was on CUNEB's National Advisory Committee and that a local committee was being organized in Pennsylvania as well as other states to take charge of the campaign and prepare for 1925.

In Pennsylvania that committee was headed by H. Andrew Hanemann, who thus began his personal ten-year legislative effort for the credit union movement.

The Pennsylvania Legislature remained unsympathetic to the credit union concept. It turned down the bill in 1925 as quickly as it had in the previous session. The bill never emerged from its first test in the House Banking Committee. At CUNEB headquarters in Boston, Bergengren was becoming impatient. In a January 1926 internal memorandum, he let his frustrations show.

88

H. Andrew Hanemann, early leader of the Pennsylvania Credit Union Committee, founded the Pennsylvania State Employees Credit Union.

"A federal law would be valuable ... to enable us to organize credit unions in backward states (Pennsylvania, Maryland, Connecticut, Vermont, where legislators are either hopelessly reactionary or too much boss-controlled) where state legislation will always be difficult." But the time had not yet come for Bergengren to seek a federal credit union law, and the 1927 Pennsylvania credit union bill met the same fate as had its predecessors.

While the credit union movement was encountering repeated defeats in Pennsylvania, the more influential general cooperative movement was preparing for its own successful legislative campaign. It gained formal legislative consent to incorporate agricultural cooperatives from the 1929 session with Act of the General Assembly No. 394. The act provided "for the incorporation and regulation of cooperative agricultural associations having capital stock." It defined agriculture as "including persons engaged in agriculture, dairying, live-

89

stock raising, poultry raising, floriculture, mushroom grow-ing, beekeeping, horticulture, and other allied occupations."

This act reflected the rural credit needs of the agricultural community, enabling formation of multi-service coopera-tives. It was sponsored by a group of Central Pennsylvania legislators, and supported by the State and National Grange, *The Pennsylvania Farmer*, and the Department of Agriculture.[5]

The success of this act could have seriously hurt the future of the Pennsylvania credit union movement. That it did not do so points out most vividly the importance of Desjardins' decision to combine the activities of the rural cooperative credit associations and the People's Banks in a single institu-tional network. The Agricultural Cooperatives Act met most of the needs of the rural community. Had its sponsors desired, the act could well have met all their credit needs as well. In fact that same coalition that had persuaded the legislature to pass the Agricultural Cooperatives Act would later prove instrumental in the successful legislative campaign for a credit union law.

Although the cooperative movement was successful in ob-taining the agricultural act in 1929, the credit union move-ment suffered yet another failure in its attempt to gain approval of a credit union law by the same session of the legislature. The 1929 campaign, like its predecessors in 1925

5. The agricultural cooperatives were empowered to sell stock (shares), to borrow money (accept deposits), and to issue notes. Their defined business activities went far beyond financial services. They were empowered to buy and sell land, crops, livestock—and the stock of other corporations engaged in buying or selling agricultural products "when such purchase and hold-ing shall be in keeping with the purposes for which the association was formed."

While granting credit to members was clearly within the powers pro-vided by the legislature, such was not intended to be a primary activity of the agricultural cooperatives. The secretary of banking was given no au-thority over the new associations. Instead, the legislation placed the cooper-atives under the supervision of the secretary of agriculture and the dean of the School of Agriculture at the Pennsylvania State College [now Univer-sity].

and 1927, was locally led by Hanemann. In addition, the 1929 effort had the active support from Bergengren and CUNEB.

Letters from Bergengren to Filene in September and December of 1928 indicated that winning a Pennsylvania law was CUNEB's top priority. Bergengren's 1929 Report to the Trustees of the Twentieth-Century Fund (the source of CUNEB's financing) included mention of the pending legislation in Pennsylvania. Bergengren knew that any optimism he may have expressed to the trustees was excessive. Peter Cameron still occupied the Pennsylvania Secretary of Banking seat, and he was still strongly opposed to the credit union concept.

Bergengren responded to this problem with an attempt to enlist the support of former governor Gifford Pinchot, then a private citizen living in Washington, D.C. In a lengthy letter, he told Pinchot of the legislation's progress to date. "The Pennsylvania bill was referred to a Committee [Banking Committee of the House].... The matter is one of new impression to Mr. Cameron, but his first reaction was that the law which you have in Pennsylvania has already solved the problem."

Such an attitude was regrettable but it says much about the real and pressing need for credit union legislation. Existing Pennsylvania law permitted licensed private lenders to charge a maximum of 3.5% interest per month on small loans, an annual percentage rate of 42%. There were 600 lenders licensed under provisions of the law.

Bergengren appealed to Pinchot's well-known sympathies of rural cooperative activities: "The bill offered this year was really at the instigation of the Third Cooperative Conference held at State College some months ago, which I was invited to address," wrote Bergengren to Pinchot. "These folks are very much interested in the development of rural credit unions." He concluded with a request that Pinchot write the secretary of banking in support of the legislation.

Apparently Pinchot's Washington interests left him no time for legislative problems back in Harrisburg. In any event, neither the records of CUNEB nor the Pinchot Papers show any response to this request.

The 1929 bill was defeated, and CUNEB immediately began work preparing for the 1931 session of the legislature. As early as December 1929, Bergengren was writing to credit union organizer Thomas W. Doig that "the only states of any real importance without credit union laws at present are Pennsylvania, Connecticut, Ohio and Washington and we have the preliminary campaigns well advanced in all of these states."

The following April, Bergengren's letter to Pinchot and the other members of CUNEB's Board of Advisors noted that there were few legislatures in session during 1930, and that CUNEB was using the year to build its organization and prepare for the legislative campaigns of 1931. Two campaigns of major importance were coming up, Connecticut and Pennsylvania. Pinchot did not reply as he was in the midst of his own campaign at the time. He was seeking reelection as governor of Pennsylvania.

By December 1930, work to pass a Pennsylvania credit union law in 1931 was in full swing. The newly elected governor Pinchot was put on notice early when he received a letter from Edward Filene. "It occurs to me that recommendation, in your annual message, of a credit union law for Pennsylvania would not only be timely, but would doubtless result in making possible credit union service, which is now proving so effective in many other states."

It is surprising that Pinchot and Filene were not better acquainted. They had several mutual friends, and numerous overlapping interests. Both Filene and Pinchot were politically active and influential in national affairs. Pinchot had been chief forester of the United States during the administration of President William Howard Taft and he was a close associate of Theodore Roosevelt. Filene was a close friend of Franklin D. Roosevelt. Both were friends and admirers of Louis Brandeis. Yet all indications are that the two had never met, and never before corresponded.

The letter from Filene served to remind Pinchot that he was still a member of the National Advisory Council of CUNEB. While the signature is Filene's the letter was actually written by Bergengren. It lacks the more polished and thoughtful Filene style; it does not even congratulate Pinchot on his recent election to a second term as governor!

A second letter from Filene to Pinchot, dated January 12, 1931, added a firmer request for support from the governor. This letter, too, was probably written for Filene by Bergengren. It informed Pinchot that Bergengren had been actively campaigning for credit union legislation in Harrisburg, "where he has been in consultation with various folks, particularly in the State Agricultural College and the State Department of Agriculture."

Filene brought Pinchot up to date on Bergengren's other activities in Pennsylvania as well, including his meetings with secretary of banking Cameron. The letter concluded with a request that Pinchot meet with Bergengren "at any time between now and the nineteenth" and consider making the credit union bill an official administration measure.

At the same time Bergengren also wrote to Pinchot under his own name. Several passages of his letter include language that is suspiciously identical to that used in the Filene letter. Bergengren also marshalled his other forces. His letter mentioned support from Penn State College, the first assistant postmaster general (postal credit unions were at the 250 mark), "railroads and large public service corporations, nationally developed industrial units, etc. which include Pennsylvania units, where credit union organization would be of great service."

Pinchot quickly responded to Bergengren and Filene, apologetically noting to each that their original letters had just been brought to his attention. "I have been unable to read the material you sent me but hope to reach it ere long," Pinchot wrote to Bergengren. "As a member of the National Advisory Council of the Credit Union National Extension Bureau, I am very much interested in the efforts of the Bureau to have enacted in Pennsylvania a law that will give credit union service to its citizens," he wrote to Filene.

Pinchot's political and administrative caution overruled his devotion to the cause of cooperation. He noted that banking secretary Cameron and Bergengren had met recently to draft "a satisfactory credit union bill." That legislation, wrote Pinchot, "will be presented to the Pennsylvania Legislature during the present session." No commitments, no promises were forthcoming.

Bergengren knew how to put the best face on any situation. He wrote Pinchot thanking him for his "very fine cooperative attitude towards the credit union law in the current session of the Pennsylvania Legislature." He enthusiastically reported to the governor that CUNEB and secretary Cameron had worked out a bill that would be introduced in the Senate by Senator Leon Prince of Carlisle "who is thoroughly convinced of the value of this legislation," and in the House by Representative Rhodes of McKeesport.

In his February 20 letter to the Governor, Bergengren took note of the coalition that would eventually be responsible for passing Pennsylvania credit union legislation. "In addition to a rapidly developing interest in credit unions on the part of urban groups of wage workers," he wrote, "during the past year the major rural organizations have increasingly come to appreciate the value of rural cooperative credit. I feel convinced that in the event the Pennsylvania bill is enacted, it will be utilized by both urban and rural groups, and prove of very great value."

The two bills, Senate Bill 160 and House Bill 536, were filed separately. Bergengren wrote the governor again in late April, enclosing a copy of his *Cooperative Banking*, published in 1923. The governor thanked him for the gift, noted that the press of state business was such that he had no time to read the book, and assured Bergengren that "if the bills you mention are passed by the Legislature and come to me for my approval they shall have my most serious consideration." Again no promises, nocommitments were forthcoming.

Bergengren was optimistic about the 1931 Pennsylvania campaign. He expected the bills to pass, expected the governor to sign them, expected to be able to add Pennsylvania to his trophy cabinet. But Pennsylvania politics is a complex art, and Bergengren had not done his homework. He had inadequate support from the East, and the credit union movement was still attracting opposition from the mining and steel interests, groups which confused labor unions with credit unions.

By May, Bergengren was relearning the realities of Pennsylvania politics. He became aware of the concerted and well-financed attacks from the small loan companies. This was not an unusual situation. Credit union legislation had faced such opposition in virtually every state. But Bergengren was becoming increasingly irritated at another problem unique to the Commonwealth. "The greater difficulty in Pennsylvania," he wrote to the governor, "is to develop enough drive behind the bill to get it out of Committee and before the House, where I am convinced there is a favorable majority.

At the end of the month, Bergengren was still mildly optimistic about the Pennsylvania situation. He had made the Keystone State his top priority. "The only important states remaining, from a population viewpoint, are Pennsylvania and Connecticut," he wrote in a report to Filene. "Pennsylvania contains one-half of all the people now living outside of credit union territory."

The 1931 Pennsylvania credit union bill eventually gained approval by the House Banking Committee and by the full House. The bill stalled in the Senate Banking Committee (and approval by the full Senate appeared to be unlikely). As the end of the session neared, Bergengren realized that he was facing a major legislative defeat. He turned one last time to the governor for help. "The difficulty seems to be that while many folks want credit unions in Pennsylvania, no one seems to want the credit union badly enough to make a determined fight for it."

Writing to Filene, Bergengren was less philosophical and more realistic. "For the first time we got a bill through the Pennsylvania House of Representatives, only to lose it in the Senate from the opposition of the Russell Sage 42% lenders."

Bergengren was understandably bitter. The reform work of the Russell Sage Foundation had succeeded in licensing and regulating small lenders. The legislation passed in the name of reform still allowed charges of 3.5% interest per month while defusing demands for lower-rate sources of credit such as credit unions.

In the legislative session of 1933, that situation would change. A powerful coalition assembled by Bergengren and others would take charge of the credit union bill. With the help of Pennsylvania leaders from business, industry, agriculture and labor; with the assistance and encouragement of an association of 53 citizens from across the Commonwealth; the legislature and governor would finally approve the Pennsylvania Credit Union Act.

IV

The Campaign for a State Law

"Passage of the years has thinned the ranks of the men and women who led the fight for credit union legislation in most of the states and it may be that the present day leaders of the movement have forgotten, if they ever knew, the story of the struggle which the Extension Bureau faced."

Claude Orchard, 1963

THE TELEGRAM ARRIVED in the late afternoon of May 25, 1933. To Roy Bergengren, managing director of the Credit Union National Extension Bureau, it contained most welcome news. "BILL SIGNED TODAY" it said. "FULL SPEED AHEAD." Datelined Harrisburg and signed by Anthony Smith, an assistant to Pennsylvania Governor Gifford Pinchot, the telegram informed Bergengren that Governor Pinchot had just signed the credit union law.

The final, ultimately successful campaign started quickly on the heels of the 1931 defeat. Bergengren felt that much of the problem in Pennsylvania lay with a lack of concerted local leadership. While H. Andrew Hanemann had been working on obtaining a Pennsylvania law since 1923, he had not been able to organize a cohesive and powerful group that could actively help in the legislative effort. That, thought Bergengren, would be rectified this time around.

With Hanemann's help, CUNEB began work to create The Credit Union Association of Pennsylvania. William S. Middleton served as secretary of the group which was headquartered at 233 Market Street in Harrisburg. Its leading members included Frank Shellhamer, Lawrence Hardman, John Hamlin and others who had previous experience in the Pennsylvania legislative wars as well as a group of new recruits.[1] By

---

1. The full list of members of this organization is as follows: Lewis S. Erickson, chairman, Harrisburg; H.E. Gayman, Harrisburg; Frank Parker, Philadelphia; H. A. Hanneman, Camp Hill; John R. Hamlin, McKeesport; R. H. Spare, Pottstown; G.R. Kreider, Jr., Lebanon; Joseph F. McCarthy, Upper Darby; Carl E. Sheldon, Bradford; A. T. Larson, Kane; Leonard W. Williams, Haverford; H. Alexander Dean, Pittsburgh; Howard J. Martin, Meadville; Rev. Joseph Schmidt, Carlisle; Carley L. Yost, Pittsburgh; John T. Jones, Wilkes-Barre; Fred H. Black, Pittsburgh; John S. Koehler, Leba-

the time the bills were actually submitted to the legislature, this group was in place to make their desires known. "The purpose of this Association is to further the enactment of a credit union law in Pennsylvania," said a line at the top of their letterhead. "We urge the enactment of House Bill 536 (Senate Bill 160) to authorize credit union organization in Pennsylvania," it repeated at the bottom.

At the beginning of the 1933 legislative season, Bergengren must have thought Pennsylvania was a lost cause. The state was in the midst of the Great Depression. The Senate Banking Committee had proven itself to be under the control of major commercial banking interests from Pittsburgh and Philadelphia. The State Banking Department was not particularly sympathetic to the credit union movement and the Pennsylvania Credit Union Association had never become effective. In more than ten years of organizing work, Bergengren had been unable to find a dynamic leader for the Pennsylvania credit union movement.

Bergengren kicked off the 1933 campaign on November 7, 1932, with a letter to Governor Pinchot. With a modesty as remarkable as it was false, Bergengren took a hurt, puzzled, almost defeated tone as he combined his request for help from the governor's office with the more typical and traditional technique of waving the credit union flag.

non; Lawrence F. Hardman, Erie; Samuel G. Parker, Philadelphia; John I. Correll, Bangor; Louis D. Anderson, Lancaster; J. O. Bearstler, Pottsville; E. E. Dilliner, Uniontown; McKinley H. Stevens, Upper Darby; Rt. Rev. Andrew Ignasiak, Erie; G. H. Younger, Philadelphia; Stephen A. Bodkin, Pittsburgh, L. B. Snedden, McKeesport; William A. Staudt, Reading; Henry J. Volz, Pittsburgh, H. L. Shank, Lancaster, John R. Devlin, Pittsburgh; Ralph K. Garrahan, Kingston; E. A. Clayton, Philadelphia; Joseph B. Arleans, Pittsburgh; Charles H. Fleming, Pittsburgh; J. M. Clark, Braddock; Marcus A. McKnight, Carlisle; Matthew Geiger, Philadelphia; M. C. Black, Allison Park; B. M. Fairchild, Lewisburg; Joseph H. Goldman, Pittsburgh; J. W. Porter, Wilkinsburg; W. E. Foye, Uniontown; Milton Miller, Pen Argyl; William J. Carson, Philadelphia; P. P. Weaver, State College; Frank Shellhamer, Harrisburg; H. M. Brooks, Pittsburgh; Daniel Reamer, Monessen.

"Pennsylvania is about the only important state left which has no law of this sort, and I am somewhat in doubt as to the wisdom of attempting further legislation in that state. We got our bill through the House during the 1931 session, but were not able to make any progress at all in the Senate. Would it, in your judgment, be a waste of energy to attempt a renewal of this effort to get a Pennsylvania credit union law in the coming session, having in mind that there are now such laws in 35 states, that the depression has emphasized in tremendous measure the need of the people for the credit union, and that the credit unions have shown an extraordinary capacity to survive the rigors of the depression. Your opinion in this matter will be greatly appreciated."

Fortunately, Pinchot did not choose to tell Bergengren to forget about organizing Pennsylvania. Instead, he turned the issue over to his young assistant, Anthony Smith. Smith was on leave from Yale Law School, assisting Governor Pinchot with his overwhelming correspondence. The governor did, however, make sure that Bergengren understood that credit union legislation would not have the administration's top priority. "Governor Pinchot has been so busy with unemployment relief matters that he has asked me to write you so that you may have an answer before too long to your courteous letter of November 7th." wrote Smith as he assumed administration responsibility for credit union activities.

Pinchot was not simply ducking the issue. Pennsylvania unemployment was the worst in the nation. The coal mines had virtually shut down. The steel mills were running at a fraction of their capacity. At the time Smith wrote to Bergengren, the situation was the worst it had ever been—and it was still worsening. Within a few months the state's economy would hit its darkest point. Franklin D. Roosevelt had just been elected President but had not yet been inaugurated. Herbert Hoover was still in the White House. Almost one-third of Pennsylvania's work force was unemployed. It is certainly understandable that the governor chose to turn a bothersome chore such as dealing with Bergengren over to his young and enthusiastic — if inexperienced — assistant.

Smith's immediate supervisor, Duncan McCallum, was a veteran politician with extensive experience as a loyal and devoted aide. Under more normal circumstances, McCallum would have taken responsibility for handling the work involved in guiding the credit union bill through the Banking Department and the legislature. But McCallum was busy. He provided what support he could, and offered substantial guidance. The task of corresponding with Bergengren and providing administration assistance to the credit union bill was the responsibility of Smith.

The credit union bill offered a major opportunity to Smith. He was sympathetic to the goals of the credit union movement and he welcomed the opportunity to serve as the administration's point man in a real legislative effort. It would be his job to coordinate the efforts of administration leaders, sponsoring legislators, and others interested in the bill.

First Smith wrote to Senator Frank J. Harris of Pittsburgh, a ranking member of the Senate Banking committee. "If, as a member of the Senate Committee on Banks and Building and Loan Associations, you can advise us what the objections to the Bill were and from whom they came, the favor will be appreciated greatly."

An identical letter went to Senator George T. Weingartner of New Castle. Weingartner's reply confirmed Bergengren's earlier assumptions: as the senator recalled, "the objection to the bill was that there was already sufficient banking facilities in Pennsylvania to cover the situation, that with our building and loan associations, savings accounts and various other accounts in banks and trust companies that there was no particular need for this kind of legislation in Pennsylvania."

In other words, the opposition of the registered small loan companies ("the Russell Sage 42% lenders") had carried the day.

Another hurdle came from the State Banking Department. Peter Cameron, the secretary of banking who had opposed every credit union bill since 1923, was gone. Friends of the credit union movement had little cause for celebration; his replacement was secretary of banking William D. Gordon and O. B. Lippman, his conservative commissioner. Neither of them was enthusiastic about credit unions. Without the support, or at least the acquiescence of Lippman and Gordon, Smith knew, the credit union bill would never make it through the Senate.

Five days later Smith was taking a more cautious line. He needed an administration sponsor and the Banking Department would not cooperate. The answer came from the roots of the credit union movement itself and from its promise of providing a source of credit to farmers and other rural Americans. Smith asked John McSparran, Pennsylvania secretary of agriculture and a long-time friend of the credit union movement, to sponsor the measure for the administration.

McSparran was an experienced politician. He was not about to take on the fight without some troops behind him. The credit union movement in Pennsylvania did not have the best reputation for being able to field an army of active supporters. McSparran asked for time to consult with leaders of the National Grange.

When informed of that development, Bergengren was quick to claim friendship with Louis J. Taber, master of the National Grange. "I addressed the Grange at two of its sessions on the subject of possible cooperation on the part of the Grange in behalf of rural credit union development," wrote Bergengren.

Apparently those meetings with the national leadership were productive despite strong opposition to the Pinchot administration by the master of the Pennsylvania Grange. McSparran was hesitant to interfere in legislation which primarily affected another department even though his own interest in the credit union movement was well established and he knew that the governor supported the credit union concept.

Senator George Weingartner, who had led Senate opposition to previous credit union bills, was no longer in office. And while the representative who had sponsored the 1931 bill in the House had lost his seat, Representative Louis Schwartz of Philadelphia had expressed interest in credit unions and a willingness to sponsor the legislation.

Secretary McSparran was the main administration champion of the bill. He became even more supportive when the State Grange elected a new master who was much more friendly to the Pinchot administration. The Banking Department, however reluctantly, was willing to go along if Bergengren and his friends would make a few changes in the bill.

Grange support gave McSparran the backing of his primary constituency. He agreed to make the credit union bills official administration measures, supported by the Department of Agriculture—if they conformed to demands from the banking department. McSparran's enthusiastic support—and Pinchot's backing—would prove extremely valuable to Smith as he worked to hold Lippman, Gordon, and other reluctant supporters in line.

Smith set up a meeting in McSparran's office, the first of several critical sessions. It included Smith, McSparran, Bergengren, Gordon, Lippman, and the attorney general. By the end of that meeting, the status of the 1933 Pennsylvania campaign was becoming clear. For the first time, it appeared that credit union legislation had a real chance of passing.

In a lengthy letter written just after Christmas 1932, Bergengren provided Smith with material to counter the objections to credit unions expressed during the mid-December meeting. The letter stresses several arguments that illuminate the fears expressed by the banking department, and perhaps by others in the state. Bergengren goes to great lengths to explain:

> "that there is nothing new, strange, radical or experimental about the credit union.
>
> 'credit union experience in the [35] states in which there are credit union laws has been uniformly successful, and there has

never been an effort to repeal such a law after it had been enacted.[2]

"that credit unions do not compete with banks, but that they are supplements to the bank system.

"that they fill a tremendous credit gap in the banking system, which when not properly bridged by credit unions leaves the masses of the people to the exactions of high-rate money lenders in time of credit necessity.

"Credit unions have value both (a) to urban groups of city wage workers , and (b) to farmers.

"If any form of banking should have yielded by now to the strain of the depression because of the intimate personal effect of the depression on its members, it should have been the credit unions.

"none of the credit unions organized by the Credit Union National Extension Bureau (at least 90% of the whole) have failed or been closed up....

"It can be proved.... that the credit unions have established the finest record during the industrial depression of any bank operating under any laws in any country at any time, under conditions of similar stress."

Two days later, Bergengren was writing directly to Pinchot. Either he was unaware that all credit union correspondence was being routed to Smith, or he simply thought it polite and politic personally to bring the governor up to date. Smith's New Year's Eve response to Bergengren's position paper was brief and chatty. The governor's January 6, 1933 response (written by Smith) was more to the point. It augured well for the new year.

"The fact that Credit Unions have stood up so well during the depression leads me to feel that Pennsylvania should join the list of states having laws which make such organizations possible.

2. Actually, West Virginia repealed its credit union law in 1931. Some rapid and fancy footwork resurrected it in short order, but Bergengren's claim involved convenient memory, not fact.

"I know that Secretary McSparran feels that we should have such a law, and I am sure the Department of Agriculture would be glad to add its influence to put it upon our statute books."

This letter marks the first time Pinchot was willing to go on the public record as supporting the Pennsylvania Credit Union Bill. As of January 6, 1933, the Pinchot administration formally adopted the Pennsylvania Credit Union Bill as an administration measure. The fight was far from over, but Bergengren was about to get substantial help from the home team.

In a memorandum dated January 6, 1933, Smith took on the Banking Department. "I am writing because I know you have no time to talk to me personally," he wrote to Secretary Gordon. "The Governor has given his approval to the plan of having the Department of Agriculture push a bill for the creation of Credit Unions. The Unions have been endorsed by the National Grange and Secretary McSparran is very favorable." The rest of the memo went on to outline the plan of action and request Gordon's presence at a conference to draft a coalition bill. Smith also wrote to Bergengren, notifying him that Schwartz would sponsor the legislation in the House for the Department of Agriculture, and requesting that CUNEB provide Schwartz with appropriate materials. Bergengren immediately wrote to Smith and Schwartz sending copies of the 1931 bill and a list of requested changes. They were needed, said Bergengren, to bring the Pennsylvania bill into conformity with general credit union practice. They included requested changes in the fee structure, examination procedure, and charter approval procedures. The governor's copy of that letter indicates that most of those requests were found unacceptable.

Previous commitments forced Bergengren to decline Smith's invitation to attend the projected meeting with McSparran and Gordon. Smith was also reluctant to involve Schwartz before Bergengren, McSparran, and Gordon had a chance to work out their own consensus bill. As a result, drafting a final edition for submission to the House was postponed. Bergengren, not informed of the delay, left for his western tour in full expectation that the bill would be filed momentarily.

As the month wore on, Agnes Gartland, Bergengren's assistant at CUNEB, became anxious about the bill. Smith was probably enjoying the unusual break from CUNEB pressure. It did not last. In Bergengren's absence, Gartland took over the typewriter. "I think the only thing we need fear is that the bill may be late getting in and will not be reached," she wrote to Smith. "Therefore I am stressing the importance of quick action in this case, and anything you can do to impress upon Mr. Schwartz the importance of getting the bill filed will be helpful." Smith wrote Gartland immediately to explain the delay. He also told her that Bergengren would be invited to participate in the final drafting of the bill and that the legislature would be in session until June.

The Pennsylvania Credit Union Bill was really created at a Harrisburg meeting of Representative Louis Schwartz, Secretary McSparran, Secretary Gordon, Commissioner Lippman, Bergengren, and Smith. The meeting, held February 20, was called by Smith on behalf of the administration. By its end, all had agreed to support a compromise bill, and the administration stood, fully unified, behind H-1131.

Schwartz had been selected by Smith to sponsor the bill in the House. A loyal and influential Republican from Philadelphia, Schwartz had supported the credit union bill during the 1931 session and was actively interested in seeing it become law this time around. Even before the meeting with Dr. Gordon, Secretary McSparran and the others, Schwartz became a major problem for Smith and Bergengren.

Representative Schwartz saw credit unions as a great money-making scheme. With only a few modifications, he wrote Bergengren, it would be possible for an individual to control a credit union and operate it most profitably. Schwartz himself was interested in opening such an operation as part of his real estate brokerage office.

While Bergengren contacted Schwartz in an attempt to explain the real mission of credit unions (while keeping his sponsorship, interest, and substantial influence behind the bill), Smith prepared fall-back positions. The Banking Department still refused to support the bill actively or to help find a new sponsor. But Secretary McSparran did offer to help if necessary, and several "railroad interests" also indicated that their support was available. Schwartz, faced with losing his sponsorship of an increasingly popular bill, concurred with Bergengren and stopped insisting on the changes.

So there was real reason behind Bergengren's rare optimistic mood as he wrote to Smith at the end of February 1933. "It seems to me that we are gradually clearing away the difficulties, and that there is a real chance for this bill," he said. But Bergengren's optimism remained tempered by long experience in Pennsylvania.

In a report to Filene and the Twentieth Century Fund, he outlined the year's goals for CUNEB, and expressed his hopes and hesitations as he discussed the coming legislative campaign in the Keystone State. "We are, as you know, concentrating this year on Pennsylvania. You know also something of the abnormal difficulties incidental to getting a credit union law enacted in that state. Right now it looks as though we have some of these difficulties ironed out, and to this effort will be given our very best efforts until it is disposed of one way or the other."

At the beginning of March, Roosevelt assumed the presidency. A frightened nation took heart as they sat close to their radios and heard his precise, paternal voice announcing that "The only thing we have to fear, is fear itself!" In March he demonstrated that he was willing to act as firmly as he spoke. To stem a growing tide of bank failures and rising panic, he temporarily closed all of the banks. With the nation's faith in its thrift institutions at its all-time nadir, Bergengren planned a trip to Harrisburg. As he reported to Filene, "If banks open up sufficiently so that, somehow or other, we can get some money, I plan to go to Harrisburg Tuesday, as our Pennsylvania bill is beginning to make a little progress."

There was still trouble ahead. In the House Banking Committee, chairman Ellwood J. Turner was placing new barriers in the way of the credit union bill. Turner had once served as an attorney for the installment loan companies' trade association and still supported their interests. He had actively opposed the 1931 bill and was outspoken in his opposition to H-1131. Turner eventually released the bill after Bergengren made two special trips to Harrisburg for conferences with him, and then only after the direct intervention of the governor's office in the person of Tony Smith.

Bergengren was unaware of Smith's activities, and wrote Smith that the Turner situation was under control. Smith was polite enough not to inform Bergengren that to whatever extent Turner was under control, the governor's office was, in fact, the restraining force. Throughout the five-month process, Bergengren never fully understood the extent of Pinchot's support. Even though Pinchot's sympathies for cooperative endeavors were well known, even though Pinchot had been on CUNEB's advisory board for ten years, and even though Smith was obviously working with the blessing of Pinchot, Bergengren remained fearful that the governor had little interest in the credit union bill.

Perhaps Bergengren had seen too many state acts go down to defeat at the eleventh hour. In one case when a legislature reconsidered, Bergengren had seen a bill defeated after it had been passed. Perhaps his experience with the state of Washington where the governor routinely vetoed credit union bills had embittered Bergengren. Or perhaps he had learned to be cautious and never to assume that anything was certain in political life. In any case, as the bill worked its way through the legislative process, Bergengren watched with anxious care. He remained in constant touch with all three principles —Smith, McSparran, and Schwartz—throughout the crisis.

Such watchful attention was necessary. Representative Schwartz almost caused the administration to withdraw its support by attempting to pressure Smith and Pinchot into unnamed "favors" in return for continued sponsorship of the credit union bill. Again it was Secretary McSparran who came to the rescue, this time by offering Schwartz support for his "Sunday Sports" bill.

Bergengren's attention to Pennsylvania activities is most remarkable given the hectic events going on around him. President Franklin Roosevelt was just starting his New Deal administration. The bank holiday was disrupting financial affairs and business activity throughout the nation as banks of deposit closed. Credit unions found themselves denied access to their own assets, and even CUNEB was unable to obtain cash from its accounts. The negative publicity generated by bank closings was forcing an extensive public relations campaign on Bergengren, who was also burdened with lobbying for a national credit union act as well as state laws in Idaho, Washington and Oklahoma.

None of that prevented Bergengren from contacting Smith on an almost daily basis. Occasionally he would send two or more letters or telegrams in a single day, typically requesting information about the status of the bill or urging Smith to greater diligence or speedier action. Several times Bergengren made the long trip from Boston to Harrisburg to give the bill personal attention.

At Smith's direction and with Bergengren in Harrisburg to help work through the crisis, Pennsylvania labor threw its support behind the credit unions. In late March, while Schwartz was tied up in negotiations over his bill to legalize Sunday sports, Turner recommitted the credit union bill to the House Banking Committee. This time John Phillips, president of the Pennsylvania Federation of Labor, came to the bill's rescue.

Bergengren returned to Boston, and CUNEB sent letters to all Pennsylvania contacts requesting that they write their legislators. Now anticipating House approval, Bergengren began calling on friends of the credit union movement, asking them to contact their senators. "There is a real chance to get

Governor Gifford Pinchot signed the Pennsylvania Credit Union Act in 1933.

House Bill 1131 enacted into law if we all work persistently and promptly together," he wrote.

In early April, Bergengren's optimism again began to droop. He had lined up support from John Flynn, president of the Pennsylvania Manufacturer's Association, but the bill remained tied up in the House Banking Committee. "WHAT IS PRESENT DIFFICULTY" asks a frustrated Bergengren in an April 8 telegram to Smith. "DIFFICULTIES HEAVY CALENDAR OF CONTROVERSIAL MEASURES INTERTIA AND POSSIBLY TURNER" reads the equally frustrated reply.

Anthony Wayne Smith, assistant to Governor Pinchot, coordinated efforts to pass the 1933 Pennsylvania Credit Union Act.

A. J. Sordoni, Pennsylvania industrialist and statesman, provided support vital to passage of the Pennsylvania Credit Union Law.

By April 12, the bill had been reported out of committee and had passed two readings in the house. Bergengren's efforts to line up support were continuing. The Pennsylvania Farm Bureau, the Central Bureau of the Catholic Central Verein and DuPont Industries joined the ranks of credit union bill supporters. In an April 12 letter, Bergengren also asked Smith for his opinion of the chairman of the Senate Committee on Banks and Building and Loan Associations, A.J. Sordoni. Bergengren wrote that Sordoni "impressed me as being pre-eminently fair...and it is my impression that it might be a good plan for me to write him at length about the bill."

The Credit Union Bill passed the house on April 13. Bergengren was finally able to forget about the unpredictable Schwartz and the recalcitrant Turner. Now the Pennsylvania

Senate and Senator Sordoni's Banking Committee would become the focus of his attention.

The Senate Committee on Banks and Building and Loan Associations offered a formidable barrier. It had killed the 1931 bill, and was clearly a threat to the 1933 bill as well. "This Committee is composed of over thirty Senators, but the balance of power is probably with the State Organization, which means General Martin and the Mellons," wrote Smith to Bergengren. "By all means write to Senator Sordoni. He is a manufacturer and ought to be friendly if the Manufacturers Association can be lined up favorably."

The "Manufacturers Association" had already been lined up by Bergengren, and Sordoni proved to be a responsive and valuable contact. Bergengren's letter to Sordoni was a masterpiece of political public relations. By the time Bergengren was through with his lengthy description of the credit union movement and bill, he had discussed ways in which the organized credit union movement was working with the National Catholic Welfare Conference, Armour and Company, Swift & Company, the National Grange, the Pennsylvania Farm Bureau, Edward Filene, the banking commissioner of Massachusetts, the Manufacturers Association, the United States Postal Department, and President Roosevelt.

Bergengren was not about to lose Pennsylvania at this stage. All of Filene's friends and political powers were focused on the Pennsylvania Senate. Percy S. Brown, Filene's chief aide, orchestrated the lobbying effort. "It is very desirable to get this bill to a vote in the Senate before adjournment," wrote Filene associate L. Cooke to Senator George Woodward. "I cannot imagine anybody opposing it. I wonder whether you can do anything to advance its legislative status. If so, I will very cordially appreciate it." Another letter to Woodward came from another Filene friend, Morris E. Leeds, who duly reported to Filene that: "I approve of credit unions and have written the Senator from our district (George Woodward) urging his favorable vote on the bill."

Ironically, Brown (and presumably Filene) anticipated that

their campaign would again be a failure. "We have little hope that favorable legislation will result at this session, but feel that we at least are preparing the ground for success at the next session," wrote Brown to Leeds. Joseph H. Willits of Philadelphia's Wharton School of Finance, was equally discouraging. "I will see what I can do about the credit union bill. It ought to be passed. I don't have a large influence in the legislature but I will see what can be done," he wrote to Brown. Brown repeated his pessimistic message; "The bill has little likelihood of passing but the efforts made at this session will make it easier for us to secure additional aid at the next session."

The telegrams from Smith tell the rest of the story. On April 25 Smith wired: "SORDONI HOPES TO REPORT BILL TODAY SESSION MAY END NEXT WEEK." On April 26 Bergengren replied: "UNDERSTAND BILL REPORTED FAVORABLY CONGRATULATIONS SUPPORT OF ADMINISTRATION SENATORS VASTLY IMPORTANT ON THIRD READING." Bergengren had heard from Hanemann that the bill had cleared the committee, and wrote to Smith describing CUNEB efforts to aid the bill through its final senate reading. "Whatever happens," a worried but philosophic Bergengren wrote to Smith, "I want you to know that I tremendously appreciate all that you have done to make progress with this legislation. Hitherto we have never been able to get to first base, but you have got us all around to third base."

At the eleventh hour, on the third and final reading, the battle was almost lost as Senate opponents launched a surprise counterattack with a motion on the floor to recommit the bill. A motion to recommit is not debatable, and only some fancy parliamentary maneuvering by Senator Prince, sponsor of the Bill, saved it. He raised a point of personal privilege and used that technique to defend the measure. "It is my profound conviction that this bill, if passed, will prove to be the most meritorious and permanently helpful piece of legislation enacted by the session of 1933," he said in his impassioned plea before the Senate. The motion to recommit was withdrawn and the bill passed.

The next day came Smith's telegram confirming the home run. "BILL JUST PASSED SENATE THIRTY ONE TO NINE." Bergengren's reply was typical of his sense of political caution. "HEARTIEST CONGRATULATIONS STOP BE SURE GOVERNOR FULLY UNDERSTANDS BILL."

As his wire suggested, Bergengren was not about to relax so close to the end. He immediately wrote a supportive letter directly to Pinchot (whose staff forwarded the letter to Smith); to Smith, urging a "watch on the Senate for a day or two" to guard against reconsideration. Bergengren wrote to Smith again, forwarding Senator Sordoni's request to reserve credit union charter Number 1 for an organization to be formed by his employees; and to Smith yet again pleading that he continue working with the governor to be sure that the bill would be approved.

By May 8, a concerned Bergengren was resorting to telegrams: "CAN WE COOPERATE IN ANY FURTHER WAY" he queried Smith.

Smith tried to reassure Bergengren. "Personally I have no anxiety about what action will be taken," he wrote. Bergengren was not satisfied with Smith's lack of anxiety. He enlisted the aid of Filene to write the governor, wired the governor himself, and called up additional support from the Pennsylvania State Education Association, Secretary McSparran and others.

On May 25, the governor received the officially required opinion of the attorney general on H-1131. "The bill is in proper form and we recommend that it be approved." Pinchot signed the law that afternoon. Pennsylvania became the thirty-eighth state to approve credit unions. Bergengren could finally relax.

Bergengren would not relax. The next day he wrote to Smith suggesting a plan for implementing the new law. "It would help a whole lot if you would suggest to Mr. Lippman of the State Banking Department that I would be glad to make a very careful examination of the law, and submit to him a set of by-laws in conformity with the law, and with what has been found to be good credit union practice.... This would save Mr. Lippman some work, and would give him a tentative draft of by-laws to go by."

If Smith had thought that he was through corresponding with Bergengren, and with worrying about credit unions, he was mistaken. He replied to Bergengren, patiently telling him that Lippman would not be hurried and would prepare bylaws and regulations himself. "I suppose that he and Dr. Gordon will be the proper persons for you to keep in touch with from now on," he wrote.

Even the normally insensitive Bergengren spotted that perhaps he had neglected something. Writing again to Smith on May 29, Bergengren was a bit more personal. "As I have just written Governor Pinchot, I certainly appreciate that without your splendid cooperation we never would have succeeded."

Bergengren's gracious letter to Pinchot was sent to a weary Tony Smith to prepare the governor's reply. "I assure you that it was a real privilege to be able to sign the Credit Union Bill, particularly inasmuch as I have been a member of the Advisory Board for so long a time. I am glad that Mr. Smith was able to help you in the matter," said the letter Smith drafted for the governor's signature. "I am leaving Harrisburg in a few days in order to go back to Yale to finish my law course, and so I suppose I cannot be of much more help," wrote Smith in his own last letter to Bergengren.

Tony Smith had supplied the crucial, previously missing element to the Pennsylvania campaign. While the work of Andy Hanemann and other Pennsylvania supporters of the credit union movement had been important, it had not been sufficient to move the bill through the state legislature. Since 1923, various sponsors had seen their work smashed on the rocks of committee procedures and special interests.

Bergengren was also either unaware of or inadequately appreciative of the efforts and influence of Edward Filene. It is worth noting that neither Senator Leon Prince, sponsor of the bill, nor Sordoni overlooked Filene's interest. "I think I am as pleased as you and Mr. Filene are that the credit union bill passed the Senate," wrote Prince to Bergengren. Sordoni wrote directly to Filene, repeating a message already forwarded. "I sent your executive secretary [Bergengren!] a telegram stating, 'that the credit union bill passed the Senate of Pennsylvania yesterday,' and is now on the Governor's desk. I am sure he will sign it."

Bergengren was a dedicated and tireless worker, but he had little interpersonal skill, less understanding of the Pennsylvania legislative process, and virtually no knowledge of the personalities involved. Throughout the process, he believed that O. B. Lippman supported credit unions and that Ellwood Turner would not interfere. In fact, Turner recommitted the bill and almost killed it, while Lippman continued to distrust the credit union concept. In later years, Lippman would hinder credit union development in Pennsylvania by making organization of state chartered credit unions a difficult and tedious process.

Bergengren never fully accepted the fact that Pinchot had favored the bill from the beginning and never appreciated the extent of his continued behind-the-scenes support. Governor Pinchot had assigned Smith to coordinate the legislative campaign and it was he who provided the muscle behind Smith's memos. It was Smith who had lined up the supporters, kept them in line, and kept accurate count of Senate and House votes.

The Christmas 1933 issue of *The Bridge* had the enactment of the Pennsylvania state law as the lead story. It told of Pinchot's service on CUNEB's advisory committee, and gave full credit where credit was, in fact, due. But Bergengren was guilty of many curious omissions and misstatements in his personal account of the legislative war in Pennsylvania. The author's comments are in brackets.

"It is altogether fitting ... that the Pennsylvania credit union law should be enacted during [Pinchot's] administration, and that one of his secretaries, Anthony Smith, should have labored long and diligently, with rare ability, to help us to get a credit union law enacted during our third [actually seventh] effort in that State.

"We started in 1929 [1923]. At that time I had the good fortune to meet H. A. Hanemann, known to his friends as "Andy." During the six years [actually, eight years] Mr. Hanemann stood by the credit union ship, not only when the credit union cause had many friends, but at times of great despondency, when it seemed as though we would never succeed, and that he and I were the only two folks in the State interested in credit unions....

"[In 1931] we tried again, and then things began to break better. To begin with, Representative Louis Schwartz became favorably interested in the bill. To that single circumstance we owe its enactment. He succeeded in getting the bill through the House in 1931 [Schwartz did vote for the 1931 bill, but had nothing more to do with it.] .... "In this year's session Mr. Schwartz was again in charge in the House and ... the bill won the approval and cordial support of the new Chairman of the Senate Banks committee, Hon. Andrew J. Sordoni. The combination of Representative Schwartz and Senators Sordoni and Prince proved the winning combination....

"As I have noted, Anthony Smith worked indefatigably for the bill, as did the Pennsylvania credit union veteran, Andy Hanemann. Meantime the cause had enlisted many new and most valuable friends, including particularly the Secretary of Agriculture, Hon. John A. McSparran, President J. Herbert Kelley of the Pennsylvania State Education Association, the representatives of the various postal credit unions in Pennsylvania, the Pennsylvania Credit Union Committee which had been organized during the 1931 campaign and many others....

Ten years later, while writing *Crusade*, Bergengren would not remember Smith, McSparran, Pinchot, Sordoni, Prince, nor even Schwartz (who was probably better off forgotten). He did remember Hanemann whom he mentions several times and nominates as "the father of the Pennsylvania credit union movement." For many years, he would refer to Pennsylvania as one of CUNEB's most difficult challenges. It was also, as Bergengren frequently noted, one of CUNEB's most important challenges. Once organized, Pennsylvania soon became a leading credit union state. Ironically it would be the large number of credit unions chartered under federal law, however, not under the hard-fought state law, that would take Pennsylvania to national prominence in the credit union movement.

Bergengren quickly realized that the fight to organize a credit union movement in Pennsylvania did not end with the ceremonial signing of the new law. It was too full of compromises, several of which made Pennsylvania an expensive and difficult state in which to organize a credit union. Others placed new charters on the desk of Lippman. And the banking commissioner—perhaps in response to pressures from the existing banking establishment—found himself increasingly opposed to the new institutions.[3]

One compromise, mandated by state law, made it necessary to advertise in a local paper the intention to charter a credit union. The Pennsylvania Department of Justice later ruled in a formal opinion that it would also be necessary to publish such intention to apply for a charter "in the legal journal of the proper county ... in addition to publication in a newspaper of general circulation." The state even required a special form, a "publisher's certificate," as part of the paperwork required for the application. This need to publish such advertisements added significantly to the expenses faced by potential applicants for state credit union charters.

The law required also that full bylaws be written and directors be selected before the application could even be submit-

3. Banking commissioner Lippman made himself a legend in the Pennsylvania credit union movement. Years later managing director Michael Judge would recall having been told, as a young field representative for the Pennsylvania League, that the only way to get Lippman to approve a credit union charter, was to prove to him that the group was so wealthy and powerful that its members really didn't need a credit union.

ted. This was an involved process which had to be completed with no assurance of state approval. Furthermore, even after the Department of Banking issued a "certificate of approval," all papers had to be forwarded to the governor's office for approval. With Pinchot in office, that would present no real difficulty, but it opened the door for many potential future problems.

The obligation to McSparran, the Department of Agriculture, the National Grange and other agrarian interest groups showed up in an unusual provision that empowered Pennsylvania credit unions "to make loans to such cooperative society or societies ... having membership in the credit union as are organized under the laws of this Commonwealth." This provision makes it clear that McSparran and his associates saw credit unions as a way to complement rural comperatives by making additional funds available to them.

A concession to Gordon and Lippman is clear in the Act's provision that "Credit unions shall report to [the Department of Banking] as often as may be required by the Secretary of Banking and at least annually. Supplementary reports may be required by the Secretary from time to time. Credit unions shall be examined as often as may be required by the Secretary of Banking and at least annually and the Department may use such other method of assuring itself of the condition of the credit unions as it shall deem advisable." This provision left the credit unions open to potential continual expensive harassment by the banking department. Most other states required only annual reports or examinations.

The Pennsylvania law also required that the credit unions carry·all expense for such examinations. Bergengren argued that such an expense would be much too heavy for small institutions serving limited numbers of members. While the original provision stood, Bergengren did succeed in persuading Gordon to exempt credit unions from examination charges during their first six months of operation on the very real grounds that few would be able to afford it at that stage. He did not succeed in getting the state to bear such costs itself. The bill required a credit union "pay annually its proportionate share of the overhead expense of the said Department of Banking."

Even the small loan industry won a concession in the Pennsylvania Credit Union Law. A special provision at the end of the act ruled that "Nothing contained in this act shall apply to any person or persons or corporations engaged in the business of loaning money under the terms of [the small loan act]." The 42% lenders might be adversely affected by credit unions, but they would not be directly affected by the act itself.

In most other ways the Pennsylvania law went along familiar lines. It mandated that members share a common bond "whether of occupation, association, or residence within a well defined neighborhood, community, or rural district." It distinguished between deposits and shares, setting a maximum par value on shares of $10.00. It gave the credit union an automatic lien on all shares and deposits held by a member for any sum due to the credit union. It set a maximum entrance fee of $1.00. A reserve fund of 20% of net annual earnings was mandated. Credit unions, like all other Pennsylvania institutions for savings, were exempted from all taxes including the stock transfer tax.

There was dissatisfaction with the Pennsylvania act from the beginning: even before the celebrations at CUNEB headquarters ended, work was underway to amend the law. Bergengren was also busy in another quarter. He had already decided that the next logical step—the best way to enable credit unions in the states that still lacked laws and best way to provide the movement with a way around uncooperative secretaries of banking—was a federal credit union law. The Pennsylvania experience provided part of the motivation for Bergengren's decision that it was time to seek a federal credit union law.

We now know that the Pennsylvania law was inadquate. The combination of high expense and lengthy procedures kept all but a few credit unions from even applying for a state

charter.[4] Those that did apply, tended to be the better organized and better financed efforts. They included the postal
employee credit unions which had been operating without
benefit of charter for several years, and industrial credit unions, organized with the encouragement (and often financial
support) of an industrial sponsor. While organization under
Pennsylvania law was more difficult than Bergengren would
have wished, it was far from impossible.

THE PENNSYLVANIA LAW was signed on May 25,
1933. Just a few days before, Bergengren had watched
as three bills were filed with the United States Congress, then meeting in special session. While that package
would not pass, it was the first firm step towards securing
federal credit union legislation.

Within days of Pinchot's final approval of the Pennsylvania
Act, Bergengren was back in the state laying the foundations
for the formation of the Pennsylvania Credit Union League.
In typical fashion, he did not even pause to admire his legislative handiwork. That was yesterday's news, and Bergengren
was always much more concerned about tomorrow's accomplishment. Yesterday had witnessed the long-awaited birth of
the Pennsylvania credit union movement. Today's task was to

---

4. Among the few that did apply—and that eventually survived the delaying tactics of the banking department to actually complete the chartering
process—were a credit union for state employees (organized by Andrew
Hanemann) and a credit union for the employees of Senator Sordoni who
had led the Senate banking committee to its approval of the 1933 law.
Representative Schwartz who had talked frequently of organizing a credit
union in Philadelphia, never did so. Other credit unions that won early
state charters include: Allentown Teachers; Erie Postal Workers; Walworth Employees, Greensburg; Harrisburg Postal Employees; Pennsylvania State Employees, Harrisburg; Swift Harrisburg Employees;
Lancaster Postal Employees; Lancaster Teachers; McKeesport Postal Employees; Dill & Collins Employees, Philadelphia; Philadelphia Teachers;
Sears, Roebuck Philadelphia Employees; Armour Philadelphia Employees;
Supplee-Biddle, Philadelphia; Carbon County Teachers, Wilkes-Barre; Armour Newberry; Kemba Employees, Pittsburgh; Ingram Employees, Pittsburgh; Building and Needle Trades, Philadelphia; St. Basil Parish,
Pittsburgh; Swift Pittsburgh Employees; Ageco of Pennsylvania, Reading;
and Scranton Federal Employees.

make Pennsylvania part of a nationwide organized credit union movement. On the agenda lay the formation of the Pennsylvania League, creation of the Credit Union National Association, and adoption of the Federal Credit Union Act.

Many difficulties lay ahead. The majority of Pennsylvania's credit unions would be chartered under federal rather than state law. Developing a cohesive and viable league in Pennsylvania would prove almost as challenging as winning a law had been. And the leaders of the Pennsylvania credit union movement would soon prove themselves almost as fractious as the state's politicians.

Nevertheless CUNEB's greatest challenge was now its greatest single accomplishment. There was a Pennsylvania Credit Union Act. There was a Pennsylvania credit union movement.

V

Creating the League

"It is our plan to build the credit union from the ground up, not from the top down. Our first work ... has been the formation of laws and the organization of the credit unions. The first stop ... is the organization of state credit union leagues."

Thomas W. Doig

THE CREDIT UNION MOVEMENT in the United States achieved three of Roy Bergengren's goals in 1934: in June, President Franklin D. Roosevelt signed the Federal Credit Union Act; in August, credit union and league delegates from throughout the nation formed the Credit Union National Association; December witnessed the creation of the Pennsylvania Credit Union League.

The accomplishment of CUNEB and Bergengren in winning the 1933 legislative battle of Pennsylvania had been impressive. As the second most populous state in the nation, Pennsylvania had been worth the extended, expensive and exhausting fight. Here was potential for a great and constructive future for the credit union movement. But the Pennsylvania law was not a good credit union law. It mandated costly and complicated procedures for charter applicants. It permitted excessive supervision. In short, it would allow the movement to develop slowly, but would do nothing to encourage or accelerate it.

Bergengren realized that further development of the credit union movement both in individual states and at the national level required a federal credit union law. But it was not easy to shift the efforts of CUNEB from seeking state laws to working at the national level. That was a substantial shift in policy, and the action was taken only after long deliberation.[1]

---

1. One good account of the history of the Federal Credit Union law is well told in Fite and Moody's *The Credit Union Movement*. A more passionate and personal perspective is offered in Bergengren's own autobiographical *Crusade*. The former offers a reliable and complete account of the progress of the legislation in Washington. The latter offers unique, valuable insight to Bergengren's perceptions and changing moods.

In April 1933, the bank holiday of the previous month was a recent memory and the chances for legislative success in Pennsylvania still seemed bleak. Bergengren began to pressure Filene for help on a federal credit union law. Pennsylvania, he pointed out, was the second most populous state in the union, yet CUNEB seemed unable to obtain needed legislation. Furthermore, the state legislature met only every other year, and if they failed in 1933, as then appeared likely, they would not have another chance until 1935. "Having in mind that the National Association of Credit Union Leagues [eventually renamed Credit Union National Association] will be organized in 1934 and that the National Association will probably not have the resources or the time necessary for promoting legislation in new states, it becomes obviously important to accomplish some legislation which would make credit union organization possible in these remaining states. This, of course, could only be done by Congressional action."

The ten-year Pennsylvania experience was, therefore, an important part of Bergengren's decision to seek federal legislation. As a veteran of the Pennsylvania war, he felt that taking on the United States Congress would be simple.

Actually, Bergengren had been considering federal action for many years. In *Crusade*, he acknowledges that he first considered the federal legislative route in 1921. "We decided to attempt state legislation because we felt that the educational work would have to be done in each state anyway, and that there would be of necessity a measure of education effort connected with each attempt to secure state legislation."

Bergengren's decision to "go to Washington" in 1933 was motivated by a number of factors, including: the bank holiday; the near loss of West Virginia through a repeal measure; the coming organization of the national association; and memories of difficulties encountered in a few states, "Pennsylvania in particular." Continuing problems in Connecticut and unresolved difficulties with the banking departments of several states contributed to CUNEB's decision. The decision was taken despite strenuous objections from Filene.

The Boston merchant had no love for federal regulatory agencies. The self-help concept of state laws and leagues appealed to his individualistic personality. Federal legislation, he feared, would eventually and inevitably alter the nature of credit unions. As a result of this attitude, Filene did not at first play a major role in developing the federal legislation. He did line up some support from a few senators and did contact the administration.

Filene was well known and respected by the administration. He often served as the New Deal's spokesperson in the business community. The administration owed many favors to Filene. He had powerful friends. He could have made Bergengren's task much easier. As it was, he asked no special favors of the administration. As the issue advanced, however, Filene began to deploy his forces. As usual, Bergengren remained virtually unaware of Filene's quietly persuasive diplomacy.

The Roosevelt administration at first resisted placing its imprimatur on the Federal Credit Union Bill. It was almost a replay of the Pennsylvania situation. Roosevelt, like Pinchot, was a longterm supporter of credit unions. As a state senator, F. D. R. had actually sponsored the first New York Credit Union Law. Now it was only after an exhaustive process involving reviews by cabinet-level officials and recommendations by several agencies that the official administration support was finally forthcoming.

Fortunately, the bill's process through Congress differed greatly from the Pennsylvania experience. The first package of bills submitted by CUNEB was abandoned in committee, but subsequent progress was rapid. Unfortunately congressional adjournment was approaching more rapidly than congressional consideration of the credit union bill. Congress had announced plans to go home on June 16. On June 15, the *Christian Science Monitor* reported:

"Among the bills that hang in the balance as the congressional session draws to a close is one which has not had the benefit

of the publicity given to certain other measures of wide importance.

"The measure referred to is a bill introduced into the senate
providing for an act to set up credit unions under federal
charter. Back of this bill lies the long story of the credit union
movement, whose growth has been attended by many bitter
battles in state legislatures where, at times, the money lenders'
lobbies have opposed this democratic system of financing....

"The credit union idea has swept across the nation until
today millions of dollars of workers' money is invested in
them. Thirty-eight states have credit union laws. Ten states,
for one reason or another, have held back. In some cases, such
lack of legislation can be traced directly to powerful opposition by money-lending agencies, charging usurious interest
rates, and certain to lose much profit by such enactment."

With the support of Texans Morris Sheppard in the Senate
and Wright Patman in the House, along with the hard-won
support of Henry Steagall, chairman of the House Banking
Committee, and through a series of unorthodox but fascinating parliamentary techniques, the Federal Credit Union Bill
survived.

The years of wrangling with state legislatures in general—
and with Pennsylvania and Connecticut in particular—had
endowed Bergengren with patience, persistence, and had
earned him an advanced degree of ability in lobbying techniques. He needed the full range of those skills in Washington, and he used them well in pursuit of the grand prize.

On June 16, last day of the 73d Congress, Rep. Steagall won
the unanimous consent of the House to consider the Credit
Union Bill as a "committee of the whole." This unusual procedure was required because there was insufficient time for
routine processing. The bill passed with only two dissents,
despite the representatives' widespread ignorance of credit
unions. The unanimous recommendation of Steagall's Banking Committee proved sufficient to guarantee passage.

Over in the Senate, Sheppard called unanimous consent to pass the bill, "as amended [by the House] unread." Here too, the recommendation of its committee and the support of the administration proved adequate, assisted perhaps, by the pressure of time and the lure of summer days at home. The Senate passed the bill without dissent—the only way in which its rules permitted such an unusual process. President Franklin Delano Roosevelt signed the Federal Credit Union Act on June 26, 1934.

The *Christian Science Monitor* welcomed the new federal credit union law with an enthusiasm that rivaled the rhetoric of Bergengren himself.[2]

> "A Henry Ford has come to the banking field. The coming of the automobile with the advent of the old Model T furnished a parallel to the promise which the credit union movement now holds out to the masses with the passage in Washington of the Sheppard Bill making possible the formation of credit unions under federal charter....
>
> "In the past, says Mr. Bergengren, the credit union has been demonstrating the practicality of bringing bank credit to the workers. In thousands of industries throughout the country where credit unions have been set up by employees, certain definite results have been obtained and unmistakable proofs advanced."

The bill placed jurisdiction over federally chartered credit unions in a special section of the Farm Credit Administration (FCA). The FCA governor assumed the role held by secretaries of banking at the state level. Leadership of the Credit Union Section was assigned to Herbert Emmerich, first assistant to FCA Governor W. I. Myers. Emmerich, in turn, sought Bergengren's advice regarding the appointment of an assistant

2. Reference to Henry Ford and the enthusiasm of the report make it likely that much of the copy for this article was supplied by a CUNEB press release written by either Bergengren himself or by Agnes Gartland.

director who would eventually take over the agency. That appointment went to Claude Orchard.[3]

Orchard had joined the movement in 1929 when he helped organize a credit union for the employees of an Armour meat packing plant in Omaha. Armour officials were so pleased with the results that they released Orchard to devote full time to organizing similar groups throughout the company. Thus while Orchard was technically a credit union volunteer, he was actually a full-time employee of Armour, working exclusively on credit union business.

Orchard requested a one-year leave of absence from Armour and Co. to head the Credit Union Section of FCA. He assumed his post on August 20, and promulgated a series of policies which dramatically affected the path of the Pennsylvania movement. It was Orchard who ordered that his agency actively encourage the organization of both federal and state credit unions. The type of charter would be selected by each individual credit union itself.

The policy's phrasing clearly reflects the CUNEB experience in Pennsylvania and a growing irritation with the inhibiting procedures of Pennsylvania banking commissioner O. B. Lippman. The choice of charter, ordered Orchard, should be made "in the light of the cost of organization and the workability of the State Law involved...." There was little doubt about which form of charter was preferable in Pennsylvania.

In most states, federal organizers assisted with the formation of both state and federal credit unions. In Pennsylvania, virtually all efforts were directed towards obtaining federal charters. It would not take long before their work began to bear rich fruit, and Pennsylvania began to fulfill its potential.

3. Tom Doig was bitterly disappointed when he did not get the federal job. His antagonism towards Bergengren may well date from this incident. In *Crusade*, Bergengren recalled that he provided a list of seven candidates, "including Tom Doig of Minnesota." Bergengren says that he "hoped Tom wouldn't take it," but would stay with the prospective national association where he was badly needed. In a contemporary letter to Filene, however, Bergengren admitted that Doig was never nominated.

The Keystone State would soon become the leading federal credit union state in the nation.

Before that could happen, Orchard had to develop his own staff and organization. For Orchard, this was the beginning of an exciting and dynamic year. Even while establishing his Credit Union Section, he was called on to assist Bergengren, first in the creation of the Credit Union National Association and second in the formation of the Pennsylvania Credit Union League.

Some 70 credit union leaders were invited to a conference at Estes Park, Colorado, in the summer of 1934 to establish the Credit Union National Association. The list included representatives of the existing leagues and of typical credit unions such as parish, postal, packing-house, rural, and similar types of organizations. The final list included people from 27 states. More than 50 credit union leaders accepted Bergengren's invitation, but the Estes Park Conference included no representative of Pennsylvania's credit unions.[4]

Membership in the new association would be through the leagues, although individual credit unions were allowed to join in states where no league yet existed. A proposal by Bergengren for a set dues structure ("each credit union member to pay ten cents a year until the fourth annual meeting") was rejected by the delegates, who deferred the matter to the board of directors.

The delegates showed no reluctance to slap the hand that had fed them. Edward Filene had advocated, led, and financed the credit union movement for more than 20 years. Now he wanted to be elected the first president of CUNA. Instead, he

4. "When we assembled for the first time on August 8 we found that the largest delegation was from Illinois, twelve all told, vigorously led by Tim O'Shaughnessy. There were five of us from Massachusetts and four from New York, including the president and the managing director of the New York League. There were twenty-one present from three states, or 40 percent of the whole. The states that responded to the first roll call were New York, Washington, Illinois, Minnesota, Missouri, Iowa, Massachusetts, California, Alabama, Texas, Wisconsin, Kentucky, North Carolina, Tennessee, Arkansas, Ohio, Nebraska, Colorado, Michigan, Indiana and the District of Columbia." *Crusade*, p. 239.

had to settle for the title "Founder." CUNA presidents would be elected by the board of directors. Bergengren would be the first managing director of the new national association.

Bergengren himself was well aware of the tight financial control credit union leaders like to maintain. When Filene wanted him to leave his payroll and become a full-time employee of CUNA, Bergengren insisted that he could better serve the credit union movement from outside, and requested that Filene remain his personal financier. They compromised. Filene agreed to continue Twentieth-Century Fund responsibility for Bergengren, through CUNEB, for one year. Bergengren would then become the employee of CUNA and his salary would be the responsibility of its board of directors. This arrangement also gave Bergengren time to win required ratification of the CUNA constitution and establish needed organization structures.

The system of state leagues, a national association, and an international organization, which is now the organized credit union movement, existed in Bergengren's mind and in Filene's heart long before it took more tangible form.

The constitution specified that it would become effective when ratified by 15 leagues. The problem was that at the time there were only five self-sustaining, professionally staffed credit union leagues: Massachusetts, New York, Illinois, Minnesota and Missouri. Other states had leagues on paper or informal league-like associations. The task for Bergengren, then, was either to create new leagues or to strengthen those that existed. Until the leagues were powerful enough to collect dues from member credit unions and pay them to CUNA, there was no real national association.

Bergengren and Doig were soon able to get all but one of the existing leagues to ratify the constitution, and to create several new ones for the purpose. Ironically, they encountered major difficulty in Massachusetts where MCUL predated CUNEB and felt slighted by the developments at Estes Park. In Pennsylvania, a league was created in December 1934 with almost the sole purpose of ratifying the CUNA constitution.

Dora Maxwell, pioneering credit union organizer from New York, played an important role in organizing the Pennsylvania League.

The Pennsylvania League was the last to take that official action.

In Massachusetts, CUNEB had been the heir of a loosely organized league. As the movement began to grow in the late 1920s, the Massachusetts Credit Union League not only became an increasingly powerful and useful organization in its own light, but became the model for similar organizations in other states.

Bergengren's difficulties in gaining ratification from the Massachusetts group reflected his failure to recognize either the accomplishments of other credit union leaders or of the league as distinct from CUNEB. The Massachusetts league was the oldest in the nation. It had made numerous contributions to credit union history long before Bergengren came on the scene. Many Bay State leaders questioned the legitimacy of Bergengren's position in the national movement, as well as their own lack of status and authority.

135

Bergengren's ultimate response was to form a second state organization. Since the name Massachusetts Credit Union League was already taken, the new group took the name Raiffeisen Associates. At root of the dispute was the inability of cooperators to cooperate. It was not that they had sharply differing ideas about philosophy, mission, procedures, or organization. Rather, they were split by jealousy over who should get credit for achievements. Such personality conflicts showed up not only in Massachusetts credit unionism, but throughout credit unionism, in the general cooperative movement, and in many other voluntary associations.

The New York League quickly ratified the Estes Park agreement, largely because of substantial work done well before the meeting. At the start of the decade, the New York League had faced serious internal problems and possible collapse. From CUNEB's viewpoint, the New York credit union movement had experienced serious, potentially disabling problems from its inception.[5]

New York was the home of the Russell Sage foundation, an organization which Bergengren had always seen as destructive competition. He felt they were too abstract and aloof for real credit union work, that they had no understanding of the fundamental nature of the issues involved.

Russell Sage leaders did tend to compromise on issues more readily than did Bergengren. The model law for a uniform small loan act tolerated interest rates as high as 3.5% per month, an amount that Bergengren and other credit union people found totally unacceptable. Furthermore, lenders operating under such uniform small loan acts often presented concerted opposition to credit union laws, as they did so successfully for many years in Pennsylvania.

5. The New York experience is important because it was resolved by Dora Maxwell, and Maxwell would become an important organizer and advisor in Pennsylvania.

Even Filene warned Bergengren to tred lightly where the Russell Sage foundation was concerned, especially in New York. Bergengren could never accept such advice. Instead, he opened a New York office of CUNEB to try to undo what he saw as the mismanagement and improper conduct of the Russell Sage group. To manage the new office, Bergengren selected Basil Mallicoat. Mallicoat soon withdrew, and his job went to Dora Maxwell, the outstanding organizer from the Consumer's Cooperative Credit Union.

Maxwell proved herself highly effective, not only in working with crowds but in working with individual politicians and executives. Her friends soon included then New York Governor Franklin D. Roosevelt and his agricultural commissioner, Henry Morgenthau, Jr. Maxwell was especially effective organizing rural credit unions in agricultural areas.

In Minnesota Doig led the formation of a credit union league in 1927. Lithe, energetic, and wiry, Doig was blessed with a fine voice and outstanding oratorical skill. Like Bergengren, Doig proved to be a master organizer who could work a crowd and stir them to action. It was Doig who handled the legislative campaign in Minnesota and saw it to its quick success in 1925, obtained the first state charter for his own credit union, then turned to forming credit union chapters, leagues, and assisting Bergengren with the national association. He was a stenographer in the office of the Minneapolis postmaster Arch Coleman and treasurer of the Minneapolis Postal Employees Credit Union. Doig became increasingly fascinated with the concept as he learned more about both the theory and the practice at first hand. Tom Doig would become an important influence on credit union affairs in Pennsylvania.

While Maxwell was organizing rural credit unions in New York, Doig became involved with parish credit unions in the Midwest. Bergengren, always an inspirational speaker, continued his own organizing efforts. Wherever he travelled, Bergengren left a trail of new credit unions in his wake.

Claude Orchard, a credit union organizer from Nebraska, helped organize the Pennsylvania League and many early federal credit unions in the Commonwealth.

Orchard, before he accepted federal appointment, and Maxwell took charge of organizing Pennsylvania. Thirty years later, in 1964, Orchard remembered those early days of credit union activities in the Keystone State:

"Well, in the spring of 1934 there was a considerable amount of organization work going on. The credit union law in the State of Pennsylvania had been passed by the legislature of that State in the summer of 1933 and laws in that State become effective 90 days after the legislature adjourns as I remember. So some of us—Mr. Bergengren, Dora Maxwell, who was then working for the Extension Bureau, and I went into the State of Pennsylvania late in the fall of 1933, began to get applications for charter for credit unions, from groups which had helped to get the law passed, particularly groups in post offices, state

Tom Doig, assistant to the managing director of CUNA, choreographed the reorganization of the Pennsylvania Credit Union League.

employees, employees of Armour and Company, employees of Swift and Company by that time, and employees of the man who owned the Sterling Hotel in Wilkesbury [sic] who had been the father of the credit union law. His name slips me at the moment [State Sen. A. J. Sordoni, chrm. of the Senate Banking Committee].... While we established no credit unions that I remember of in 1933, in the early spring of 1934 we had quite a crop in the State of Pennsylvania."

At the end of that year, Orchard and Bergengren returned to Pennsylvania to harvest the crop which they had prepared with such care.

Saturday, December 8, 1934 was a cold and damp day in Harrisburg. But spirits and hopes were high among the delegates and credit union representatives meeting in the State Council Chamber, Room 319 of the Education Building. They

139

were there in response to an invitation from Roy Bergengren to all credit unions operating in the State of Pennsylvania.[6] The stated purpose of the meeting was "organizing a State League and its possible affiliation with the National Association."

CUNA was little more than a name, a constitution, bylaws, and a dream when Bergengren arrived in Harrisburg for the league organization meeting. With him were Claude Orchard, now with the Federal Credit Union Section of FCA, Doig, Tim O'Shaunessy from the Illinois League and Earl Rentfro. Rentfro was an employee of the Rock Island Line Railroad and with O'Shaughnessy, an organizer of their efficient network of credit unions. He was a leader of the Missouri League.

The meeting convened following a "delightful" dinner served by the Y.W.C.A. It was chaired by H. Andrew Hanemann, treasurer of the Pennsylvania State Employees Credit Union and veteran of the ten-year legislative war. Bergengren spoke to the group about the history of the credit union movement.[7]

6. There is no single reliable and comprehensive list of credit unions then operating in the state. The following list is a compilation based on records in several different sources, including the records of the Pennsylvania League, CUNA, and state archives. In the order in which they were organized, credit unions operating at the time the League was formed include: Reading Postal Employees (1929); Allentown Teachers, Bradford Postal Employees, Pennsylvania State Employees, Philadelphia Postal Employees (1930); Teachers Credit Union of Greater Philadelphia (1932); Armour Philadelphia Employees, Armour Pittsburgh Employees, Armour Wilkes-Barre Employees, Building and Needle Trade Workers, Carbon County Teachers, Dill and Collins Employees, Ingram Employees, Lancaster Postal Employees, McKeesport Postal Employees, Scranton Federal Employees (1933); Altoona Postal Employees, Altoona Schools, Armour Newberry Employees, Bridesburg Philadelphia Employees, Erie Postal Employees, Employees Swift Harrisburg, Employees Swift Philadelphia, Employees Swift Pittsburgh, Federation, Ingals Employees, Kemba Pittsburgh Employees, New Castle Postal Employees North Bend, Oil City Postal Employees, Perry Furnace, Pittsburgh Teachers, Pittsburgh Provision and Packing Employees, Public School Employees of Philadelphia, St. Basil Parish, The Second Street, The Walworth Employees, Utilities Employees, Vogts Employees, West Market, Williamsport Teachers, Your Money's Worth (1934).

As the League worked its way through the process of organizing itself, Hanemann was elected president and Ira Kreider of Lancaster was elected secretary. They were to serve until the new board of directors would have an opportunity to meet and formally select League officers.

The CUNA people had come fully prepared with a League constitution and complete set of bylaws. With appropriate legal solemnity, their adoption was moved and seconded. Then the script started to go awry. First came an amendment to change the number of directors from the standard nine to 14. This would allow each of the credit unions that were represented at the meeting to elect one director. Then the delegates threw away the script entirely. They changed the section on "League finances," deleted a provision providing for payment of salaries by the League ("as established by the board of directors") as well as a provision establishing standing dues.[8]

One representative insisted that no dues should be paid to CUNA, but Doig, Rentfro, and the others successfully argued that working with CUNA in the sale of supplies and other support services would be a real money-maker for the group.

7. According to the official minutes of the meeting, more than 70 credit union delegates responded to Bergengren's invitation. Unfortunately, there is no list of the attendees. We do have a list of the "directors" selected by each credit union to represent it at the League, and of their credit unions. That list is as follows: Allentown Teachers Credit Union, Edwin D. Clauss; Building and Needle Trade Workers Credit Union, R. J. Brodsky; Harrisburg Postal Employees Credit Union, Earl L. Blatt; Kemba Pittsburgh Employees Credit Union, W. R. Koester; Lancaster Postal Employees' Credit Union, Ira W. Kreider; McKeesport Postal Employees' Credit Union, Charles Blend; Pennsylvania State Employees Credit Union, H. A. Hanemann; Philadelphia Teachers Credit Union, Isadore D. Karchin; Pittsburgh Teachers Credit Union, R. H. Henderson; Swift Harrisburg Credit Union, K. W. Dry; Swift Philadelphia Employees Credit Union, L. C. Gilbert; West Market Credit Union, N. H. Berman; Williamsport Teachers Credit Union, J. C. Hoshauer; Reading Postal Employees Credit Union, Ralph Gilbert.
8. The deleted dues entitlement would have given the League annual dues amounting to the lessor of 0.5% of the member credit union's assets, or one-sixth of any dividend paid by the member credit union. From that income, the League would have been responsible for paying dues to CUNA.

The final decision was a compromise. It meant that for the immediate future, at least, Pennsylvania's contribution to the CUNA coffers would be unpredictable:

> "This League shall derive revenue from such central activities as it may maintain in accordance with the determination of the Board of Directors and resulting from its association in the Credit Union National Association.
>
> "Except as said League shall raise each year for said Credit Union National Association in such way and manner as the Board of Directors of the League in any given year shall determine and for so long as this League is affiliated with said National Association, such proportionate part of the dues of said National Association as may be apportioned in any given year to credit unions affiliated in this League, there shall be no dues assesed for the support of this League in excess of a sum not to exceed in any given year three hundred dollars until such time as there shall be one hundred credit unions operating in the state of Pennsylvania."

In other words, as long as CUNA gave the money back to the League, the League would assess dues. But the League would not contribute more than $300 to CUNA for the use of CUNA.

Bergengren did not like the compromise and left the meeting. When, as the next order of business, the new League finally ratified the CUNA Constitution and formally applied for CUNA membership, Doig, Rentfro, and O'Shaughnessy became the CUNA signatories. So it was without the benefit of Bergengren's signature that Pennsylvania became the last state League to ratify the CUNA Constitution, leading Orchard to comment later that he was pleased to have witnessed both the first and last ratification votes. Doubtless, Bergengren was also pleased to have seen (if not witnessed) the last of them.

Signing the ratification and application agreement for the new League were:

John Hoshauer   Wm. R. Koester
Isadore D. Karchin   Ira W. Kreider

Charles M. Blend	R. H. Henderson
Ralph Gilbert	Laurence C. Gilbert
N. Horace Berman	Earl L. Blatt
Ralph J. Brodsky	H. A. Hanemann

Signing the constitution and bylaws of the Pennsylvania Credit Union League were:

Edwin D. Clauss, Allentown Teachers
Fred E. Fisbeck, Swift Philadelphia Employees
Henry E. Keugh, Pennsylvania State Employees
John C. Hoshauer, Williamsport Teachers
Ralph J. Brodsky, Building and Needle Trade Workers
Albert L. Jackel, McKeesport Postal Employees
William A. Staudt, Reading Postal Employees
Henry E. Stafford, Lancaster Postal Employees
R. H. Henderson, Pittsburgh Teachers
N. Horace Berman, West Market
Isadore D. Karchin, Philadelphia Teachers
Earl L. Blatt, Harrisburg Postal Employees
Wm. R. Koester, Kemba Pittsburgh
H. R. Petrie, Swift Harrisburg Employees

The 1934 meeting of the Pennsylvania Credit Union League adjourned at 10:00 p.m. It was followed immediately by the first meeting of the board of directors.

At the directors' meeting, H. Andrew Hanemann was elected president and managing director. N. Horace Berman of Philadelphia's West Market Credit Union was elected vice president; William R. Koester, Kemba Pittsburgh, treasurer; John Hoshauer, Williamsport Teachers, secretary.

Hanemann's election as both managing director and president was unusual. It may have been unique. It was certainly an appropriate honor. As Bergengren later recalled, "Mr. Hanemann was primarily responsible for the [Pennsylvania] law and for the first credit union, and it is altogether fitting that he take his place among the pioneers as the 'father of the credit union in Pennsylvania.'"

The first resolution passed by the board was a dues assessment: "Each credit union shall send in, within thirty days, one cent for each member to cover initial expenses." Harrisburg was selected as the place for the next meeting; it would be held at the call of the president. The final motion, passed unanimously, allowed all business of the board of directors to be conducted by mail, unless three or more members objected.

To a remarkable degree, this first meeting followed patterns that would become part of the credit union movement. The officers were from four locations; they were selected to represent Philadelphia, Pittsburgh, North Central and South Central just as they represented their credit unions.

The League clearly demonstrated from its birth that it would not take orders from CUNA. It altered the standard bylaws in two critical areas: selection of a board of directors and the payment of dues. These would prove continually troublesome areas, and the tradition of rejecting demands from Bergengren and the CUNA executive would become routine business in Pennsylvania.

The group had, unfortunately, rejected good advice and procedure. Having stripped itself of operating funds, it would be in for several difficult years. Hanemann was unable to obtain secretarial help and solicitation of membership quickly fell to nothing. Similarly, the new League could undertake no organizing activities. It had forced itself to rely on CUNA and on Orchard's staff at the Federal Credit Union Section. While the federal organizing effort was substantial and successful, credit unions organized by the federal agency proved to be neither particularly loyal to the League nor interested in supporting its activities.

The Credit Union National Association quickly learned that organizing a league in Pennsylvania had been premature. The new League was formally admitted to CUNA on December 16, 1934, and while no official vote for a national director was recorded in Harrisburg, CUNA recognized Hanemann as Pennsylvania's first national delegate. But for the next 18 months, there would be no mention of the Pennsylvania credit union movement or of the Pennsylvania League at an official CUNA function.

The critical nature of the Pennsylvania problem became evident to Bergengren when he attended the second annual meeting of the Pennsylvania Credit Union League. It was held in Harrisburg on May 3, 1935, attended by only 26 members representing six credit unions.[9] President Hanemann chaired the meeting; visitors included Bergengren, Maxwell, and Orchard.

Bergengren was in Harrisburg specifically to raise money and support for CUNA. As the featured speaker for the evening, Bergengren took as his subject "The Purposes of the National Association and its Functions." He explained that the dues went primarily to support credit union organizing activities, much of which was needed in Pennsylvania, and educational work. He asked that 0.5% of assets per year be committed to the League and indirectly to CUNA as dues. The meeting was recessed for informal discussion, and perhaps a little arm twisting. When the group reconvened, the delegates voted unanimously to support Bergengren and CUNA.

Hanemann himself had other interests. He was actively pursuing improvement of the state law through amendment. He called the attention of the delegates to House Bills 2338 and 2337, requesting that they contact their state representatives and senators seeking support for the bills. The meeting quickly adjourned. In the absence of a quorum, there could be no meeting of the board of directors. The Pennsylvania League was still a paper organization.

While the second annual meeting had approved the payment of dues to CUNA, the League had no funds, made almost no collections and made no payment to CUNA. The directors, while empowered to conduct business by mail, never did so.

9. The credit unions represented at the May 3, 1935 meeting were: Harrisburg Postal Employees; Pennsylvania State Employees; Armour Newberry Employees; Williamsport Teachers; Swift and Company Harrisburg Employees; and Lancaster Postal Employees.

They never formally adopted a budget. They never sent a delegate to Madison, Wisconsin, to meet with CUNA.

Fresh life was breathed into the Pennsylvania credit union movement through the work of Orchard and his organizers at the Federal Credit Union Section. Orchard doubtlessly welcomed the reinforcement, but he was a veteran of organizing campaigns in Pennsylvania well before his federal appointment. In a 1962 letter to then League executive director William Pratt, Orchard recalled the early days in Pennsylvania:

"I seem to remember that I talked to the folks in the post office at Lancaster and at Allentown and of a fruitless visit I made to the International Correspondence Schools at Scranton....

"I also remember being with Mr. Bergengren in Harrisburg. We worked there with employees of the State (Andrew Hanemann) and with the teachers. I believe that the folks in the post office met with me later at the Penn Harris.

"Then I clearly recall that Mr. Bergengren and I were driven one evening from Pittsburgh to McKeesport where he organized the Post Office C.U. and I met for the first time with that veteran of the Penna credit union wars Rudy Goetz. I seem to remember that Dora [Maxwell] and I met with the Pittsburgh teachers in a Methodist Church downtown and that the three of us spent some time with one faction of the Philadelphia Teachers.

"Selfishly I would like to live over the credit union beginnings in Pennsylvania and will be pleased indeed if you decide to press Dora and Agnes [Gartland] along with Matt Pottiger, Rudy Goetz, even Andrew Hanemann and others who were a part of that early endeavor to put their recollections down in writing.

"Some day the Credit Union Movement in Pennsylvania will be so large and so helpful to its citizens, that there will be a demand for the story of its beginnings."

146

The day when that credit union movement in Pennsylvania would be "so large and so helpful to its citizens" was greatly accelerated by the work of Orchard and his leading Pennsylvania organizers, Jimmy Dacus and Julia Connor.

According to the official records of the Federal Credit Union Section of the Farm Credit Administration, Fried and Reineman Employees FCU in Pittsburgh was the state's first federal credit union. It was chartered in November 1934. Organizing activities picked up quickly. In December, several federal credit union charters were granted to organizations throughout the state. They included, in order, Allentown Postal Employees FCU, Allis-Chalmers Pittsburgh Works Employees FCU, Pittsburgh Fairmont Creamery FCU, Employees of the Philadelphia Navy Yard FCU, and Pittsburgh Press FCU.

By the end of the year, there were 149 federal credit unions chartered in Pennsylvania, more than any other state in the nation; New York was second with 110; Texas was a distant third with 63. That first year's crop of federal credit unions included several that would provide the League with powerful leadership.[10]

10. Among the earliest federal credit unions chartered were: Warren (Pa.) United States Employees FCU; Springfield (Delaware County) Pa. FCU; Bridesburgh Philadelphia Employees FCU; Mercer County (Pa.) United States Employees FCU; Pittsburgh Whitaker Employees FCU; Pittsburgh District Reorganized L.D.S. FCU; Pittsburgh District Western Union Employees FCU; Hope Pittsburgh Office Employees FCU; Peoples Natural Gas Forbes Station Employees FCU; Sander Markets Employees FCU; St. Augustine's Parish; People's Natural Gas General Office Employees FCU; Allegheny County Y.M.C.A. Employees FCU; Allegheny County (Pa.) U.S. Government Employees FCU; Standard Sanitary Pittsburgh FCU; Chromalux FCU; Circle E. Employees Oakmont FCU; Donora Wire Works Employees FCU; Joseph Horne Company Employees Pittsburgh FCU; Mackintosh-Hemphill Employees No. 1 FCU; Pittsburgh Firemen's FCU; Tacu Employees New Kensington Pa. FCU; Apollo Steel Employees FCU; Philadelphia DuPont Grasseli Employees FCU; Frank & Seder Employees FCU; P.& W.V. Railway Employees FCU; Philadelphia Breyer Ice Cream Co. Employees FCU; Harris Stores Employees FCU; Pittsburgh Credit Bureau Employees FCU; Bucyrus-Erie Employees of Pennsylvania FCU; Pittsburgh Coal Employees FCU; Westinghouse Micarta Products Employees FCU; U.S.Northern Penitentiary Employees FCU; Elks FCU; A.T.&T. Employees Pittsburgh Pa. FCU; Westinghouse Foundry Employees Trafford, Pa. FCU; Pittsburgh P.R.C.Employees FCU; U.S.Bureau of Mines, Pittsburgh Employees FCU; Gimbel Pittsburgh Employees FCU; Yorkco York Employees FCU. The above were all chartered by the end of May, 1935.

147

By the end of 1935, its first full year of operation, Claude Orchard well deserved the plaudits he was receiving in the credit union movement. His end-of-year report told the story well.

> "The Credit Union Section now has 19 field investigators who are prepared to give prompt assistance to groups anywhere in the United States desiring to form a credit union. Our investigators are particularly eager to assist any director, committeeman or member who needs help in forming a new credit union."

The record in Pennsylvania spoke loudly for the administrative skill behind those words. And Orchard did not confine his activities to the work of the Federal Credit Union Section. Functionally, he became an active organizer for CUNA. He and his staff became CUNA activists; Orchard, Dacus, and Connor were all important players in CUNA's attempt to bring the Pennsylvania League to a higher level of activity.

In Pittsburgh, Orchard, Maxwell and Doig had even managed to form a chapter—without any involvement from Hanemann and the Pennsylvania League. Under presidents J. Frank Beaman (then Financial Editor of the *Pittsburgh Press*) and Howard H. Hook, this chapter was responsible for the rapid growth of the movement in the Pittsburgh area. With Doig's urging and planning, it would soon be responsible for much more. This Pittsburgh Chapter would become the basis for reorganizing the Pennsylvania League.

To credit union leaders throughout western Pennsylvania, there was nothing extraordinary about the newly formed chapter. Future League director Lawrence Hardman later recalled those days:

> "After a few Federal Credit Unions were organized, a call was sent out by the Extension Bureau [actually, by CUNA] for Pennsylvania credit unions to meet in Pittsburgh at the Board of Education Building. Erie Postal was represented by four

members of our Board. It was at this meeting that I became acquainted with Otto Herklotz and Rudy Goetz.

"Shortly thereafter Tom Doig came to Erie, and was instrumental in organizing the Chapter here. I was elected secretary at that time, and representative of the Erie Chapter—which office was resolved into a directorship, which I held for many years."

In January 1936, Hanemann wrote to the Pennsylvania credit unions announcing that the third annual meeting of the Pennsylvania Credit Union League would be held March 7, 1936, in Harrisburg. The invitation was sent on Pennsylvania Farm Bureau Cooperative Association letterhead. Hanemann had left the state's Agriculture Department to work for the agricultural cooperative, but retained both his membership and office with the State Employees Credit Union.

The letter must have annoyed the leaders in Madison when copies reached them. Hanemann took advantage of his mailing to the credit unions to solicit business on behalf of the cooperative's Farm Bureau Mutual Automobile Insurance Company. Hanemann's letter was enthusiastic about the coming credit union league meeting: "We hope that a delegation from your Credit Union will attend. In fact, we hope this will be the largest Credit Union gathering ever held in Pennsylvania." He was even more enthusiastic about Farm Bureau Insurance. "Here is an opportunity for your members to make very material savings in their automobile insurance, which could be handled for those members who are interested, through designated agents within your credit union."

Originally scheduled for March 7, the third annual [1936] meeting was actually held Saturday, April 18 at the Penn Harris Hotel, Harrisburg. It convened at 6:30 p.m. on a clear spring night, full of the promise of reawakening and renewal. The business meeting followed the banquet. Spirits were running high with enthusiasm and excitement for the growing Pennsylvania credit union movement.[11]

Visitors at this meeting included an impressive list of people who would become important leaders of the Pennsylvania credit union movement. One delegate from Philadelphia Dupont-Grasselli Employees FCU was William Pratt, a future director and executive director of the League. Claude Orchard was there with his wife representing his Federal Credit Union Section. With him was Julia Connor, the former correspondent [administrative assistant] at FCA who had become his leading credit union organizer in Pennsylvania. Connor would soon become Pennsylvania's first full-time credit union professional, the League's first full-time managing director. James A. [Jimmy] Dacus, another federal credit union organizer, was also there with the Orchard party. Representing CUNA were Doig and Ralph C. Christie. Christie, a CUNA "field secretary," was a colleague of Maxwell.

This meeting was called on behalf of CUNA's leadership as a major attempt to bring the Pennsylvania League to life—and to dues-paying status. In his introductory comments, Hanemann stated that the order of business would be "to decide whether to emulate the Midwestern credit unions in their league and chapter organization and to learn the connection between the State League and the National Association."

The meeting was conducted on the most fundamental level. It was as if the delegates had had no previous experience with

---

11. Credit unions represented at the April 18, 1936 meeting (and the number of delegates from each in parentheses) were as follows: Allentown Postal Employees FCU (4); Allentown Teachers CU (4); Building and Needle Trade Workers CU (4); Harrisburg Postal Employees CU (4); Lancaster Postal Employees CU (1); McKeesport Postal Employees CU (4); Pennsylvania State Employees Credit Union (7); Philadelphia Teachers CU (5); Swift Harrisburg CU (7); Williamsport Teachers CU (1); Armour Newberry CU (5); New Way Employees FCU. (4). Philadelphia Dupont-Grasselli Employees FCU. (5); Bradford Postal Employees CU (2); Shenango Pottery Employees FCU (3); St. Basil Parish Credit Union of Pittsburgh (3); National Casket Pittsburgh Employees FCU. (4); Harrisburg Teachers FCU. (3); Westinghouse Micarta Products FCU. (2); Culbreth FCU (1); Your Money's Worth CU (1); Lancaster County Teachers CU (1).

credit union activities, and, in fact, most of them were new to the movement.

Orchard spoke about the status of the credit union movement, stressing the rapid expansion of the federal credit union system. He emphasized the need for a state league and a national association as the only practical way to coordinate their growth and activities. Doig was the featured speaker of the evening. He opened with greetings from Bergengren, "and then delivered a very inspiring and instructive address. He discussed the History and Purposes of the Credit Union, emphasizing the fact that the real purpose of the Credit Union is to eliminate usury. Mr. Doig explained very clearly the need of a State League and the National Association and suggested a dues schedule of 1/2 of 1 per cent of assets for dues." Ralph Christie, introduced as a chapter organizer, then concluded the program with comments on the meaning of the CUNA trade mark, the recently adopted Little Man Under the Umbrella.

For the third time, the Pennsylvania League took up the question of dues. After extended debate, the delegates agreed:

> "That the dues of the Credit Unions of Pennsylvania in the Pennsylvania Credit Union League shall be fixed at one-half of one per cent of the assets of the Credit Union as of December 31, 1935, with minimum dues of ten cents for each member of the Credit Union affiliated, except that no Credit Union which paid a dividend of less than three per cent shall pay dues."

A second resolution was passed requiring that those credit unions exempted from dues still pay an entrance fee of $2.00 for membership in the League. Delegates from three credit unions, Allentown Teachers, Philadelphia Dupont Grasselli and Harrisburg Teachers, agreed to send in checks at once. Hanemann agreed to place the question before the directors of the Pennsylvania State Employees Credit Union immediately with a recommendation that they too remit the required payment. This appeared to be a simple request. It would later have major implications.

At last it appeared that the Pennsylvania League was ready to assume a full and responsible role in the organized credit union movement. Doig suggested that chapters be formed and that each chapter appoint three persons to serve as a State League membership committee. That recommendation was duly moved and seconded. So too was his recommendation that a membership meeting be scheduled for Saturday July 18, 1936, "to elect a Board of Directors for next year, and transact such other business as may come before the League."

While it appeared that things were finally going well in Pennsylvania, the representatives from CUNA and from the Federal Credit Union Section were neither pleased nor satisfied. There were three months before the special July 18 meeting would convene in Harrisburg. The national association leaders determined to use that time period to seek new leadership for the Pennsylvania credit union movement.

VI

Reconstruction and Restart

"Tom Doig and Dora Maxwell came to Pittsburgh and requested us to send representatives to Harrisburg to help with the reorganization of the Pennsylvania League. The League had been set up about a year before. But it was extremely inactive and there was much dissatisfaction with it. So we went to work and reorganized the Pennsylvania League."

Joe Moore

SATURDAY NIGHT, JULY 18, was a violently hot, sticky evening in Harrisburg. It was an evening that would see tempers in the Penn Harris Hotel rise as high as the thermometer. The deeds done that night would result in a new start for the Pennsylvania Credit Union League. Officially, this was the second session of the third annual meeting of the League. In the future, many Pennsylvania credit union leaders would regard it as the first meeting of the League.

For Tom Doig, Dora Maxwell and a few others, it was an evening they had long anticipated. To a large group of credit union leaders, especially a boisterous group from the western part of the state, it promised to be an eventful evening of fun and excitement. In the entire Pennsylvania credit union movement only the infant League's incumbent officers and directors and a few delegates from member credit unions did not know that major changes were about to take place.

Despite the oppressive heat, the meeting was well attended. It was by far the largest group of credit union representatives ever gathered in the Commonwealth.[1] As had already become

1. Eight chapters were represented at the meeting; they were Bradford, Erie, Harrisburg, Lancaster, Metropolitan (Philadelphia), Pittsburgh, Wilkes-Barre, and Williamsport. Credit unions represented at the meeting were: Allentown Teachers CU.; Ambridge Pennsylvania School Teachers FCU; Spang Chalfont Ambridge Employees FCU; Hotel Bethlehem Employees FCU; McCourt Label FCU.; Donora Wire Works Employees FCU; Erie Postal Employees CU; Walworth Employees CU; Harrisburg Postal Employees CU; Harrisburg Teachers FCU; Pennsylvania State Employees CU; Swift Harrisburg Employees CU; Lancaster Postal Employees CU; Lancaster Teachers CU; McKeesport Postal Employees CU; Enterprise Can Company Employees FCU; Shenango Pottery Employees FCU; Circle E Employees Oakmont FCU; Atlantic Refining Company Employees FCU; Carl

traditional, the evening started with a lavish banquet, but the main dish to be devoured that evening would be H. Andrew Hanneman, his fellow officers, and the directors.

Roy Bergengren would recall that hot night in Harrisburg many years later. "On July 18 there was an important meeting on a very hot night when Tom [Doig], Dora [Maxwell], Julia Connor, Jimmy Dacus (the latter two of the federal section), and I reorganized the Pennsylvania Credit Union League at Harrisburg. The meeting started at 6:30 pm. It hadn't gone far when we had our coats off. It adjourned at 1:15 am. The thermometer registered 90 degrees throughout, and I noted that Tom's shirt was as wet as though he had been ducked in the creek. Just below zero weather could not stop the national board in Madison in February, so 90 degrees in the coolest spot in Harrisburg could not prevent reorganization of the Pennsylvania League in July."

The featured after-dinner speaker was Claude Clark, president of CUNA. He spoke on "Benefits of a State League." Then League president Hanemann introduced Bergengren who gave "an inspirational" talk about the importance of the national organization. Routinely the meeting moved on to election of directors.

Memories differ somewhat about the following sequence of

Mackley Houses FCU; Dill and Collins CU; New Way Laundry Employees FCU; Philadelphia Consumer Coop Club FCU; Philadelphia DuPont-Grasselli Employees FCU; Philadelphia Long Lines FCU; Philadelphia Navy Yard FCU; Philadelphia Teachers CU; Philco Employees FCU; Sears, Roebuck Philadelphia CU; Western Union Philadelphia District Employees FCU; Allegheny County U.S. Government Employees FCU; Allis Chalmers Pittsburgh Works Employees FCU; ATT Pittsburgh Pennsylvania Employees FCU; Heppenstall Employees FCU; Hope Pittsburgh Office Employees FCU; Joseph Horne Company Employees Pittsburgh FCU; Koppers Pittsburgh Employees FCU; Mackintosh-Hemphill Employees No. 1 FCU; Peoples Natural Gas General Office Employees FCU; Pittsburgh Firemen's FCU; St. Basil Parish CU; St. Joseph Parish Mt. Oliver Pennsylvania FCU; Spear Employees FCU; Swift Pittsburgh Employees CU; Western Electric Shippers FCU; Waestern General Division Employees East Pittsburgh FCU; Western Section K Employees FCU; Ageco Credit Union of Pennsylvania; Scranton Federal Employees CU; Western Micarta Products Employees FCU; Nelson Brothers Wilkes-Barre Employees FCU; Triangle Employees FCU; Armour-Newberry Employees FCU; and Williamsport Teachers CU.

Howard Hook served as president of the Pennsylvania Credit Union League, 1936–1940.

events. The official record tells a simple but incomplete story. The people who were there recall the evening's full range of activities, but their memories are far more complex than the official records.

According to the minutes:

> "A motion (2) was made, seconded and passed, 'That the previous motion [election of directors] be tabled until we find out who is entitled to vote.'
>
> "Mr. Thomas Doig read the list of credit unions which had signed up for the State League and given a check for dues.
>
> "The following motion was then made and seconded; 'That the Secretary call the roll of those entitled to vote and in answering to the roll call each credit union should cast its vote either in favor of election of directors by ballot or by roll call.' Motion carried."

In accordance with that motion, the meeting voted to proceed with the election of directors by secret ballot.

157

The reorganization originally planned by Tom Doig when he had suggested the July meeting was suddenly visible to Hanemann and the other incumbent League leadership. It was too late for them to do anything about it. Doig and Maxwell—perhaps Connor and Dacus as well—had spent the past several months contacting credit unions throughout the state in preparation for this meeting. Doig had personally recruited the many delegates from the Pittsburgh area. All were told of League activities and of the problems CUNA had been having. They were formed into a well-coached cadre. The parliamentary maneuvering was carefully planned and perfectly executed.

Among those credit unions which had not paid their dues was the Pennsylvania State Employees CU. Its delegates, including president Hanemann, were declared ineligible to vote or be nominated as director. Of the incumbent officers, only secretary John Hoshauer was renominated.[2] Jimmy Dacus of the Federal Credit Union Section and Mattis Pottiger of Harrisburg Postal Employees were appointed as tellers.

At this point the official record breaks off; apparently president Hanemann left the meeting and secretary Hoshauer stopped taking notes. Eyewitness A. R. Thompson, a delegate from Allegheny County (Pa.) U. S. Government Employees FCU, later wrote that Tom Doig temporarily assumed the chair, and S. Gurbarg took over as acting secretary.

2. The officially accepted nominations for director were:Edwin Schecter, Philadelphia Teachers; Anthony Zeller, New Way; G. A. Palmer, Joseph Horne Co. Employees Pittsburgh; William Pratt, Dupont Grasselli; Frank Tokay, Donora Wire; John T. McClintock, Harrisburg Teachers; William Robinson; Gerard Nicholas, Scranton Postal; A. R. Thompson, Allegheny County Federal Employees; Samuel Gurbarg, Philadelphia Consumers Coop; H. E. Stafford, Lancaster Postal; Otto Herklotz, McKeesport Postal; David Oblon, Wilkes-Barre; Earl Blatt, Harrisburg Postal; John Hoshauer, Williamsport Teachers; Thomas Caldwell, Westinghouse Employees; John Tegley, Enterprise Can; J. P. Byers, Shenango Pottery; Joseph A. Moore, Pittsburgh Firemen; Nevin Loch, Allentown Teachers; Earl Shaffer, Swift & Co. Harrisburg; Albert Rosenfelt, Carl Mackley, Houses Philadelphia; Leo Taggert, Ambridge Teachers; F. Kersting, Pittsburgh; R. C. Andrews, Swift & Co. Pittsburgh; Lynn Starret, Erie Postal; James Copley, Oakmont; E. I. Mills, Westinghouse.

Doig's script continued to play as written. The resumed official minutes record that "It was moved and seconded that first 8 nominees declared elected be elected for two (2) years, the other for one (1) year."

Elected for two-year terms were:

J. A. Moore	R. G. Andrews
O. Herklotz	E. I. Mills
G. A. Palmer, Jr.	A. R. Thompson
L. R. Taggart	Frank Tokay

Elected to one-year terms were:

J. W. Copley[3]	F. G. Caldwell
L. N. Sterrett	J. P. Byers
S. J. Gurbarg.	F. W. Kersting
J. M. Tegley	

The story behind that decision is a complicated reflection of Pennsylvania politics and geographical problems that would long plague the League. The first eight were all Pittsburgh-area delegates. The Pittsburgh group was large and well-organized. It was evident to all assembled that they could easily control the entire meeting. The decision to allow the Philadelphia area some representation (the one-year directors) was a compromise won by Doig in consultation with a hastily called caucus of the Pittsburgh group.

Eight directors were also elected who were not listed in the minutes of the general meeting, but who were seated at the directors meeting immediately following the plenary session. According to other accounts, they were selected to represent the chapters on the board of directors. This technique, presumably suggested by Doig, insured at least some representation of non-Pittsburgh, non-Philadelphia credit unions.

3. J. W. Copley resigned from the board when he was elected managing director at the board meeting which immediately followed the general session. E. Shechter was elected to fill his seat.

These "chapter directors" included:

D. J. Shannon (Philadelphia)
M. A. Pottiger (Harrisburg)
H. H. Hook (Pittsburgh)
J. C. Hoshauer (Williamsport)
L. F. Hardman (Erie)
I. W. Kreider (Lancaster)
E. D. Clauss (Allentown)
C. E. Sheldon (Bradford)[4]

John Hoshauer and E. D. Clauss thus became the only survivers of the founding group of officers and directors. They witnessed the overthrow of their friends and associates; Hoshauer lost his position as secretary; but the two did retain their seats on the board. Both continued to serve the board with distinction; neither was subsequently elected to League office.

The official minutes contain no record of the selection of chapter directors. As far as the record is concerned, their names appear as official members of the board at the next meeting. The minutes also do not record the compromise that gave the Pittsburgh-area directors two-year terms and directors from other areas, one-year terms.

That incomplete record reflects the chaotic disorder of the conduct of the evening's business. It also reflects the abrupt transfer of power as Hoshauer's record of the early part of the evening is replaced by Samuel Gurbarg's notes on the election, then by Pottiger's minutes of the Board meeting.

Fortunately other sources supply some of the missing narrative. Among other accounts are the recollections of A. R. Thompson who was elected to the board of directors that night. An attorney with the Veterans Administration and

---

4. A. R. Thompson's account of this meeting in the 1952 annual meeting booklet identifies C. E. Sheldon as elected to the board to represent the Bradford Chapter, but Sheldon is not listed in the minutes of the subsequent board meeting.

president of Allegheny County (Pa.) U. S. Government Employees FCU, he made many contributions to the League as an editor of League publications, as League president, and as author of many League bylaws. He remembers the entire reorganization well. In a 1982 interview he told of the entire episode:

> "Now how Tom Doig got hold of my name, I don't know. But sometime early in 1936....he came to my office and introduced himself and we had quite a conversation. Afterwards he contacted Al Palmer over at Hornes [Department Store], so we arranged for a luncheon meeting, the three of us, Al Palmer, Tom Doig, and myself....
>
> "Tom explained what he had in mind.... He said what he was trying to do was ... well they had a state organization in Pennsylvania but it was inactive and no one was doing anything about it. It was dormant. They had some officers but they hadn't had any meetings. And he wanted to get the thing revitalized....
>
> "Shortly after that time he arranged for a meeting to be held of all the Pittsburgh credit unions together [presumably the first meeting of the Pittsburgh Chapter]. This was sometime before the announced meeting in Harrisburg was scheduled....
>
> "It was a hot summer night. Howard Hook who was president of Koppers Credit Union, arranged space for the meeting. So we all gathered to elect representatives to go to Harrisburg for this so-called reorganization meeting. That's where we all met each other. Joe Moore, Howard Hook, Al Palmer, all the rest of them that were around at the start of the credit union from Pittsburgh....
>
> "Now Pittsburgh was so active at that time because of Tom Doig's influence and the fact that we had a number of people who were interested in promoting this. They were a little disgusted with the people from the East because they had done so little with this organization. So we went down to Harrisburg with enough representatives to control the meeting completely....

"This doesn't show in the records, of course, not the official records. We elected the entire board of directors. All from Pittsburgh. Well, we knew that wouldn't stand up, but we had to show our power. Our interest was in getting the organization established so that it would operate and not become a dormant paper thing....

"We had our own caucus meeting and decided that we would let a few of those elected remain, and then voluntarily we let them from the eastern part of the state select who they wanted to be in there, including Matt Pottiger from Harrisburg and Ed Thompson and some of those early names....

"Remember that no one knew anybody. We knew very little about each other. Now for the board of directors, we elected all of the Pittsburgh people for two-year terms. Then the ones that were elected later got one-year terms.

From the point of view of Tom Doig, Dora Maxwell, and the Pittsburgh group, the evening was a great success. To Hanemann, it was the end of his 13-year association with the Pennsylvania credit union movement. He left the meeting and the organized credit union movement. Only long after he had retired from active leadership of Pennsylvania State Employees Credit Union did his credit union reaffiliate (1977). The other "old guard" officers also withdrew. Several of them did, however, resume active roles at later dates.

Joseph Moore's memories of the re-organization, recorded in a 1967 interview with Howard Custer of CUNA Mutual, were similar to Art Thompson's:

"Tom Doig and Dora Maxwell came to Pittsburgh and requested us to send representatives to Harrisburg to help with the reorganization of the Pennsylvania League. The League had been set up about a year before. But it was extremely inactive and there was much dissatisfaction with it. So we went to work and reorganized the Pennsylvania League.

"Many new credit unions had been chartered in Pittsburgh and western Pennsylvania. We sent a considerable delegation to the Harrisburg meeting. But we didn't understand what it

Joe Moore, pioneering credit union leader from the Pittsburgh area played a leading behind-the-scenes role in the Pennsylvania League's reorganization. He served as president of the League, 1946–1949.

was all about. I was elected to the state and national boards at this meeting."

Moore's election as Pennsylvania's first national delegate to the CUNA board of directors came at the League directors' meeting that same night. H. H. Hook was elected president of the League. D. J. Shannon was elected vice president; Matt Pottiger was elected secretary; Frank Tokay was elected treasurer; J. W. Copley was elected managing director.

Hook, president of Koppers Pittsburgh Employees FCU, was new to the credit union movement, as were Tokay of Donora Wire Works Employees FCU and Moore of the Pittsburgh Firemen FCU. All were active members of the Pittsburgh caucus, hand-picked for the job of helping to reorganize the Pennsylvania League by Doig and Maxwell.

Moore was chief clerk of the Pittsburgh Fire Bureau. He was recruited for the credit union movement by Claude Orchard who had been referred to Moore after Pittsburgh's fire chief decided that he could not understand what the visitor from Washington was after.

Pottiger was an assistant to the Harrisburg postmaster and

an active member of Harrisburg Postal Employees CU, one
of the first credit unions chartered under the Pennsylvania
law. His credit union had been organized by Orchard and
Bergengren; Pottiger had attended the first League meeting
in December 1934. Of the group that took over the League,
Pottiger was the only officer whose personal experience went
back to that early date. In a 1967 interview he recalled that the
League "did not—you might say—get off the ground with
this thing at that time.

> "In April of '36 they came back. At that time it was Doig and
> Orchard and I think that they actually had some assistance
> from some of the federal examiners. Miss [Julia] Connor was
> then working for Farm Credit, and I believe Bill Covington,
> who now has the Chicago region or is a director of one of the
> regions of the Federal Bureau."

Pottiger was a representative of the Harrisburg Chapter
during the 1936 reorganization. Thus the addition of the
"chapter directors" provided a seat on the board for him. He
viewed the events of that evening from a slightly different
perspective, but his recorded memories of the events fit well
with the other accounts.

> "Art Thompson was on the first board in '36. He came to the
> meeting in July. That was when most of us got together. Frank
> Tokay and Joe Moore and Bill Pratt showed up at that meeting
> also.... But they had this thing pretty well planned that they
> would try to get it off the ground. There was Doig and the
> delegates from the Pittsburgh area. So as a result of that meet-
> ing, Howard Hook from Koppers Company in Pittsburgh was
> our first League president. Frank Tokay was elected trea-
> surer."

This group meant business, and knew how to go about
putting their organization on a sound and active footing. At
the suggestion of Treasurer Tokay, they selected the Union
National Bank of Donora as depository for League funds,
directed the treasurer to secure bonding (at League expense),

Mattis Pottiger, first editor of the Pennsylvania Credit Union League's newsletter, volunteer managing director of the League, and long-term secretary of the League was president of the League, 1951–1953.

and determined that dues previously paid to the League should be considered as covering the year ending December 31, 1936.

The question of CUNA dues was referred to a new committee on revision of the bylaws. For the moment, at least, Doig had

165

to be satisfied with $10.00 appropriated to him personally as reimbursement for the cost of the band he had hired for the evening. The new League officers were serving notice that they would not necessarily dance to CUNA's tune, but would rather pay the piper themselves.

Except for the immediate question of dues, Doig's plan was a great success. "I was very pleased indeed with the Pennsylvania meeting and feel sure that now we have the basis on which a very strong and useful league can be developed," wrote Bergengren to Frank Tokay in August.

The Pennsylvania Credit Union League was fully launched. Never again would extended periods go by without meetings of the board (except for a one-year period during a major struggle over redistricting and control of the board). The new directors voted to reconvene September 19. Loyal to the interests of their city, they selected Pittsburgh as the site for their next meeting. The old order, based in Harrisburg, was out. The power had gone west.

Moore quickly and quietly drew the League reins into his own hands. He had done his homework well. Moore was a practiced politician, and he assumed control of the League in an almost casual way. Art Thompson remembers that Moore's selection as national director seemed to be an afterthought.

> "In that July 1936 meeting—what I call the first meeting— we only elected one national director. We later learned we could have four. And during the evening a number of my people wanted to know if I wanted to take that job. No one really wanted it particularly. Finally Joe said he was willing to take it. Once we got someone who was willing to take it, well that settled it. So Joe was elected at that meeting. Now I guess subsequently it was determined that Pennsylvania was entitled to four, so we elected Matt Pottiger, Bill Pratt, and Frank Tokay. We didn't know there should be anyone. It was Tom, Tom Doig, who pointed out that there was a national association and there should be a national director."

Moore retained tight control over the board for many years thereafter. Art Thompson and Matt Pottiger were well aware of Moore's unofficial power, and the cost of crossing him. As Thompson recalled:

> "It wasn't too long until Joe Moore took power—took over. He was from the Pittsburgh area and the Pittsburgh area was highly political. It was Democratic in nature at that time—during the Roosevelt administration—and everything in Pittsburgh was controlled by the political voice. Joe was a politician.
>
> "Everything was controlled by influence. You had influence, you got what you wanted. And it wasn't too long until Joe began to call the shots. And he called them to the point where if you disagreed with him, well you were out of the picture and he seemed to be able to maneuver enough people to believe this. He was a very forceful individual.
>
> "He was doing it for the good of the credit union. He believed in the credit union. Maybe the results justified the means. If I had taken opposition to him openly and not tried to be strategic—I probably would have been defeated for the board of directors. He decided who was going to be on the board of directors for the Pittsburgh area."

As Pottiger recalled, Moore's influence extended beyond the Pittsburgh area. "Because of a little difference of opinion I lost my position as national director and League secretary for one year because Joe Moore was quite disturbed because we wouldn't abide by his wishes."[5]

---

5. Pottiger's dispute with Moore came when Moore sought election to the CUNA vice presidency, Eastern District. Pottiger refused to support him in this ambition. As Pottiger later told the story, "Joe went out and lined up a coalition between Philadelphia and Pittsburgh [Pottiger was from Harrisburg] and had me thrown out as a national director and secretary. He couldn't do anything to my position as a director of the league, however. Prior to the next year, this thing, without me saying anything at all, cleared itself up. Instead of going back to secretary, I was moved up to vice president."

Few people have been as zealous in their leadership of a cause as Joe Moore was in his commitment to the Pennsylvania credit union movement. He was a tireless worker and a skilled speaker. His clipping and note files give evidence of voracious reading and an organized approach to his frequent speeches.

Moore was a strong leader, a man of strong opinions. He was devoted to the Catholic Church and to the credit union movement. Both were deep personal commitments, and he fought hard in defense of his beliefs. The power of Joe Moore over the Pennsylvania credit union movement, a power that would last for many years, was an important and enduring result of Doig's reorganization.

At CUNA, news of the reorganization was greeted with rejoicing. "I was very pleased indeed with the Pennsylvania meeting and feel sure that now we have the basis on which a very strong and useful league can be developed," wrote Bergengren to Frank Tokay. CUNA had good reasons to rejoice. Tokay had just sent Doig a check for $500.00 "to cover partial payment on 1936 dues to the National Association. This amount is being forwarded to you at this time in order that the Pennsylvania League will not be considered among those delinquent on August 1st." The new leaders of the Pennsylvania League had just seen what happened to those who were delinquent. They had no wish to follow Hanemann into premature retirement from credit union activity.

Tokay immediately raised fresh questions. He asked that CUNA grant a dues remission in cases where credit unions had grown rapidly and the 10-cents per member assessment took them over 0.5% of total assets. Doig proved equal to the challenge. Suddenly he found much merit in the actions of the old (pre-reorganization) leadership.

"The decision regarding this matter was really made by the Pennsylvania League itself at the meeting on April 18th.... Possibly this was a mistake.... However, since I do very much appreciate the way you boys in Pittsburgh have come along

Frank Tokay of Donora, elected treasurer of the League at the 1936 reorganization, had a long and influential impact on history of the League.

with our program I am going to leave it to you to decide just what to do in cases of this kind during this first year."

The pleasure of CUNA's leadership at the reorganization in Pennsylvania was expressed in many other ways as well. President Claude Clarke had no formal report at the August 1936 meeting of the executive committee, but did take the time to say that he "felt the reorganization of the Pennsylvania League was one of the finest things that the National Association had done." The same meeting voted "to accept Mr. Joseph A. Moore as National Director from Pennsylvania in place of Mr. Hanemann, resigned."

The honeymoon between CUNA and the Pennsylvania directors was destined to be short. By 1937, the Pennsylvania delegation was filing objections to CUNA's dues schedules. As CUNA's board of directors minutes record:

> "The fixing of a dues schedule was next discussed. Mr. Pratt of Pennsylvania presented a report on the basis of assessing dues, the result of a study by the Pennsylvania Credit Union League, stating that the League did not believe the present method of assessment was equitable, and requesting the Executive Committee to consider the report, which was not read because of its length, in detail. On motion of Mr. Doig, duly seconded, it was:
>
> "VOTED; That the report of the Pennsylvania delegation relative to dues be received and referred to the Executive Committee for study and consideration."

Bill Pratt became a League director at the 1937 annual meeting, January 30, Lewistown.[6] He was elected with Pottiger

6. Chapters from Allentown, Bradford, Erie, Harrisburg, Lancaster, Philadelphia, and Pittsburgh sent delegates to the Fourth Annual (Lewistown) meeting of January 30, 1937. They were joined by representatives of 39 credit unions, including: Allegheny Co., Pa., U. S. Government Employees FCU; Allentown Teachers CU; Allis-Chalmers Pittsburgh Works Employees FCU; Altoona Postal Employees CU; Armour Newberry CU; Armour Philadelphia CU; Bradford Postal Workers CU; Carl Mackley Houses FCU; Circle C Oakmont FCU; Donora Wire Works Employees FCU; Elks FCU; Enterprise Can Co. Employees FCU; Erie Postal Employees CU; Franklin C P T FCU; Hamilton Watch Employees FCU; Harrisburg Postal Employees CU; Heppenstall Employees FCU; Joseph Horne Co. Employees Pittsburgh FCU; Kaufmann Employees FCU; Kaufmann Store Employees FCU; Koppers Pittsburgh Employees FCU; Lancaster Postal Employees CU; Mackintosh-Hemphill Employees No. 1 FCU; McKeesport Postal Employees CU; National Works Employees FCU; New Way Laundry Employees FCU; Philadelphia Con. Coop Club FCU; Philadelphia DuPont Grasselli FCU; Philadelphia Navy Yard FCU; Philadelphia Teachers' CU; Pittsburgh City Hall Employees FCU; Pittsburgh Firemen's FCU; Sears, Roebuck Philadelphia FCU; Shenango Pottery Employees FCU; Swift Harrisburg Employees CU; Swift Pittsburgh Employees CU; Western Electric Shippers FCU; Western General Division Employees East Pittsburgh FCU

and Tokay to join Joe Moore as national directors. These four represented Pennsylvania at the first annual meeting of the Credit Union National Association board of directors held later that year in Washington. Pratt, a Philadelphian, quickly became a leading personality of the Pennsylvania League. Art Thompson remembers him well:

> "Of course Bill Pratt was a very strong operator too. But he was more of the compromiser type. He got his way more by persuasive powers than by out-and-out political work. With Bill, he got what he wanted, but he had the greatest power of persuasion. He convinced you; he didn't force you; he persuaded you."

Essentially, Pratt became eastern Pennsylvania's balance to the powerful skills and regional interests of Pittsburgh's Joe Moore. They had totally different personalities, but shared a deep devotion to the credit union movement and respect for each other's powers and capabilities. Together, they formed a powerful and politically potent team; their strength was recognized throughout the national credit union movement; their joint power over the Pennsylvania credit union movement would endure for more than a quarter of a century.

Pratt's interest in credit unions was simple and cogent. He knew little of Raiffeisen and cooperative credit theory. He had had little exposure to loan sharks, either at first hand or by repute. He found Bergengren to be an inspiring speaker who spoke directly to one important issue. As Pratt later recalled: "Bergengren did talk about the money lenders and the difference in rates. It was quite obvious if we could do this for ourselves at a low rate, why not? And I said we had enough management people in there and supervisors and a couple of people from the rank and file. There was a blending of minds."

Dorothy Pratt remembers the crushing poverty of her husband's childhood. Bill Pratt had to leave school at a young age to help support his family and was almost entirely self-taught. Exceptionally careful with money for his entire life, Pratt

171

Art Thompson, elected a member of the League Board at the 1936 reorganization, authored many League bylaws and served as president of the Pennsylvania Credit Union League, 1955–1957.

would spend much of his credit union career fighting for lower CUNA dues.

Pratt was a director of Philadelphia DuPont-Grasselli FCU and also served as the credit union's president. He never worked directly with credit union members, and he was not an active organizer. He was a big man with a commanding presence whose skills were, as Art Thompson recalled, largely rhetorical and persuasive. Pratt provided a practical, simplistic approach to the problems of League administration.

Pratt was attracted to the credit union movement by its philosophy of self-help. He consistently thought that people

172

should do things for themselves and not rely on others. And if a group of people could take better care of their own financial needs more efficiently and at lower cost than outsiders, that suited him perfectly. He understood the concept "cost-effective" long before he had ever heard the words.

Pratt's first attempt to alter the dues structure came at the League's 1937 annual meeting—the meeting which moments before had elected him to the board. He proposed setting dues at 5% of gross earnings with a minimum membership fee of $5.00. The established CUNA dues schedule was based on gross assets, not gross income.

Other suggestions came from the floor. Edwin Schechter proposed dues based on the number of fully paid shares held by credit union members. Art Thompson pressed a plan based on numbers of members.

The board members were in a mood to compromise. They resolved the issue by empowering Pratt to present his proposal to the CUNA board of directors. At the same time, the Schecter proposal was supported by the board for presentation to CUNA as a new way of assessing national dues. For the League, the directors approved the Thompson plan.

This marks the beginning of the Pennsylvania League's practice of assessing dues in a manner determined by its own directors—not in accordance with practice suggested by CUNA. The League established dues at 15 cents per credit union member (as of December 31 of the previous year), provided, that new credit unions paying a dividend of less that 3% pay a membership fee of $5.00, and that credit unions paying no dividend pay membership fees of $2.00. No credit union would pay dues higher than a $300.00 maximum established in the first dues action.[7]

---

7. During the debate, a visitor from New York recommended that Pennsylvania imitate the New York League and adopt a dues policy based on total assets. The response was quickly heard that even after 15 years of operations, the New York League still faced continuous argument over dues. That experience, declared one Pennsylvania director, would not be repeated in the Keystone State.

Even as Bill Pratt was demanding that CUNA find ways to cut expenses and lower dues, the CUNA leadership was working to convince the Pennsylvania League that the time had come for it to hire a full-time, professional managing director. Tom Doig pointed out to the CUNA executive committee at their November 1937 meeting that nine states, six of them with fewer credit unions than Pennsylvania, all had full-time managing directors. Doig knew that Pennsylvania's 5% dues schedule should be sufficient to support a full-time executive. "We must act immediately in those states which are in a position to afford a managing director," Doig told the CUNA executive committee. He later reported to them that "Mr. [Clifford] Skorstad and Miss Maxwell spent the month of October in Pennsylvania doing contact work which we hope will place that League in a position to employ a full-time Managing Director next year."

Skorstad was the CUNA field organizer primarily responsible for rural credit unions. He was in Pennsylvania frequently during the early years, but his success here was limited. Actually, the American credit union movement never really penetrated rural communities. A 1936 survey of credit unions in rural America found that fewer than 5% of the nation's 5,100 credit unions were serving rural communities. Farmers, the report noted, typically needed large production loans, not small personal loans. Second, the report noted that many rural communities had special banking institutions that had been created specifically to meet the needs of farmers. Finally, the report noted that the organized credit union movement had expended little effort to organize in rural areas.

This pattern was repeated in Pennsylvania. Despite Skorstad's work, only a few Pennsylvania credit unions were organized to help in rural areas. As the League and Farm Credit Administration took increasing responsibility for organizing Pennsylvania and CUNA's Organization and Contacts Department concentrated more on working with leagues, Skorstad had even less success in the state. Federal Credit Union Section organizers concentrated heavily on industrial plants and virtually ignored rural communities.

Organization of rural credit unions was one benefit that CUNA hoped would come with a full-time managing director. It had become obvious that without such direction, organizing Pennsylvania credit unions would continue to lag well behind expectations. With no money and no help, the League's first managing director, Andy Hanemann, had not been able to accomplish anything in the post. J. W. Copley, Hanemann's successor elected at the July 18, 1936 meeting, also found organization work more difficult and time-consuming than he had anticipated.

Like Hanemann, Copley was a volunteer. The time that he could devote to League activities was limited. He was the treasurer of the Pittsburgh Chapter and proved to be a skilled chapter organizer. By September 1936, there were active chapters in Pittsburgh, Philadelphia, Erie, Bradford, Lancaster, Allentown, and Harrisburg. Although he had the inclination, he had neither the time nor the skill to handle all of these demands.

Copley spent most of his report at the next meeting explaining that he had insufficient time to accomplish any of the tasks assigned at the previous meeting. He had spent most of his time seeking to expand membership and assisting in the ongoing credit union organization activities. Over the past three months, he had visited more than 50 different industrial plants to encourage credit union membership. At the June 1937 meeting of the directors, Copley resigned.

At the same meeting, Matt Pottiger, League secretary, was elected managing director. Pottiger took on the responsibilities of that post in addition to his duties as editor of the new monthly league publication, *Keystone State News*, and in addition to his responsibilities as secretary of the League.

Pottiger was also selected by the board to be the voting representative of the League at CUNA Supply Cooperative, a new affiliate of the Credit Union National Association that was being organized to provide office supplies, forms, and other materials needed by credit unions. The Pennsylvania League voted to join the cooperative at the June 1937 directors meeting.

The managing director was ordered by the board to seek further publicity for League activities and to promote the additional contact and organization of credit unions. He was directed to continue publication of the monthly news letter.

This would not have been a complete board of directors meeting without consideration of a "dues" resolution. Accordingly, Bill Pratt revived his recommendation from six months before. This time he was successful, and a revised dues structure went into effect for the Pennsylvania Credit Union League:

> "The annual dues of the credit union members of the Pennsylvania Credit Union League shall be five percent (5%) of their gross earnings as of December 31 of the previous year, but not less than five dollars ($5), except that credit unions paying no dividend shall pay a membership fee of five dollars ($5), and each member credit union shall submit annually to the Treasurer of the League a certified copy of its financial statement as of December 31 of the previous year."

This policy was declared retroactive to the previous annual meeting. Thus the Thompson plan based on number of members was discarded and the Pratt plan based on gross earning revived and reinstated.

Since January 1937, 25 new credit unions had been organized in the state. They included 24 federal charters and only one state charter; 15 of the new organizations had affiliated with the league and there were 99 dues-paying member credit unions. The League had a bank balance of $1054.54. It owed $409.95 to CUNA.

Pottiger served as managing director until February 1938 when the board employed Julia D. Connor as the League's first full-time professional executive.

By 1935, Orchard had nineteen men working in the field, organizing and supervising credit unions. One of those nineteen "men" was Connor, an assistant investigator with the Credit Union Section of the Farm Credit Administration. The only woman (with 18 men) doing the job, Connor was appointed at her request shortly after the passage of the federal credit union law, promoted from being chief of the correspondents' section (an executive administrative assistant) at FCA.

When interviewed at the time, she commented that: "I do not consider that it is a man's work any more than a woman's; for I have met with men as well as women, many a time going right into the workroom, whether it be a glass plant, an enamel factory, a shoe factory, or a ladies' shop; there is no line of sex or color when we talk about the common problems of men and women."

Connor's job with the Credit Union Section was described in the *Philadelphia Inquirer* as "spreading information and creating interest in credit unions as a means of promoting thrift and making it possible for salaried men and women to take care of their own credit problems, at reasonable rates of interest."

Connor brought energy, zeal, and dedication to her organizing work with the Federal Credit Union Section. "Every employer is familiar with the financial problems of his employees as reflected by wage assignments, garnishments and company loans to employees. These problems occupy no inconsiderable attention of employers and involve no insignificant sums of company funds. They vary only in proportion to the number of employees. In their number are many who are on the borderline of want, who, through any emergency requiring the expenditure of funds, are either forced to seek charity, or to turn to the money lenders to tide them over," she told the *Inquirer* reporter.

Connor had been a correspondent (administrative assistant) with FCA when the Credit Union Section was created. She was

177

fascinated by the concept of credit unions, and quickly sought transfer to the new department. Claude Orchard was impressed by her zeal, by her accomplishments with FCA, and by her understanding of credit unions and desire to serve. It was thus Orchard who brought Connor into federal credit union work.

Roy Bergengren published an early article about Connor in *The Bridge*. Her comments went to all who knew and cared about the credit union movement. "Here is work which, in the future, more women will find to their liking. It involves more than business alone, more than banking; it holds the element which gives value and significance to everything that interests the feminine business idealist, the element of human values."

"Miss Connor," wrote Eleanor Morton, the reporter for the Philadelphia paper, "is the first in a long line of women who will create history in the field of finance." Actually Julia Connor was far from the first woman credit union leader. Other women leaders of the credit union movement included Agnes Gartland and Dora Maxwell at CUNA, Harriet Berry in North Carolina, Louise McCarren [Herring] in Ohio, Angela Melville in Tennessee and Kentucky, Elizabeth Lynch, Helen Logue and many others.

In Pennsylvania, Agnes Gartland had played an active role throughout CUNEB's attempts to win the Pennsylvania law, and Dora Maxwell, traveling and working with Tom Doig, had played an important part in early League affairs, especially the 1936 reorganization.

Connor's decision to accept the offered position of managing director of the Pennsylvania League in February 1938 marks a turning point in League history. It is a moment as important as the July 18 reorganization meeting.

Connor's move from the Federal Credit Union Section to the Pennsylvania League was especially critical because of changing federal policies which were about to curtail FCA organizing activities. Had the League not been ready to hire Connor and assume responsibility for organizing credit unions, the Pennsylvania movement might well have died then and there.

First, the Bureau of the Budget challenged the right of federal officials to organize private financial institutions such as credit unions. For a government agency to encourage the organization of financial institutions which they would also supervise seemed to be a conflict of interest. When FCA's chief examiner found shortages in two state-chartered credit unions organized by Federal Credit Union Section officials, he recommended that FCA Governor Myers curtail federal organizing activities.

Myers responded by placing tight limits on FCA organizers. They could no longer initiate credit union formation, although they would be permitted to continue to respond to requests from interested groups for information and assistance. They could no longer assist credit unions forming under state charter. For Jimmie Dacus, Julia Connor, and Milton Rhye—the Federal Credit Union Section organizers with primary responsibility for Pennsylvania—these restrictions were less onerous than for others at FCA. Pennsylvania credit unions overwhelmingly preferred federal charters, and the League was strong enough to serve as a referral agency. But the new limitations doubtless made the possibility of working for the League an attractive proposition for the active and ambitious Connor.

The League had become a viable trade association in 1936, but it was capable of little more than self-support. Through the work of Pottiger, it had created a monthly newsletter and organized several campaigns for legislative reform. There were almost no other League programs.

The League existed because CUNA had organized it and a few people like Moore, Pratt, Thompson, Tokay, and some of the others enjoyed League activities. Since Hanemann and his group had been ousted, there had been no leaders in Pennsylvania who understood the history and philosophy of the credit union movement. The League was functioning in an ideological vacuum.

Pratt's understanding of the credit union's mission was pragmatic, not philosophical. He understood the need to make low-cost loans available, and the advantages inherent in people helping themselves. He did not appreciate that credit unions need not constantly seek to maximize profits. And where the availability of information, educational programs, or other movement activities conflicted with the goal of lowering operational costs, Pratt stood ready to sacrifice programs. His main interest lay in efficient, cost-effective management.

Moore's main interest was in the political affairs of the credit union movement. A fireman, he was dedicated professionally and personally to helping people in need. Where Pratt was intrigued by the credit union's potential for self-help, Moore was attracted by the institutional capabilities of an organization set up to provide help. He was fascinated by CUNA and its political possibilites, and perceived his own role to be that of social benefactor. The credit union gave him the opportunity to do good on a grand scale.

Moore was in total control of the Pittsburgh contingent of the League, and sought continually to expand his own influence on state and national credit union affairs. His abilities helped make Pennsylvania's voice a strong one in the national credit union movement. Like Pratt, he had relatively little interest in the substance and programs of the movement.

Connor's interest in credit union activities predated her work with the Pennsylvania League. It was her interest in rural values and cooperative credit that had originally taken her to FCA. It was her fascination with the credit union concept that led her to request transfer from the Correspondents' Section to the Federal Credit Union Section when the latter was formed in 1934.

Connor's commitment and dedication to credit unions made her an effective organizer in Pennsylvania. While working with Orchard she had personally been responsible for organizing many of the federal credit unions in the eastern district.

So when it became apparent that the federal government would be withdrawing from the organizing business and building up its supervisory functions, Connor actively sought to move from the Federal Credit Union Section to the Pennsylvania League. Recognizing that organizing activities would have to become the responsibility of either the state government, as in Wisconsin, or the state leagues, CUNA had been trying to persuade Pennsylvania to hire a full-time director since August 1937. At the directors' meeting, Doig pointed out that the dues schedule was adequate to support a full-time executive and that the potential for League growth was promising.

On several occasions, Connor had accompanied Orchard, Doig, Maxwell, and others from CUNA and the Federal Credit Union Section to League meetings. She was there both as the only individual familiar to many of the delegates from newly organized credit unions, and as the unofficial establishment nominee for Pennsylvania managing director.

Connor was present at the January 22, 1938 meeting of the board of directors, accompanied by Milton Rhye of the Federal Credit Union Section who had recently joined her in the field. At that meeting, Pottiger informed the group that he thought it "necessary and imperative" that a full-time managing director be employed. Furthermore, Pottiger said that he did not wish to be considered (he already knew the salary that was contemplated and that he could not afford to accept it). On a motion from the floor, it was decided to hire a full-time managing director and the meeting adjourned for dinner.

The few remaining questions and doubts were taken care of at the dinner tables. When the meeting reconvened, the directors voted to accept Pottiger's resignation, effective with the hiring of a full-time managing director. It was then voted that Connor be elected to the position at a salary of $200.00 per month, subject to termination by either the board or Miss Connor on 30 days' written notice. Connor decided to leave her federal post and accept the offered position effective the following month. She thus became the first senior official of the League with any substantial organizing experience.

When she joined the League, the announcement in *Keystone State News* was low key:

> "For some time there has been a growing realization of the need for full time service in the development of a program of action which would insure the future of credit unions and bring credit union service to the maximum of eligible persons.... The need for a strong central organization which will actively promote the organization of new credit unions is further strengthened by the fact that emphasis of the Federal Government is being swung away from organization and will, until a change in policy, be, like that of the State, toward supervision."

The extent of Pottiger's accomplishment as acting managing director should not be underestimated. He initiated *Keystone State News* as a mimeographed newsletter and nourished it to maturity as a Pennsylvania supplement to *The Bridge*. In 1937, Pottiger led the League's legislative efforts. An attempt to amend the state law that year could have produced disastrous consequences. As a result of Pottiger's efforts, there were some positive changes made in the law and some of the changes, mostly technical adjustments, reflected desires of the credit union movement.

Pennsylvania's state chartered credit unions were released from the need to state a fixed capitalization and therefore from having to amend articles of association in order to sell shares in excess of the stated capital. They were explicity exempted from paying the bonus tax on such increased capital, an exemption previously assumed under established precedent. Procedures for amending articles of incorporation were simplified as requested by the League. And state credit union charters no longer required approval by the governor.

Other provisions in the amended credit union law were passed over the objections of the League. The requirement that charter application notices be published in both a legal and general-circulaton newspaper was strengthened. The League had sought to have the requirement abolished.

One important change altered potential membership. Under the original state law, the "common bond" was recognized as including employment, residence, and fraternal organization membership. Under the 1937 amendment, the scope of membership was restricted to employment. State charters could no longer be granted to persons whose sole bond of association was residence within the same neighborhood, community or rural district, or membership in the same fraternal, religious or social organization.

Other changes to the state credit union law included elimination of Bergengren's hard-won exemption for new credit unions from examination charges and approval of compensation for credit union officers and directors "provided that the credit union has paid a dividend of not less than 3% in the previous year. The secretary of banking was authorized to prohibit or regulate the payment of compensation when such compensation is excessive or when the financial condition of the credit union does not warrant the payment of such compensation."[8]

The League's most important legislative accomplishment was the passage of Act No. 88, exempting credit unions from payment of the capital stock bonus tax. This significantly lowered the cost of incorporation for new credit unions.

During Pottiger's administration as managing director, some significant improvements were also made in the federal law. While no particular credit is due the Pennsylvania League for these efforts, Pottiger did work to support them. Since the changes affected federally chartered credit unions,

8. Other technical changes provided by this first amendment to the Pennsylvania credit union law included: approval of borrowing privileges for directors, officers and committee members, limited to the extent of unencumbered shares held by the director, officer, or committee member; approval for crediting dividends to the members' share accounts at the option of the board of directors in lieu of payments in cash; and simplification of reserve and reporting requirements.

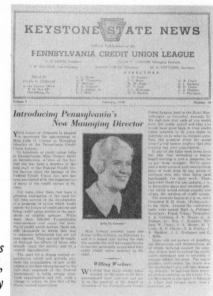

Keystone State News *was
originally written, edited,
mimeographed and mailed by
Matt Pottiger.*

they were important to the Pennsylvania credit union movement.

The amended act exempted federal credit unions from all taxation—local, state, or Federal—except for taxes on real estate and tangible personal property. An amendment offered by Rep. Everett Dirksen of Illinois protected the practice of federal departments in providing space for credit union operations.

Pottiger, as an officer in the Harrisburg Postal Employees CU was especially interested in the latter amendment. Actually, it also affected the entire League, for while Pottiger was managing director, he operated the Pennsylvania Credit Union league from his desk at the post office. The League's address for its first few years was "Harrisburg Post Office, Harrisburg, Pennsylvania." With the arrival of Julia Connor, the League address changed to Post Office Box 487. By March, the League had leased Suite 312 in Harrisburg's Kline Building.

Pottiger's record of accomplishment is considerable. His creation and regular, timely publication of the newsletter alone should stand as a major achievement. The legislative record was mixed, but the League won several important battles. Meetings of the board and of the full membership took place in such diverse locations as Pittsburgh, Lewistown, Harrisburg, and Philadelphia. All were well organized and skillfully administered.

Pottiger accomplished that remarkable record while a part-time, volunteer managing director. His full-time job was with the Harrisburg Post Office. At the same time, he was also clerk of the Harrisburg Postal Employees CU, part-time manager for a neighborhood cooperative association, national director of CUNA, delegate to CUNA Supply Cooperative, and secretary of the Pennsylvania Credit Union League. Pottiger frequently referred to the help he received from his wife, Mary Pottiger. Given the extent of his accomplishments and the probable nature of his weekly schedule, it seems likely that her work must have been a critical part of his wide-ranging activities.

The League grew during Pottiger's term as managing director, but its growth did not keep pace with the rate of increase of Pennsylvania's credit unions. New credit unions were being organized far more rapidly than they were affiliating with the League. At the end of 1936 when Pottiger assumed most responsibilities for League activities, there were 296 credit unions in Pennsylvania. Most of them were federal charters, and most of them were organized by Julia Connor, Jimmy Dacus, and Milton Rhye. Only 120 had affiliated with the League. By January 30, 1938 when Pottiger handed the reins over to Connor, there were 367 credit unions in the state; of that number, fewer than half, or 146 of them, were affiliated with the League.

Among her other accomplishments, Connor was skilled at compiling and maintaining records and reports. She was responsible for the first comprehensive survey of the geographical distribution of the credit unions of Pennsylvania.

Pennsylvania Credit Unions
May 31, 1938

County	Number of Credit Unions	
	In County	In League
Adams	1	0
Allegheny	146	52
Armstrong	1	0
Beaver	17	5
Berks	11	4
Blair	2	1
Bucks	1	0
Butler	1	0
Cambria	4	2
Center	2	0
Chester	2	1
Clearfield	2	0
Dauphin	10	6
Delaware	7	2
Elk	1	0
Erie	14	6
Fayette	2	0
Franklin	2	0
Lackawanna	5	2
Lancaster	5	4
Lawrence	5	3
Lehigh	11	5
Luzerne	12	7
Lycoming	2	2
McKean	8	4
Mercer	1	1
Monroe	1	0
Montgomery	4	1
Northampton	4	1
Philadelphia	84	28
Schuylkill	3	0
Tioga	1	0
Union	1	0
Venango	2	2
Warren	2	1
Washington	8	5
Westmoreland	18	7
York	2	1
Total for State	403	153

In four years, Pennsylvania had witnessed the creation of 400 credit unions. The fourteen credit unions that had founded the League in 1934 had grown to more than 150 dues-paying supporters. An organization with no address, no treasury, and no income now had a full-time professional managing director, an office in Harrisburg, substantial funds, and a respectable track record with the state legislature.

The Pennsylvania credit union movement's roots were now set deep in mines, the steel mills, office buildings, farms, and factories of the state. Roy Bergengren, Agnes Gartland, Tom Doig, Dora Maxwell, Claude Orchard, Jimmy Dacus, Julia Connor, Milton Rhye and the others of CUNA and the Federal Credit Union Section could congratulate themselves on their accomplishments in the Keystone State. It was now clear that they had sucessfully laid the foundations for a powerful state credit union movement.

VII

The Early Years

"Could we succeed permanently in Illinois or could you succeed permanently in Pennsylvania if the credit union movement isn't successful throughout our entire country? It would be easier for our enemies (and we have plenty of them) to destroy the credit union movement in one state than it is to destroy it in 48 states.... We must stand solidly behind those individuals who are giving all of their time to developing this thing we hold so close to our hearts."

Presley Dixon Holmes, 1938

THE FIFTH ANNUAL MEETING marks the end of the foundation phase of the Pennsylvania credit union movement and the beginning of the building era. Held June 4, 1938, at Harrisburg's Penn-Harris Hotel, this meeting set a large number of significant precedents giving it a special importance in Pennsylvania credit union history.

The meeting opened with a standing silent tribute to Edward Filene, founder of the American credit union movement, who had died September 26, 1937. Then the members were introduced to their new managing director, Julia Connor.

President Howard Hook's report gave extensive praise to the work of managing directors Copley and Pottiger, and told of the extensive organization and contact work which Connor had already initiated. The League treasury was in excellent shape with more than $4,000 cash on hand. The meeting approved a 1938 budget totaling almost $9000 including $3,500 in League dues to CUNA.

While the issue of dues to CUNA was easily handled, the question of credit union dues to the League again caused controversy. Director William W. Pratt from Philadelphia demanded establishment of a $1000 maximum. Director Joseph Moore from Pittsburgh opposed the maximum. Finally, a bylaws amendment establishing the $1000 maximum annual fee was passed:

"The annual dues of the members of the Pennsylvania Credit Union League shall be five percent (5%) of their gross earnings as of December 31 of the previous year, but not less than five dollars ($5) nor more than one thousand dollars ($1000), except that credit unions paying no dividend shall pay a membership fee of five dollars ($5). Each member credit union shall submit annually to the Treasurer of the League a certified copy of its financial statement as of December 31 of the previous year. The aforesaid annual dues shall be due and payable on or before March 1 of each year."

The newly amended dues bylaw became the standard model for Pennsylvania Credit Union League dues. While it would undergo continuous review and repeated modification in subsequent years, the basic concepts of dues based on earnings, however defined, with set minimums and maximums would remain essentially unchanged.

The membership then turned its attention to scheduling annual meetings. The 1936 reorganization meeting [the second session of the third annual meeting] had been held in July; it had been a horribly hot night, and the members had no desire to repeat that experience. The fourth annual meeting had been held on January 30, 1937 in Lewistown; it had been bitterly cold, and snow-covered roads had prevented many members from attending. The fifth annual meeting was in session June 4, 1938, and compromise was in the air. They amended the bylaws to hold future annual meetings in March or April instead of June.

As an economy measure, the members voted to limit each credit union to one voting member and one alternate delegate. In this, as in the dues and meeting schedule amendments, this fifth annual meeting established a precedent that has survived virtually unchanged except for one brief period during which each credit union was allowed two voting delegates.

The delegates were not so fortunate or foresighted when they turned their attention to a series of questions that has continually troubled the board since—establishing seats on the board of directors, apportioning them geographically, and determining procedures for electing members to fill them.

At the fifth annual meeting, the delegates passed a series of resolutions concerning the directors. They determined that there would be a total of fifteen board members who would:

- be elected by the delegates at the annual meeting from member credit unions in established districts.
- have district boundaries proportionately and equitably determined by the delegates at any annual meeting.
- include no more than one director from the same credit union.
- be elected for one-year terms,
- be reimbursed "to the extent of expenses involved in attending meetings."

The membership also set minimum expectations of two meetings of the board, including one meeting to be held with sessions preceding and following the annual membership meeting. The directors were empowered to elect "from their own number" a president, vice-president, secretary and treasurer, and "from any credit union membership," a managing director.

The session was heated. Debate raged over the requirement that officers could only be elected from among the directors, and over the need to have the managing director elected each year. The equally contentious issue of selecting district boundaries had to be deferred to a later session.

Tempers cooled somewhat over dinner, a banquet with 206 delegates and guests in attendance. With Fred C. Burris as toastmaster, speakers included Claude Orchard, Earl Rentfro of CUNA Mutual Insurance Society, Tom Doig, and P. D. Holmes, the new president of CUNA. Roy Bergengren was the featured speaker.

The membership meeting reconvened at a little after 10:00 pm. Tempers were flaring and the meeting threatened to break out of control. President Hook ordered voting delegates (limited to one from each credit union by the day's earlier vote) to one side of the room, while non-voting delegates and guests assembled on the other side of the hall.

The delegates then voted to follow CUNA's lead and establish an executive committee. It would consist of the president, vice-president, secretary, treasurer, immediate past president "and such other directors as the board may elect." The creation of this executive committee marks the first formation of a deliberately insulated group within the board, shielded from the democratic influences of the general membership. At CUNA, the executive committee gradually assumed full power for all of the board's responsibilities. Fortunately, this did not occur to the same extent in the Pennsylvania League.

Other bylaws were handled by the board as they continued to establish procedural precedents. These were essential housekeeping procedures. They are indications of the growing maturity of the League and of its legitimately perceived need to establish firm policies and behave in a formal, legal, and responsible way. They also allowed the board to put off a return to the divisive issue of its own composition.[1]

Finally the meeting was forced to return to the question of redistricting (since this was the first, they were really just "districting," not "redistricting" the League). A hastily called caucus returned to offer its formal proposal:

District 1: Erie, Crawford, Mercer and Venango counties.
District 2: Lawrence, Beaver, Butler, Clarion and Armstrong counties.
District 3: Allegheny, Washington, Greene, Fayette, Indiana, Westmoreland, Cambria and Somerset counties.
District 4: Blair, Huntingdon, Mifflin, Juniata, Perry, Bedford, Fulton, Franklin, Adams, Cumberland, York and Dauphin counties.

1. The board was empowered to "declare vacant" the office of any director whose credit union failed to pay its dues and to fill any board vacancy that might occur by reason of a director's "resignation or removal for cause." The board formed a three-person audit committee to "make a complete audit of the business, books of account, and all financial transactions of the League, which audit shall be included in the report of the committee to be read at the annual meeting." And the board received authority from the membership "to remove or recall for cause any officer, member of any committee, any national director or any employee of the League."

This 1938 group portrait of the Pennsylvania League Board of Directors is the earliest photograph in League archives. Managing Director Julia Connor sits at front center with President Al Palmer to her left and Vice President Ed Thompson to her right. Her successor as managing director, Bill Pratt, stands behind her.

District 5: Lancaster, Lebanon, Schuylkill and Berks counties.

District 6: Chester, Delaware, Montgomery, Lehigh, Northampton, Bucks and Philadelphia counties.

District 7: Tioga, Lycoming, Union, Snyder, Montour, Northumberland, Columbia, Sullivan, Bradford, Susquehanna, Wyoming, Lackawanna, Luzerne, Monroe, Pike, Wayne and Carbon counties.

District 8: Warren, Forest, Jefferson, McKean, Cameron, Elk, Clearfield, Center, Clinton and Potter counties.

In each district, the board proposed, "there shall be one director for every twenty-five (25) Credit Unions or fraction thereof organized as of December 31 of the previous year." There were major problems inherent in this solution, the most serious of which was that it concentrated the majority of Pennsylvania credit unions in two districts (Districts 3 and 6). Also it failed to provide a standing formula for apportionment, offering only an expeditious way of solving the problem immediately at hand. Despite its limitations, the compromise carried.

Directors whose terms were due to continue immediately resigned to allow the entire board to be reconstituted in accordance with the new plan. For directors J. P. Byers, S. J. Gurbarg, and Pratt, this was a temporary inconvenience; they were immediately renominated from the appropriate district. For directors Sterrett, N. T. Loch, and G. R. Foultz it meant premature and permanent departure from the board.

In seven districts, renomination and election proceeded according to plan. In District 3 there was a challenge through additional nominations from the floor. Those nominees were soundly defeated in the subsequent balloting.[2]

The members were emotionally drained from the struggle, and especially from the challenge to the Pittsburgh-area delegation. They were unable to deal with any more substantive issues. A resolution from the Philadelphia Chapter asking for financial support from the League for chapter activities was tabled. A resolution concerning examination fees charged to state-chartered credit unions was referred to committee for study.

Rentfro and Orchard sought to bring up issues relevant to Life Savings Plan insurance policies offered by CUNA Mutual (and prohibited to federal credit unions by the legal department of FCA). The issue was referred to the board for "further consideration and presentation to the legal department of the Farm Credit Administration."

As quickly as issues could be raised, they were referred to committees. A committee was formed to study the possibility of amending the federal credit union law to permit higher unsecured loans and the compensation of officers. Another was created to "study the problem of central banks." A legis-

2. The elected directors: District 1, L. F. Hardman; District 2, J. P. Byers; District 3, J. A. Moore, A. R. Thompson, R. F. Goetz, F. Tokay, G. A. Palmer, Jr., E. I. Mills and H. H. Hook; District 4, M. A. Pottiger; District 5, I. W. Kreider; District 6, E. D. Clauss, W. C. Buehler, S. J. Gurbarg and W. W. Pratt; District 7, J. C. Hoshauer; District 8, C. E. Sheldon.

lative committee was given the task of contacting gubernatorial candidates to determine their "views with respect to credit unions and credit union legislation." It was well past midnight when this annual meeting finally adjourned.

For the directors, however, the day was not over. As ordered by the annual meeting, they convened in their post-annual meeting session to reorganize for the coming year. First, all officers were reelected.[3] They also selected C. E. Sheldon as an additional member of the newly constituted executive committee.

The exhausted directors then attempted to determine a location for their next meetings. First they approved Bradford as the site for the 1939 annual meeting, then rescinded that choice as they suddenly recognized the growing size and increasingly complex needs of their expanding organization. They decided instead to select a location of greater credit union population, one more accessible to the general membership. But they were just too tired to handle it, and deferred decision for a later meeting. The directors finally adjourned at 1:15 am.

The 1938 annual meeting is notable for one final feature. The treasurer's report notes cash on hand at the time of the meeting of $4130.04. This was the last occasion for several years that Tokay would be able to report a sizeable surplus. Despite its successes—perhaps because of them—the League was about to embark on a perilous financial journey.

At the November 12, 1938 meeting of the board of directors at the Hotel Philadelphia, treasurer Tokay reported that the League's cash balance was down to $1,903.28. Worse, Tokay reported that national dues owed to CUNA which had not yet been remitted amounted to $1,380.12. If paid, Tokay informed the board, funds remaining to operate the League through February would be only $523.16.

3. President, H. H. Hook; vice-president, I. W. Kreider; secretary, M. A. Pottiger; treasurer, F. Tokay. No vote for managing director is recorded, but the position continued to be held by Julia Connor.

Tom Doig was a guest at the meeting, and president Hook explained that the League intended to defer paying its dues to CUNA. To Doig, such was totally unacceptable. The national association had not spent all that time and effort on the Pennsylvania League only to have them defer payments on dues. He argued that the dues owed CUNA were not the property of the League at all, but had been collected by the League as agent for the national association. Doig's arguments were only partly successful. The directors voted to remit dues to CUNA "as promptly as practicable." That turned out to involve considerable delay.

The second response to the approaching fiscal crisis was a suggestion from Pratt that the League limit the activities of the managing director. Connor had spent more than $1230 traveling throughout the state since her appointment. When the directors heard her report, they decided that Connor should continue "working as she had done prior to the board meeting."

In that report, Connor stated her intention to "concentrate on organization of new credit unions." She noted that she had billed the league for 9,700 miles of driving. As a result she could show 42 credit unions which had joined the League between her May 31 report and November 1. That brought League membership to 196, an increase of more than 27% in five months. She also noted the organization of 26 new credit unions (all federal charters) during the same period. Her other activities included organizing a Schuylkill Valley Chapter based in Reading and a Wyoming Valley Chapter based in Wilkes-Barre, and reorganizing the Erie Chapter.

Connor, like Copley, chose to devote substantial time to working with the chapters. Bergengren had long preached that chapter activity was the key to long-range League vitality, just as Raiffeisen (and Desjardins as well) had recognized that social activity was a crucial element in a successful credit union movement. Chapter meetings provided a forum for the exchange of information, for peer group formation, for formal and informal educational activities. Such activities added a unique new dimension to the credit union concept. In future years when directors were no longer chosen at the annual meeting, the chapters would assume an even larger importance in the credit union movement. The foundations for that subsequent era were built by these Pennsylvania pioneers.

Pennsylvania had a long but qualitatively mixed experience with its chapters. Hanemann had started a Harrisburg chapter, and Pottiger had kept it active after League reorganization. The Pittsburgh Chapter was lively and successful from its inception, partly because of the influence of Doig and Maxwell, and partly because the chapter had been self reliant until the 1936 reorganization of the League.

Other chapters had no such vitality and needed continual encouragement from the League. The Harrisburg and Lancaster chapters did not meet regularly. McKeesport and Erie chapters periodically threatened to collapse. Even the Philadelphia Chapter which formed shortly after the League was originally organized did not become active until Connor started working with it while she was with FCA.

Her experience with the Philadelphia Chapter probably influenced Connor to take advantage of their potential after she joined the League. She immediately started to strengthen the chapter network. Chapters in Bradford and Allentown became more active in March 1939 under her leadership. The Lancaster Chapter was revitalized in April. In May, an informal McKeesport group that launched a series of programs and credit unions in New Kensington, led by credit unions organized by Aluminum Company of America employees, started planning to form their own chapter.

By mid-1939, there were chapters in Erie, Pittsburgh, Harrisburg, Lancaster, Reading, Allentown, Philadelphia, Wilkes-Barre, and Bradford. Each had been visited by Connor and W. E. Allen, Chief of Membership Relations for the Federal Credit Union Section of FCA.

Unfortunately, while the number of chapters was encouraging, attendance was lower than hoped. "We are eager to learn of any means of stimulating interest resulting in larger attendance," wrote Connor in a later report. Such suggestions were not forthcoming. The chapters continued to require support from the League; their lack of ability to sustain themselves continued to vex League managing directors, both Connor and her successors. The chapters were also useful forums for stimulating credit union affiliation with the League.

The League extolled several advantages and services to convince credit unions to affiliate. One was the availability of CUNA Mutual Society insurance policies. Presumably available only to affiliated credit unions, CUNA Mutual's loan protection insurance repaid the credit union in case of death or permanent and total disability of borrowers. CUNA Supply Cooperative offered supplies to all credit unions with a 20% discount to affiliated credit unions. CUNA also offered low-cost bonding of officers and employees. These incentives might have been more effective if the CUNA affiliates had distinguished more carefully between member and nonmember credit unions. All too often, the national affiliates tended to regard all credit unions as potential customers.

The League also used less tangible arguments to convince credit unions to join the organized movement. League and CUNA spokespersons talked of protection from adverse legislation and support for favorable action. They argued that "You will be doing your bit, in recognition of what has been done by others in bringing the credit union to you, to further promote a movement which has for its purpose the elimination of usury and the improvement of our national economic life."

Matt Pottiger first used his mimeographed *Keystone State News* to make his arguments. Within a few months, the League concluded an arrangement whereby *Keystone State News* was printed as a special supplement to *The Bridge* and distributed by CUNA. Pottiger also set up meetings throughout the state in an attempt to spread the word. "It is hoped that these meetings will be the medium whereby you men and women responsible for the fine work that is being done will become better acquainted ... and will coordinate your efforts through affiliating with the State League and National Association." Speakers at these meetings typically included Orchard, Cliff Skorstad, Doig and other officers or professional staff from CUNA and the Farm Credit Administration.

Connor used extensive personal contact to convince new credit unions to affiliate with the League. She arranged for assistance whenever possible from Doig, Skorstad, or Maxwell, as well as Rhye, Dacus, Orchard, or others from FCA. Her efforts quickly produced positive results. By the end of 1938, there were 435 credit unions in Pennsylvania, and 202 of them were affiliated with the League. At the March 19, 1939 annual meeting, Connor informed the delegates that organization and affiliation were increasing rapidly, and that substantial growth could be anticipated before the next annual meeting.

The accelerating growth of the Pennsylvania credit union movement was gaining attention in other quarters as well. National delegates Pratt, Pottiger, Moore and Tokay were gaining increasing recognition at CUNA. Moore was becoming influential in the political activities at national headquarters; Pratt had been elected a CUNA vice president; Pottiger was increasingly influential with CUNA Supply Cooperative.

At CUNA headquarters there was trouble brewing. President Presley Holmes raised serious questions about Bergengren's competence to lead the association. Joe DeRamus resigned as editor of *The Bridge*, charging that Bergengren was not cooperating and was attacking the magazine all over the country.

In fact, *The Bridge* was losing money and attracting opposition throughout the state and country. Connor and Pottiger both recommended that the League stop offering *Keystone State News* as a supplement in *The Bridge*, and resume independent publication. They greatly resented the delays and major production problems that continually plagued the CUNA publication. Pottiger later recalled writing a lengthy letter of complaint to Bergengren, and attending a special session at a

CUNA annual meeting devoted to "constructive criticism" of *The Bridge*.

Pratt's "Report of the National Directors" at the 1939 Pennsylvania League annual meeting devoted extensive attention to the problems of *The Bridge*. He informed the membership that "during the past year it became necessary to change the management of our magazine and also increase the subscription price while reducing operating costs in order to reduce present indebtedness and eliminate continued increase in this debt." Pratt thought *The Bridge* a wasteful and ineffective publication that did more to further the ambitions of Bergengren than to aid credit unions and their members.

CUNA was apparently suprised when national delegates expressed resentment at these changes and when subscriptions to *The Bridge* dropped sharply. Worse yet, the close cooperation of the Leagues (whose editors and other volunteers had been providing most of the copy) also fell off. *The Bridge* was quick to retaliate. It stopped publishing the special supplements on behalf of individual leagues.

Pennsylvania thus lost its *Keystone State News* and the League was faced with the choice of resuming independent publication of a newsletter or of losing periodic communication with its member credit unions. The League ceased publication for a year, relying on *The Bridge*. Only when the CUNA executive committee suspended publication of *The Bridge* did the Pennsylvania League resume its own publication activities with a monthly magazine retitled *Key Notes*.

CUNA was also facing internal division over the question of a location for the new national headquarters. The original decision to locate in Madison, Wisconsin, had been made by Bergengren over the objections of many credit union leaders. As collections for the Filene Memorial Fund Drive progressed, the question of where to locate the new Filene House national headquarters again arose.

Moore, Pennsylvania chairman of the Filene Memorial Fund Drive, was an active participant in the dispute and remembered it well:

"I was placed on the original building committee which consisted of Messrs. Bill Reid, Claude Clarke, and myself. There were many propositions as to where we should locate our headquarters. And Bill Reid and I decided that the best proposition came from Indianapolis.... We didn't like the idea of coming up to Madison and felt that it was out of the way. I still feel that way about it.... Claude immediately rushed up and told Mr. Bergengren what the majority of the committee had decided. Mr. Bergengren told him to put in a minority report which advocated Madison. I don't need to tell you who won. The majority report wasn't accepted."

When asked "What was the sales point on which Madison was sold to the committee?" Moore replied, "Mr. Bergengren wanted it. It was never sold to the committee.... His word was pretty much law for a long time. He got accustomed to it."

Relationships between Bergengren and the Pennsylvania delegation were rarely good. Pottiger recalled that Bergengren long remembered an exchange of critical letters. Moore believed that Bergengren found him a worthy and powerful opponent. He told of hearing that Bergengren once said to a Pennsylvania field representative that "There are three things I'm allergic to: Wine, women, and Joe Moore." Moore's memory may have been slightly faulty, or he may have been exaggerating. According to his story, the encounter occurred on a plane, but Bergengren never travelled by air, always by train. Nonetheless, the story does help define the relationship between the two leaders.

Both CUNA and the Pennsylvania League were facing increasing financial difficulties. At their March 1939 annual meetings, CUNA faced a deficit of $48,000 and the League faced a deficit —its first—of almost $500.00. The most substantial single line item of the League budget, $2,950, about 35% of the whole, was CUNA dues. The ground was set for growing friction between the two organizations. In CUNA executive committee meetings, assistant managing director Doig often expressed sympathy for the problems of the Pennsylvania

League; Bergengren insisted that the League maintain its full support of national association activities and programs. The Pennsylvania national directors took this as a sign that their real enemy was Bergengren and that they had a sympathetic friend in Doig.

The national office was increasingly troubled by a growing feud between the national association and its insurance affiliate, CUNA Mutual Insurance Society. CUNA and its member leagues regarded insurance as a service offered to member credit unions, an inducement to affiliate with the League. CUNA Mutual under Renfro had more parochial concerns. The company was growing rapidly and was becoming a profitable commercial entity in its own right.

At the 1939 annual meeting national directors charged that many credit unions were buying CUNA Mutual coverage without joining the state leagues. The board directed their insurance affiliate to cancel the policies of all non-affiliated credit unions and to refuse, in the future, to write such policies. But the issue would not yield easily to such pressure. In 1940, Rentfro informed the CUNA executive committee that CUNA Mutual's responsibility to the organized credit union movement was "to render a service...but not to contribute financial support."

In Pennsylvania, a leading advertiser in *Key Notes* was the Pennsylvania Farm Bureau's insurance affiliate (which later became known as Nationwide Insurance). At Rentfro's insistence, Bergengren ordered the Pennsylvania League not to accept Farm Bureau ads for policies that competed with those offered by CUNA Mutual. This policy decision, made with Connor's blessing but over Pratt's objections, denied the Pennsylvania League a source of substantial income even as its financial difficulties deepened.

Despite the growing financial crisis, contention at the 1939 League annual meeting was largely limited to questions involving representation on the board of directors. After extensive debate on nominating and voting procedures, the board ruled that "a strict interpretation of the bylaws permits nomination from the floor by any delegate and that election must be on the basis of all delegates voting on all candidates regardless of districts." Under that rule, the nominations in Districts 2, 3, and 8 were contested from the floor. All other nominations (actually, renominations) of the committee were accepted; the nominees were declared unanimously elected. None of the floor challenges to candidates nominated by nominations committee proved successful. The board had demonstrated that it had already achieved virtual control of its own composition.[4]

A new bylaw adopted at the sixth annual membership meeting included a special provision requiring that the managing director issue a formal statement listing the "number and names of credit unions organized in this State since the previous meeting.... consideration of the status of the credit union development, and ways and means of increasing credit union organization activity in the State." This resolution indicates board recognition of the new League emphasis on organization and contact work.

Connor was becoming more secure in her position and more independent. She had a good record of organizing credit unions and securing their affiliation with the League. She had the respect and support of Bergengren and Orchard. But she understood neither the workings of the board of directors nor the bias and sensitivities of individual directors—especially such leaders as Moore and Pratt. Nor was she aware of the local significance of power struggles in Madison, where Bergengren was gradually losing his influence with the CUNA executive committee.

Thus the board requested and won a second bylaw amendment affecting the managing director. It clarified the lines of

4. When the dust settled and the shouting died down, the board of directors elected March 18, 1939 stood as follows: District 1, L. F. Hardman; District 2, J. P. Byers; District 3, H. H. Hook, G. A. Palmer, E. E. Shellkopf, F. Tokay, R. F. Goetz, J. A. Moore, A. R. Thompson; District 4, M. A. Pottiger; District 5, I. W. Kreider; District 6, W. W. Pratt, W. C. Buehler, E. A. Thompson, E. D. Clauss; District 7, E. D. Brown; District 8, M. Zias

authority and clearly subordinated the managing director to
the board, effectively reducing Connors to a clerical/adminis-
trative assistant type role. While the board acknowledged the
theoretical importance of professional executive leadership, it
limited the role of the managing director:

> "The Managing Director, under the direction of the Board of
> Directors, shall manage the business of the League. The pri-
> mary functions of the Managing Director shall be the organi-
> zation of new credit unions and securing the affiliation with
> the League of all credit unions organized within this State.
> The Managing Director shall be responsible for the invoicing
> and collection of all League dues, the compilation of statistics,
> maintenance of the League office, handling general correspon-
> dence and publicity, and shall render such other services as are
> required for the successful operation of the League. At each
> meeting of the members of the League and of its Board of
> Directors, the Managing Director shall present a complete
> report of the conduct of that office since the previous meeting,
> and shall render at any time such other reports as may be re-
> quired by the Board of Directors or the Executive Commit-
> tee."

With Connor put in her place, the board turned its attention to dues. Tired of dealing with dues through bylaw
amendments, the board moved to enable the membership fee
to be handled by resolution instead. The language of the
bylaws was changed to provide for a statutory maximum of
five percent of gross income (now "exclusive of fees and
fines"), up to $1000.00 and a minimum membership fee of
$5.00. The actual percentage would be set by the member
credit unions at their annual meeting.

A subsequent motion from the floor established the dues
schedule for 1939 at the maximum level (5% of gross income)
allowed by the bylaws.

In his "Report of the National Directors," Pratt made the
reason for such hesitant action clear. A subcommittee of the
CUNA executive committee was examining the dues issue and

was expected to produce its own report and recommendations in 1940.

> "Dues collections [for CUNA] were less than budget estimates due largely to overestimates as most of the leagues have shown an increase in growth. The C.U.N.A. budget was revised last November and a bank loan authorized to carry us through January and February."

The delegates to the League annual meeting should have been reassured. The Pennsylvania League may not have been in the best financial condition, but it was much better off than the national association. With members continuing the five percent dues schedule, the League continued to have adequate funds (although it also continued to defer payments of CUNA dues).[5]

A final bylaws amendment changed the definition of a legal quorum at regular or special meetings to consist of "duly-authorized delegates from twenty percent of the member credit unions having paid their current yearly dues prior to the membership meeting." The League was here once again following the lead of CUNA. At the national association, this change was intended to make it possible for fewer and fewer delegates to conduct more and more of the organization's business. For the League, its impact was less noticeable.

Retiring from the board at the conclusion of the 1939 meeting was director John C. Hoshauer. A veteran of the legislative wars in Pennsylvania and of the pre-law Pennsylvania Credit Union Committee, Hoshauer had been elected League

---

5. Operational expenses for the Pennsylvania League continued to increase. Disbursements in 1938 (including eleven months' salary for managing director Connor and ten months' rent on the Harrisburg office) totaled $8407.85. Expenses for 1939 totaled $11,156.62. This sharp increase was primarily a result of CUNA dues, which totaled $5,330.12 (including $930.12 overdue from 1938 and deferment of $600 due for the current year). Other increases came from the full year's salary for the managing director, small honoraria paid to the League secretary and treasurer, and $175.30 to finance independent league publication of *Key Notes*. The additional expense was absorbed by increased dues income from a growing membership.

secretary in December 1934. He had retained his seat on the board despite the 1936 reorganization. With his departure, the last link with that early phase of the Pennsylvania credit union movement was cut. That gulf widened when the board reorganized at its meeting immediately following adjournment of the annual meeting and selected new officers.

With reorganization came the retirement of H. H. Hook as president. Hook had come into the credit union movement when he organized Koppers Pittsburgh Employees FCU in July 1935. As president of that credit union, he attended the organization meeting of the Pittsburgh Chapter and was elected vice-president. When chapter president Frank Beaman resigned, Hook assumed the presidency; as Pittsburgh Chapter president he was the obvious candidate of the Pittsburgh caucus for the presidency of the reorganized League. Hook later credited his election to "the over enthusiastic campaigning of some of Pittsburgh's superlative politicians," a clear reference to Moore.

Hook had presided over the board since the July 18, 1936 reorganization when he had succeeded Hanemann. He had led the League first through the aftermath of its reorganization, and then through the tentative steps of its first three years. He had been singularly well qualified to preside over the League. An engineer by training, he was responsible for implementing many of the precise procedures which quickly brought order to all League activities. As manager of the Koppers personnel and insurance department, he was skilled and knowledgeable about many of the concerns of the League, CUNA, and CUNA Mutual. He left his successors a smoothly functioning organization.

As he left office, Hook gave a special compliment to the work of Julia Connor. "I feel certain that the membership of the league was well pleased with the program of work which you have been doing, Miss Connor," he wrote in *Keystone State News*, "and am very happy that it will be possible to have you continue that work." Recognizing the difficulties inherent in her lowered expense allotment, he continued: " I have no

G. A. (Al) Palmer served as president of the Pennsylvania Credit Union League, 1940–1943.

doubt whatever that you will be able to meet the revised budget for the year and that each and every credit union member will give you their wholehearted support in arriving at that goal."

The new league president was G. A. (Al) Palmer, Jr., employment manager of Joseph Horne Co. department store in Pittsburgh and president of Joseph Horne Company Employees FCU. Palmer had previously followed Hook as president of the Pittsburgh Chapter, where he had organized the Pittsburgh Chapter Officers FCU.

Palmer liked to joke that he organized the chapter officers' credit union because he needed a loan. "I could either borrow from my friends or from the loan sharks," he would say. On assuming office, he recognized the organizational and financial challenges ahead:

> "Credit unions are an established fact in Pennsylvania. But only the surface has been touched. Far less than ten per cent of our people have access to credit union facilities.... Nothing is too difficult if we work together in the whole-hearted cooperative spirit which is the essence of the credit union.
>
> "Our State league has grown from nothing to a sound, going concern in four years. Every effort has been made to render maximum service with minimum facilities and financial support... Our increased budget for this year permits the needed

expansion in the activities of our organization, but is still not large enough to render the kind of service in the many phases of credit union activity that we hope to offer.

"However, our League involves so much more than mere financial success. It is the moral support of every credit union, within and outside of the League, which will do most to carry on our splendid undertaking."

The election of Palmer as president was not contested. Neither were the reelections of Pottiger and Tokay as secretary and treasurer. There were three nominees for the office of vice president; I. W. Kreider, E. A. Thompson, and A. R. (Art)Thompson.

Art Thompson later remembered that the election was a confused affair in which many of the ballots were just marked "Thompson." He suggests that the tellers revealed a regional bias in deciding that the easterner, E. A. Thompson, was the intended candidate. The election went to E. A. Thompson, a director from District 6 and delegate from Philadelphia Teachers CU by one vote over I.W. Kreider, a director from District 5 and alternate delegate from Lancaster Postal Workers CU.

President Palmer was from Pittsburgh. It seems clear from the vote that E.A. Thompson was supported by the East, that Kreider was supported by Central Pennsylvania, and that part of the Pittsburgh delegation deserted their own Art Thompson in favor of statewide representation. Western Pennsylvania was already represented by president Palmer and treasurer Tokay (Donora). Central Pennsylvania was represented by secretary Pottiger. The directors from the East felt entitled to some representation. This election marks the beginning of the tradition of electing the president and vice president from opposite ends of the state, assuring that the presidency would alternate from East to West. Central Pennsylvania was accorded no significance in this equation, an oversight that would later cause great difficulty.

Another tradition that came to full flower at the sixth annual meeting was the banquet. That idea had been brought to the earliest meetings by national association leaders. It had become increasingly elaborate. The 1939 banquet made it clear that this would be a major event of all annual meetings.[6]

In November 1939, Connor took the Pennsylvania League past a critical milestone. With newly organized credit unions and newly affiliated existing credit unions, she brought League membership to over 250, representing more than half of the credit unions in the state. On January 30, 1938 when Connor took over as managing director, there were 367 credit unions in Pennsylvania of which 146 (40%) were affiliated with the League.

By December 31, 1939 there were 486 credit unions in Pennsylvania. Actually, 510 had been organized, but 24 charters had been cancelled in the five years since the beginning of the movement.[7] Of the 486 credit unions in Pennsylvania, 258

6. More than 650 delegates and guests gathered Saturday night at the William Penn Hotel. Dinner speakers were Roy Bergengren and Milton Rhye, newly promoted assistant director of the Federal Credit Union Section. Visitors included Louise McCarren, managing director of the Ohio League; A. W. Thomas, president of the District of Columbia League, Gunnar Gudmondson, president of the New Jersey Credit Union League; James D. M. Marquette, managing director of the Maryland Credit Union League; Theodore Fisher, Kenneth L. Wimer, Charles Foster, and Mr. Pace, all field representatives of the Federal Credit Union Section; and Dora Maxwell from CUNA. Following the banquet, the host Pittsburgh Chapter provided "night-club style" entertainment and dancing.
7. While the number of cancellations of charters is large and should not be passed over lightly, it should not be seen as marring the remarkably fine record by the Pennsylvania credit union movement. From October 1, 1934 to November 30, 1939, FCA had cancelled a total of 338 credit union charters; only 27 of those were in Pennsylvania. On a percentage basis, that represents far less than a proportional share of the whole. During the same period there were 86 state charters issued, of which five were liquidated. We have no way of knowing whether these liquidations were in response to credit union problems or, especially during the Great Depression, to problems faced by the sponsoring company. We do know that credit union liquidations were far less common proportionally than liquidations of banks or savings & loan associations in Pennsylvania during the same period. Connor notes in her "Report of the Managing Director" for the seventh annual meeting that "We believe that the future will show fewer liquidations in proportion to the number of credit unions organized because of the educational work being done by the Credit Union National Association and the Federal Credit Union Section."

were dues-paying, affiliated members of the Pennsylvania Credit Union League, 83 of them recruited during 1939. That total represented 54% of the Pennsylvania credit union population.

At the January 13, 1940 meeting of the board of directors, Connor presented a "Report of the Managing Director" presenting the League's achievements for the preceding year in detail. The League boasted 12 chapters including the newly-organized Midwestern Chapter (Lawrence, Beaver, Butler, Clarion and Armstrong counties), Allegheny-Kiski Valley Chapter (New Kensington area), and McKeesport Chapter. Connor had discovered that "the Credit Union Movement develops more rapidly where an active chapter is functioning.... A good, live chapter will do more to stimulate the individual credit union than almost anything else."

Yet even such successes caused problems for Connor. In assisting the McKeesport Chapter, she may have unwittingly antagonized Joe Moore, who increasingly perceived the McKeesport group as competition for his own Pittsburgh Chapter.

By 1940, Pennsylvania was a leading credit union state and national leaders were increasing their attention to activities in the Commonwealth. Rentfro of CUNA Mutual was spending extensive time in Pennsylvania, working to help the state qualify for agency status and promoting CUNA Mutual policies at chapter meetings in Erie, Beaver Falls, Pittsburgh, Harrisburg, Lancaster, Philadelphia, and Wilkes-Barre. Bergengren and his wife toured the state seeking support for the Filene Memorial Fund Drive, meeting with chapters in Erie, Pittsburgh, Harrisburg, Wilkes-Barre, and Philadelphia.

The Filene Memorial Fund was proceeding well, but it was not growing quickly enough to satisfy Bergengren. The May 11, 1939 meeting of the national directors had voted to construct the Filene Memorial Building in Madison and increased the fund drive goal from $150,000 to $250,000. With the support of the Pennsylvania delegation, proposals to purchase land and start construction immediately were rejected.

"We are sure that Mr. Filene would not approve proceeding with such a venture until it was on a sound financial basis."

There were several problems ahead. Some were visible, others, especially the coming world war, remained unseen. Two obvious problems were that managing director Connor was running out of energy and enthusiasm, and the League was running towards deepening financial difficulties. The two were reinforcing each other.

Effective in 1940, Connor was required to prepare: detailed reports of the League activities for all meetings of the directors or League members; a daily report of travel to accompany the expense account to the treasurer; a daily report to the treasurer indicating any organization and contact work; and a monthly report to the directors.

The demands of the job began to take a physical toll on Connor in late 1939 and early 1940 when she became ill and was confined to her home suffering from gastric ulcers. But by January 13, she had prepared her 24-page "Managing Director's Report" and was back in the Harrisburg office. By the March 9 annual meeting, she was in excellent form. Still, financial concerns made the directors hesitant to provide her with staff support despite repeated requests.

At the 1940 annual meeting in Philadelphia, enthusiasm was running high throughout the League. "The year has marked the advance of our organization from the experimental or temporary status to that of a well established and thriving 'going concern,'" reported president Palmer. The national directors reported enthusiastically about new CUNA bonding department programs. They were equally enthusiastic about prospects for CUNA Mutual "which is operating as a separate corporation without any direct support from the Credit Union National Association." The activities of CUNA Supply Cooperative also received strong endorsement: "You can be justly proud of the fine job being done in furnishing you with standard forms far below the price which would have to be paid through individual printing jobs."

The League's legislative committee (Pottiger, E. A.

Thompson, Kreider and Connor) reported successful efforts to amend the state law to permit state chartered credit unions to invest funds in loans to other credit unions. The amendment had passed the Senate unanimously and the House by a vote of 200 to 4. It was the League's most successful venture with the legislature to date.

The education committee (E. A. Thompson, James Hinckel, and Pratt) filed a report calling on the managing director to work with CUNA's education department to develop a series of programs for chapter meetings. The committee also suggested that the Pennsylvania Credit Union League plan, develop and issue an Information Manual. "The Manual development should be under the direction of the managing director, assisted by all League directors...."

Pratt's fellow national directors were especially enthusiastic about the job Pratt was doing on the CUNA executive committee and with the national board. At the League's annual meeting, Moore, Tokay and Pottiger filed a special " 'Minority' Report of the National Directors":

> "This ... report deals ... with the activities of our fellow director, one William W. Pratt, who has devoted an inestimable amount of time and energy as one of your national directors, and, particularly, as a member of the executive committee of CUNA, to the promotion of our economic welfare."

As one response to growing financial worries, the League again deferred part of its CUNA dues payment. The Pennsylvania League had reached the $5000 ceiling on CUNA dues, but Pratt and the other Pennsylvania national directors had argued long and hard that even with that ceiling, the Pennsylvania League was still paying more than its fair share. At their post-convention meeting, the directors voted to pay $3000 "at this time." Additional payments would require additional action. Doig and Bergengren could not assume that such action would be automatic. The board had just appropriated the $600 balance on the previous year's CUNA dues at their meeting the night before.

William W. Pratt served as executive director of the Pennsylvania Credit Union League, 1942–1965.

CUNA based its dues on numbers of credit union members, not on credit union income or assets. National director Pratt warned the board that CUNA was considering raising the $5000 ceiling. (That change was made in May 1940.) He also informed them that proposals would be coming before the CUNA board involving either a decrease in the per-capita dues requirement, or a change to gross-income basing. Either, noted Pratt, would be welcomed by the Pennsylvania directors and would result in a more equitable distribution of the dues burden.

The national directors seemingly felt that policies at CUNA were beyond their influence. Their frustration is evidenced in the Pennsylvania board's refusal to fill the additional seat on the national board to which growing membership entitled Pennsylvania. It appears that the directors felt that any increase in influence which might come through that added vote would not be worth the added expense to the League of sending another delegate to CUNA meetings.

The directors recognized that the increasing complexity of League affairs mandated continuing organization change. One was the suggestion that the Pennsylvania League follow the lead of CUNA and seek incorporation as a nonprofit association. To that end, a special committee was formed to seek legal counsel. At their initiative, attorney George M. Neal offered to advise the League for a $100.00 annual retainer, and presented a 12-page brief outlining the requirements of incorporation. It informed the directors that the primary advantage to incorporating would be relieving members of the board of any individual liability for the affairs of the League. "On motion duly made and seconded, it was voted that the committee be instructed to present its report to the annual meeting of the membership and recommend that steps be taken to incorporate the League."

An interesting byplay surrounded the board's action on Connor's request for additional league staff. Director Pratt opposed such action on grounds of excessive expense. Then a delegate informed the board that Philadelphia DuPont-Grasselli FCU had not paid its League dues. The question was raised about the legitimacy of this credit union having its delegate seated at the annual meeting. That challenged delegate was Pratt. League bylaws specifically prohibited seating a delegate from any credit union in arrears on its dues—the very provision which had originally been used to unseat Hanemann at the 1936 reorganization. The board called a brief recess; when they returned, Pratt joined other members of the board who were proposing to hire additional professional staff to assist Connor in her work. There were no further challenges to his position.

Despite Pratt's legitimate concern with the League's financial health, most of the directors recognized both the quality of leadership provided by Connor and the toll it was taking on her physical and mental condition. They gave her a $300 raise, authorized her to attend the Ohio League annual meeting at League expense, allowed her to discontinue the monthly report of activities to the directors, allowed her to hire an office assistant, and hired a "field secretary," Lloyd G. Sigafoo, who assumed primary responsibility for contact and organization work in the western part of the state.

In its enthusiasm, the League began a series of actions that inevitably hastened hard times. First, they assumed that growth would continue at the rate Connor had established in her two years as managing director. Second, they agreed to compromise with the Pratt-led faction of the board which insisted on lower membership fees. Despite their inability to meet current obligations (they again deferred payment of CUNA dues), and despite uncertainty about future obligations (CUNA seemed likely to increase dues and the League was expanding its staff), the League voted to lower 1941 dues to 4.5% of gross income.

That action was especially dangerous because CUNA was moving at the same time to increase its dues. At the May 1940 meeting of the national board CUNA passed a resolution allowing for a gradual increase of dues from leagues paying the $5000 maximum. Under its terms, the Pennsylvania League faced an annual $500 increase. And with the increases in the state's credit union population, even a drop in the per-capita CUNA dues would not prevent the League's obligation to CUNA from increasing. Even Pratt's CUNA vice-presidency and membership on the executive committee was insufficient to save the League from this increase.

CUNA's affiliates were becoming increasingly independent. Several leagues, especially New York, demanded restrictions on the affiliates, but they were already beyond the control of Bergengren. Bergengren himself was brought under direct responsibility of the increasingly assertive executive committee at its May 1940 meeting. These deep feuds running throughout the national association were bound to spill over in Pennsylvania, for virtually everything that happened at CUNA was either inadvertently reflected or deliberately duplicated in the League.

CUNA Vice President Pratt was privy to all activities at the national association. He was also increasingly involving himself in them as an active participant. In his 1940 report to the Pennsylvania board of directors, Pratt clearly allied himself with assistant managing director Doig, Rentfro of CUNA Mutual, Orrin Shipe (successor to Ralph Long as editor of the revived *Bridge*) and Maxwell against the group headed by CUNA managing director Bergengren. Similarly, Pennsylvania League secretary Pottiger was elected a director of the Supply Department of CUNA Supply Cooperative, involving him directly in the Madison power plays and intra-movement feuding.

Even as CUNA was going through its destructive growing pains, the League, too, was becoming a more elaborate organization. It found new office space and purchased its own office furniture, moving to Suite 304 in the Harrisburg's Ebner Building. Connor hired Harry E. Febich as the office assistant. And League attorney Neal was now available on a part-time basis in the League office for consultation with any credit union that had questions involving laws and regulations.

Connor was highly pleased with her new field representative. She reported that during his first six months, Sigafoo:

> "worked intently on the job, putting not only footwork, but headwork into it, and I feel sure that the results of his efforts will be far greater in the months to come.... He has established an entente cordial among credit union folks in the Western part of the State...."

Connor recommended that "Mr. Sigafoo's services be continued indefinitely." As a result he became the first long-term employee of the League, eventually retiring in 1954 after a distinguished career.

During the first nine months of 1940, 66 new credit unions were formed and 79 affiliated with the League and 26 credit unions dropped League membership. On September 28, 1940, there were 544 Pennsylvania credit unions; League membership stood at 312 or 57% of the total. Only five credit unions had liquidated.

One of the year's most important innovations came out of the Philadelphia Chapter where officials launched a special school for supervisory committee members. The program was staffed by Federal Credit Union Section personnel. This was the first formal educational activity of its type in the state. It was the forerunner to the Credit Union Institute and other educational programs eventually offered by the League.

Publication of *Key Notes* brought a new conflict. The newsletter was financed largely with ads from savings & loan associations. These advertisers became upset when CUNA went on record as opposing credit union investment in federal S & L's. Connor suggested that *Key Notes* should no longer accept advertising but should be financed entirely by the League. A decision on *Key Notes* was deferred as the board met to confer on once again relocating the League office.

At its September 28 meeting, the board decided to move the League's office to Philadelphia. With Sigafoo to handle organization and contact work in the West, Connor was spending most of her time in the East. There was no longer any need for a centrally located, Harrisburg office. President Palmer, himself a Pittsburgher, concurred. Pratt, a Philadelphian, lent his enthusiastic support to this money-saving issue.

Removing the League from Harrisburg also completed its withdrawal from the legislative arena. The League had, in effect, already abandoned its responsibility to seek legislative reform of the Pennsylvania Credit Union Act. Connor had neither the time, nor the energy, nor the skills for legislative affairs. No other League leader seems to have been interested in assuming that role. The League had no bills ready to submit to the 1941 session of the Pennsylvania legislature.

Since most Pennsylvania credit unions held federal charters and the battles with the State Banking Department were continuing, most of the League leadership argued that all relevant political activity was in Washington. National legislation, they felt, was the responsibility of CUNA. The League entertained reports on congressional activity, but showed no interest in direct participation.

The directors were much more interested in changing the legal structure of the League than of the state credit union law. They empowered attorney Neal to proceed with whatever actions were necessary towards incorporation of the League "at the earliest possible date." Other actions taken by the directors included: scheduling the 1941 annual meeting for Pittsburgh (after repeated balloting and a nearly successful challenge by the Reading delegation); ordering the treasurer to keep his records in ink, instead of pencil; and authorizing payment of the balance due on CUNA dues.

There was one ominous discussion that carried with it the storm clouds that would descend the following year. The board recorded its consensus that member credit unions should not discriminate against loan applicants between the ages of 21 and 35. The question was being asked: What happens to loans when borrowers go into military service? The next question would be: What happens to loans when borrowers do not come home? For the world was once more going to war.

VIII

The World War II Era

"The great problem that faces us here is that there is apparently a feeling on the part of many directors that management of the National Association is not willing to make a concession."

William W. Pratt, 1944

PENNSYLVANIA CREDIT UNIONS experienced
moderate growth during 1940. There were 84 new
credit unions organized (11% more than the previous
year), and there were only 12 liquidations. By now, 558 credit
unions were in operation in Pennsylvania, a gain of 15% for
the year. Eighty-seven credit unions had joined the League,
and 24 had dropped out. At the end of the year, total League
membership was 330 credit unions, a respectable affiliation
rate of 59%.

Connor's illnesses were increasing and she was becoming
increasingly frustrated. Her complaints began to take on a
tone reminiscent of Bergengren's comments during the legislative wars of the early 1930s.

> "It seems hard to believe that there is a lack of local leadership
> in the scattered sections throughout the State where chapters
> are located. Yet that is the only reason I can find for the failure
> of chapters to function. If I am present at the chapter meeting
> and take the initiative in planning for the following meeting,
> there is a following meeting; otherwise the chapter dies right
> then and there. If someone can propose a remedy for this he
> will, indeed, be the savior of the credit union movement."

At least the plans to incorporate the League were moving
smoothly as 1940 drew to a close. A required series of bylaw
amendments had been passed at the September board meeting, and copies had been mailed to the membership for ratification.

This new procedure for amending the bylaws has been
created by board member A.R. Thompson of Allegheny
County, chairman of the bylaws committee. Thompson had

begun work following the 1939 annual meeting, when he realized that the bylaws were becoming complex and that the general membership might not always be totally responsive to the will of the board. He was most concerned that such issues as districting and representation for board membership seemed to excite discussion and unpredictable reaction from the general membership.

At the 1940 annual meeting, Thompson had provided a bylaws amendment which provided:

> "This Constitution and these bylaws may be amended by a vote of three-fourths of the total membership of the board of directors at any regular or special meeting of the said board, provided that a majority of the member credit unions do not disapprove the amendment within thirty days of written notice thereof."

The implications of this amendment did not escape the general membership. After heated discussion, W.W. Pratt proposed changing "thirty days" to "sixty days," and further discussion was postponed until the afternoon session.

The board returned with an altered proposal. It provided for bylaws amendment by either the board or by the general membership:

> "This constitution and these bylaws may be amended by a vote of 4/5 of the delegates present at any regular or special meeting of the members, providing the notice for the meeting has contained a copy of the proposed amendment and a statement of its purpose, or by a vote of 3/4 of the total membership of the board of directors at any regular or special meeting of the said board. After adoption of an amendment by the board, a ballot for approval or disapproval of the board's action shall be sent to every member credit union and if, within sixty days of written notice thereof, a majority of the member credit unions have not forwarded to the league office notice of disapproval of the board's action, the said amendment shall become effective. Any amendment rejected by a majority of the mem-

ber credit unions shall not be subsequently adopted except by a vote of 3/4 of the delegates present at a regular meeting of the members."

This version of the bylaws amendment procedure was easily passed. The revision added extensive verbiage but changed little. It had become all but impossible for the membership of the League to alter their own bylaws, and for all practical purposes, it was now impossible for the general membership to stop any concerted action by the board. Control of the Pennsylvania Credit Union League had become vested in the board of directors, just as CUNA was fully controlled by its executive committee.

The first bylaws amendments passed and ratified by the new procedure provided for chartering the League as a nonprofit corporation. As of December 5, 1940, the board was administratively free to pursue its new corporate status. Also completed at the same time was the first edition of the *Pennsylvania Credit Union League Information Manual*. Unfortunately, copies of the new manual could not be mailed to all members. The fiscal year was nearing its end, and there was an early indication of the hard financial times ahead. The League did not have sufficient funds for postage.

Incorporation of the League moved a step closer at the January 1941 meeting of the board of directors, when the board appropriated $10.00 as the application fee and formally applied for registration as a nonprofit corporation. The application was signed by president Palmer, vice president Ed Thompson, secretary Pottiger, treasurer Tokay, and managing director Connor.

Incorporation of the Pennsylvania Credit Union League was completed in April. The charter was granted by the Commonwealth on April 28, 1941. The April-May 1941 issue of *Key Notes* proudly informed the membership of this "important step in League history, insuring the permanence of the organization, and safeguarding those who are interested in the development of the Credit Union Movement in Pennsylvania."

Another major commitment to the future of the League was taken with approval of new League headquarters to be located at 1504 Race Street in Philadelphia.

Despite the League's running out of operating funds at the end of 1940, and despite the lowering of the dues schedule for 1941 from 5% to 4.5% as approved at the previous annual meeting, the directors were optimistic about the League's financial future. They gambled on future growth both in membership and gross income of members and voted salary increases for all three League staff. Lest Mr. Febich misinterpret his raise as indicating total satisfaction, however, the board did suggest that Connor "encourage Mr. Febich to eliminate some of his faults, such as poor spelling."

The proposed budget allocated only $5000 for CUNA dues, disregarding the anticipated assessment increase. The League seems to have been determined to resist CUNA's financial needs, including the actual 1941 dues assessment of $5,600. The board even passed a resolution calling on the national association to place a $100,000 absolute cap on its budget. And the board once again resolved not to fill its own fifth seat on the CUNA board of directors to which it was fully entitled.

The Pennsylvania board remained more concerned with federal law than with state legislation, but never connected this interest with increased support of the national association and its legislative relations program. The League contined to ignore requests and increasingly strident demands from its state-chartered members for help to obtain relief from the more restrictive provisions of the state credit union law.

Several state-chartered credit unions went so far as to have their own bills submitted to the 1941 Pennsylvania legislature. Yet the League, having moved from Harrisburg, displayed no interest in these credit unions or their demands. Such bills included state credit union law amendments to: allow interlending between state and federal credit unions; broaden the allowed fields of membership; and permit payment of a "patronage dividend" [loan interest rebate] by state credit unions.

The board did find time and energy to concern itself with national issues, including two areas affected by CUNA's proposed amendments to the Federal Credit Union Act. Pennsylvania actively supported legislation permitting payment of "patronage dividends" by federal credit unions as proposed by CUNA (while ignoring the same issue before the Pennsylvania legislature), and opposed CUNA's support of a revitalized FCA.

The CUNA proposal would have put the Federal Credit Union Section back in the organizing business. The Pennsylvania directors argued that such activity would be too expensive and would be reflected in higher federal examination fees. Ironically, it was precisely such activities which had made Pennsylvania a leading credit union state. Apparently it bothered none or few of the board members that their own credit unions had originally been organized by FCA yet they were denying the same opportunity to other potential newcomers.

These early Pennsylvania credit union leaders were dedicated to their movement. Part of that dedication came from a total commitment to the principles of thrift. To them, one of the greatest values of the movement was its ability to both teach andpractice those principles. They were faced with an unresolvable dilemma. To the extent that they supported costly dissemination of information and organizing activities, they incurred expense and violated one of their prime values. Yet they realized that to increase League activities, it would be necessary to provide financial support. The real and difficult question was how to best serve the interests of their individual credit unions and the interests of the movement.

In preparation for the next day's annual meeting, the March 21 board meeting recommended that League dues once again be lowered. They had no experience with the 4.5% of gross income schedule then in effect. The 5% schedule of the previous year had emptied the League treasury by late December. Yet on March 21, the board voted to assess dues at 4% of gross income for 1942.

Art Thompson recalls the discussions that continually swirled around the dues issue:

> "The big conflict, as I remember in those days, developed between the small credit unions and the large.
>
> "Now you had a number of members of the board of directors (I think maybe more from Philadelphia than from Pittsburgh) that were going to fight any dues structure that would make them appear to be supporting the league by themselves.
>
> "On the other hand you had the small credit unions that wanted a dues schedule that would be as favorable to them as they could because they were operating on a small budget and they couldn't afford a lot of dues. As long as you have big credit unions and small credit unions I guess it's always going to be that way."

The League was growing rapidly through the organization of a large number of smaller credit unions. Because the League operated on a "one credit union, one vote" basis, these newer, smaller credit unions could potentially control the annual meeting. The older and wealthier credit unions controlled the Pittsburgh Chapter and Philadelphia Chapter. With no other consistently active chapters, these two groups controlled the board. And the board with its executive committee and bylaws control had effectively insulated itself from the general membership.

Lower membership fees were not in the best interest of the smaller credit unions. They needed the kinds of help that only a well-staffed, well-financed league could offer. They needed assistance in bookkeeping, promotion, and other activities. The high rate of League disaffiliation indicates that the League was not providing necessary services.

The $1000 ceiling on League dues exclusively benefitted the large credit unions. To their enduring credit, the 1941 board saw beyond an even more self-serving temptation and voted down a motion to lower that ceiling to $900. They simultaneously voted to hire an additional field secretary and allow the managing director to devote less time to organization activities and more to administrative affairs.

The final budget brought before the 1941 annual meeting proposed expenditures of $20,220, compared to $16,750 for 1940,and called for lower dues.

It was a naively optimistic time for all Americans. Many leaders looked out on a troubled world and saw nothing amiss. Europe was already in turmoil and soon the United States would be involved in World War II. But to the board of directors as to most other Americans, optimism seemed the appropriate mood of the day. The depression was easing; unemployment was dropping; industrial production was accelerating. Few people realized that these developments were but the silver lining to the growing clouds and reflected an accelerating shift of the American economy to a wartime basis. They saw only reason for gaiety as the League met at Pittsburgh's William Penn Hotel. Banquet tickets, including dancing, were $2.75 each.

An early report accepted by the meeting, Joe Moore's report as state chairman of the Filene Memorial Campaign, should have warned the League to be on guard against financial optimism. Moore reported that Pennsylvania had contributed $4,000.09 ($2,962.14 in cash, $1,037.95 in purchase of Filene memorial stamps—mostly by the League), only 26.7% of the state quota. Nationally the drive had achieved a mere 48% of its $150,000 initial goal.

Other reports were routine; only the refusal of past president H. H. Hook to run for reelection to the board of directors caused a stir. Hook nominated E. A. Kistler as a replacement, but a caucus of Pittsburgh area credit unions selected E. R. Sheakley instead. H. Van Brookhoven, Jr. was elected from District 5, replacing C. A. Bowman who retired.

The membership also voted to adopt a recommendation of the Pittsburgh Chapter and to schedule future annual meetings a little later in the year. They anticipated that warmer weather would allow more members to attend. The appropriate bylaw amendment moved the annual meeting date to April.

The most controversial issue of the meeting was the CUNA proposal that the Federal Credit Union Section resume its organizing activities. Despite the fact that a majority of the 108 credit unions represented at the eighth annual meeting had been organized by Federal Credit Union Section staff, the delegates voted to oppose the CUNA plan.

The real issue was not ingratitude, but the growing schism between rural and urban credit unions "the city boys *vs.* the country boys" as John McCullough, a future League president, would describe it. The rural and urban credit unions had different needs and different values. Once they had had different credit union systems. Desjardins and the American credit union movement had unified them. In the forum provided by the League, those differences all too easily became clashes.

The early credit union movement was based on unity and cooperation. That was true of Desjardins' pioneering work synthesizing competing ideologies; it was a vital part of Bergengren's vision of a coordinated national concept; it was crucial in Pennsylvania, where the state law was passed only through an extraordinary cooperative effort and the League grew through the cooperation of CUNA and Farm Credit Administration.

That cooperative spirit was fading everywhere in the world in 1941, not just in the credit union movement. Confrontation was the order of the day. Where cooperation had been the hallmark of the credit union movement, internal conflicts had become more important to an increasing range of policies and decisions. The same pattern affected both the national and state organizations.

Conflict was everywhere: Philadelphia vs. Pittsburgh; city *vs.* country; big *vs.* small; Bergengren *vs.* Doig; CUNA *vs.* CUNA Affiliates; newcomers *vs.* old guard; volunteers like Pratt, Moore, and CUNA President R. A. ['Doc'] West *vs.* full-time credit union professionals like Connor and Bergengren.

Relationships between CUNA and the Pennsylvania League were also strained. The League was routinely in arrears on its national dues. Pennsylvania collections for the Filene Memorial Fund not only lagged behind quotas, but also behind collection rates in other states. Worse, the Pennsylvania delegation continually argued with CUNA over the location of the new headquarters. Moore had originally demanded that CUNA's headquarters should be in Indianapolis; in 1941, Pennsylvania's national delegates were insisting that CUNA relocate from Madison to Washington, D.C.

Ideally, the gap between CUNA and the League should have been bridged by the powerful personality of William Pratt. A former president of the Philadelphia Chapter, League director, national delegate, CUNA Eastern District vice president, member of the CUNA executive committee and a director of CUNA Mutual, Pratt was an imposing and influential figure at both organizations and their affiliates.

He was also a member of several important CUNA committees, including: affiliates committee; control of CUNA Mutual committee; dues committee; FCA contact committee; pension plan committee; and surety bond committee. Other Pennsylvania representation on CUNA committees came through Matt Pottiger's seat on the tax and legislation committee. Such representation might well have given Pennsylvania an influential voice in national affairs.

It seems instead to have heightened friction between the national association and the state league. Pratt's policies on the size of the CUNA board of directors, CUNA dues, the relationship of CUNA Mutual to the national association, the location of Filene House, and establishment of a national credit union collection agency were all minority positions at CUNA, and all adopted as official policies of the League. There is no evidence of interest in compromise.

In one area, Doig did try to follow Pratt's lead. He sought to get the CUNA executive committee to follow the Pennsylvania system whereby delegates to CUNA would not be seated unless a credit union had fully paid its annual dues. Doig's speech seemed at first to have come at a good time. By May 1941, Pennsylvania had fully paid its $5600.00 CUNA dues; the League's national delegation was actively seeking to improve its standing at headquarters. But at the CUNA board meeting Pratt lost his bid for re-election to his vice presidency and thereby lost his seat on the executive committee.

In Philadelphia, the League was preparing for a productive year. The combination of increased membership and higher average assets brought record dues collections. The new field secretary, Henry Hullinger, extended the organizing activities dramatically.

Then Europe was at war and the United States moved to a wartime economy, producing war materials for lend-lease distribution to the Allies and preparing to enter the conflict.[1]

The League proved that *Key Notes* would become an important tool for credit unions, as it transformed the journal into a newsletter of advice and explanation of complex federal regulations designed to cope with wartime stresses on the national economy.

On August 9, President Roosevelt issued Executive Order No. 8843 governing consumer credit. Its intent was to limit wartime inflation and speculation by limiting consumer access to credit. The order included Regulation W, limiting the duration and amount of instalment loan contracts. Regulation W hobbled the entire thrift industry. It nearly destroyed the credit union movement by restricting or stopping the most popular and important income-producing types of activity.

Regulation W was intended to reduce consumer demand and inflation pressure on durable consumer goods manufactured from materials needed for national defense. Such items

1. The first wartime measure potentially affecting credit unions was Executive Order No. 8785 which froze all financial assets held by foreign nationals in the United States. It became unlawful for credit unions to release any funds held by resident aliens (other than citizens of Ireland, Great Britain, and Turkey) without special license issued by the Department of the Treasury.

included radios, refrigerators, furniture, automobiles, vacuum cleaners, washing machines, stoves, and a wide variety of other items. The federal government had no desire to hurt lending institutions. They made every attempt to ease the impact of Regulation W. Doig and CUNA president William Reid were consulted in its creation; the regulation was promulgated with full consideration for the problems and practices of credit unions.

Regulation W required credit unions to register with the Federal Reserve and generated a whole new series of forms, legal opinions, and supporting regulations. For the next four years, *Key Notes* would prove invaluable for keeping credit unions informed about policies and procedures involved with Regulation W, sales of war bonds and rules involving loans to military personnel.

On December 7, 1941, the Japanese attacked Pearl Harbor. The United States was at war. The "little man under the umbrella" symbol of the American credit union was changed for the duration. He went into uniform, put his umbrella aside and shouldered a rifle. The credit union movement would do what it could to support the war effort.

"It is superfluous to point out that the New Year will probably be the most difficult one that the credit unions will ever be called upon to face," wrote president Palmer. "On behalf of your state League I want to pledge the highest degree of cooperation and service."

The League's first contribution to the war effort was office secretary Febich who resigned to enter military service. The League had no intention of moving to a lean staff for the duration. Febich was replaced by Paula Lloyd as office assistant to the managing director and the field staff was strengthened with the addition of Bob Steinke who started working in the Philadelphia area in February. Steinke had excellent credentials and recommendations for the post. He was a charter member and the treasurer of Remrandco [Remington-Rand Corp.] FCU. He was also treasurer of the Philadelphia Chapter CU.

233

The first wartime meeting of the League board was held January 10 at Philadelphia's Warwick Hotel. The treasurer's report showed that the gambles taken in previous years had paid off. Increasing credit union growth and increasing League membership had enabled the League to meet its obligations. Accordingly, the board voted to again lower dues. The 1943 schedule called for a fee assessment of 3.5% of gross income. The board also approved hiring a supply clerk, Mario Cervone.

The most serious loss to the League experienced at this outbreak of war came with the resignation of Julia Connor. Her letter informing CUNA of her resignation told part of the story: "It is with great regret that I shall leave the work I love and this League which I have helped to build." In the *Bridge*, editor Shipe took note of her record and accomplishments: "The records of the Credit Union National Association, which go back to January 1, 1938, show that since that date 340 new credit unions have been chartered in Pennsylvania. The total of credit unions in the state is 639."

Connor returned to service at FCA, accepting a position as chief of the general administrative files. As the federal government dispersed its offices throughout the nation, the Farm Credit Administration moved to Kansas City. For Connor, that was the silver lining. Kansas City was her hometown.[2]

Connor's own farewell message in *Key Notes* was brief and terse. "It is with genuine regret that I say to you, my friends, Farewell! For your hearty cooperation during the four years that I have served as managing director of the Pennsylvania Credit Union League, I thank you."

President Palmer was effusive in his praise:

"The Credit Union Movement, and particularly our Pennsylvania Credit Union League, suffers an almost irreparable loss

2. She also left the credit union movement at the same time. An Executive Order effective three days before her resignation removed the Federal Credit Union Section from FCA and placed it under authority of the Federal Deposit Insurance Corporation.

with the resignation of Miss Julia D. Connor, managing director, to be effective April 25, 1942....

"Miss Connor was elected managing director in January, 1938, coming to us from the Credit Union Section of the Farm Credit Administration. At that time there were less than 350 credit unions in the State, and fewer than 200 in the League. The budget was less than $5,000. The program and services rendered by the League were at a minimum....

"Today there are close to 650 credit unions, 62% of them League members. Our budget this year is $27,000. Under her leadership a central office has been established, and legal incorporation completed. The field force has been increased by three additional members. Every type of service is now available to credit unions."

Palmer also identified at least part of the reason that Connor chose to return to federal service when he took note of the difficulty of working "successfully for a board of directors consisting of seventeen members, frequently representing seventeen divergent opinions, and under the critical scrutiny of several hundred member credit unions."[3]

Neither Matt Pottiger nor Bill Pratt had great affection or respect for Connor. In 1967 interviews with Howard Custer of CUNA Mutual, neither would discuss her in any detail. Pottiger recalled only that she had come from Farm Credit Administration and returned to the agency at the outbreak of the War. Pratt's recollections of Connor were somewhat more detailed:

"She was a good managing director and she made some suggestions basically in operations. But she didn't get involved too much with the politics as to what should be resolved and this

3. Connor was not a physically strong person, and her health worsened sharply during her four years of League leadership. Louise Herring remembers her as timid and cautious, hesitant to go out and organize— more interested in writing records than in setting records. Connor's legacy did include comprehensive statistical records of her work with the League. They chart an outstanding record of growth in credit union organization and League affiliation.

sort of thing. Because, let's say, she grew up with these [credit union] people to a certain degree where I had ten years of living with them as a board member and four years of being a managing director too, see, and still being on the board."

Pratt was never comfortable with the women leaders of the credit union movement, including Connor. "It's pretty hard for a bunch of men to let a woman get out in front and lead them," he told Howard Custer.

Connor had many supporters among the directors. The majority appreciated her efforts and rewarded them, often over the objections of a small but vocal group. She was underpaid, but she had been given moderate raises. As the League grew, she was provided with additional staff including two (briefly three) field secretaries as well as full-time office assistance and a supply clerk. It is equally clear that she was never accorded great support or respect by League leadership.

None of the board leaders with the possible exceptions of presidents Hook and Palmer seem to have appreciated the magnitude of her accomplishments. They did not realize the work involved in compiling her detailed and statistically reliable reports. They did not realize the value of her methodical approach to organization and contact work. When Lloyd Sigafoo joined the field staff, he was able to maintain her pace of organization and affiliation work in his region—but not to improve on it. The same thing happened when field staff were added in the East.

At the end of her administration, the League was growing more slowly despite the efforts of two field staffers (with Connor confined to administrative work) than Connor had accomplished working alone. Yet Art Thompson, Pratt, Moore and the other board members were not appreciative. They seem to have believed that the League's growth was due to natural forces rather than Connor's dedicated efforts. "I think this was natural growth," said Pratt of the Connor years. Perhaps, but the "natural" growth slowed sharply—then reversed—after Connor left the League.

Connor officially tendered her resignation at a specially-called March 29 meeting of the executive committee.[4] Her resignation was officially "accepted with regret." Field assistant Steinke was directed to devote more of his time to administering the affairs of the central office; Connor's resignation took effect April 30, 1942.

The full board was officially informed of Connor's resignation and of executive committee actions at the April 17 regular pre-convention meeting in Erie. At that same meeting, T. Walter McGrath of Philadelphia was elected to fill the unexpired term of W.C. Buehler who had resigned from the board. McGrath would soon become an active director and officer. He also became a powerful ally of Pratt. Miss Connor was excused from the meeting. Pratt suggested that the directors buy a gold watch to present to her at the next evening's banquet. Treasurer Tokay handled the collection.

Replacing Connor (especially at her salary) turned out to be more difficult than the board had anticipated.[5] "After considerable discussion of the matter, it appeared to be the consensus that the position should not be filled until after more publicity had been given the existing vacancy and an effort made to secure more applicants...."

At the April 18 regular meeting of the board, newly-elected president E. A. Thompson agreed to serve as managing director pro tem with the assistance of Pratt as his colleague on an ad hoc administrative committee of the board. Such a power

4. In the confusion following Connor's resignation, the quality of League records degenerated seriously. The official records are incomplete. A copy of the executive committee minutes is available in the A. R. Thompson papers in the research collection of the League. Copies of most reports including managing director Connor's final reports are all lost, as are copies of the final report of president Palmer. Subsequent descriptions of meetings rely heavily on the Thompson papers and articles in *Key Notes* in addition to the official records of the League.
5. Applications were received from: A. Lansdale, assistant managing director of the New Jersey League; two of the Pennsylvania field assistants, Lloyd Sigafoo and Robert Steinke; Thomas Curran of Philadelphia; Thomas Furman of Reading; Carl Simmons of Lancaster; and Edna S. Boyer of Philadelphia.

shift within the board was bound to cause ripples. From the Pittsburgh perspective, too much power was being concentrated in Philadelphia. Moore countered by standing for election as vice president.

Pratt sought to secure Philadelphia's ascendance. He argued that the vice-presidency should go to someone outside both the Philadelphia and Pittsburgh districts. E. R. Sheakley was then nominated for vice-president, but Moore was easily elected. Pottiger and Tokay were re-elected as secretary and treasurer, respectively, and as delegate and alternate to CUNA Supply. Palmer joined Moore, Pratt, Pottiger, and Tokay as a fifth national director with L. F. Hardman as alternate.

It was not an auspicious beginning for president E. A. Thompson. He was a charter director of Philadelphia Teachers Credit Union and president of that group since 1938. He was a member of the committee on credit unions of the National Education Association, and was principal of Philadelphia's prestigious G. W. Childs School.

He would need a full range of skills to guide the Pennsylvania credit union movement through the coming storm. The clouds were dense at the July 11 Harrisburg meeting of the executive committee. For the previous two years, League fiscal policy had become increasingly short-sighted. A financial crisis was inevitable. By June 1942 it had arrived. Credit union income was down sharply, reduced by Regulation W, by the unavailability of consumer goods and by general lack of demand for loans caused by the War.

Many credit unions were in arrears on League dues. While they appreciated the information service provided by *Key Notes*, they were well aware that the publication was distributed to all credit unions, affiliated and non-affiliated alike. Virtually all other League services had ceased with the departure of the managing director.

The executive committee approved salary increases for office secretary Lloyd, supply clerk Cervone, and office manager Steinke. The committee then postponed the scheduled September board meeting because of the League's increasing

E. A. (Ed) Thompson, served as president of the Pennsylvania Credit Union League, 1943–1946.

financial difficulty, rescheduled the 1943 annual meeting for Pittsburgh instead of Wilkes-Barre to cut costs and increase attendance; cut the mailing list for *Key Notes*; and requested that the directors seek expense compensation for attending meetings from their credit unions and try to preserve League funds.

In their most significant cost-savings move, the League decided not to appoint a new full-time managing director. President Thompson immediately announced that he would not continue to act in that capacity, and Pratt was appointed as acting managing director, effective July 16, at the nominal compensation of $50.00 per month. As Pratt recalled those days:

> "We had two fieldmen and one girl in the office [and a third field secretary, Lloyd Sigafoo, in Pittsburgh] and a supply boy and I went down at night whenever I could. I was in the paint and chemical plant but I was also supervising loading munitions for the war in a [tape is garbled].... So when I could get

239

down there, I'd do it. We didn't do much work and I scribbled off letters and she typed them. Bummed the rest of the time to go through the war."

With Hullinger and Steinke as field assistants serving the areas around Philadelphia and Pittsburgh; with Steinke helping out in the office and the full-time work of Lloyd and Cervone, and with a sharply curtailed menu of League services, there was little left for Pratt to do. As acting managing director for the remainder of the war years, he signed checks and handled League correspondence, answering letters when necessary, referring them when possible.

At the September 18, 1943 meeting, Pratt announced that Steinke had requested a leave of absence to take a defense job. His request was denied so Steinke resigned. Much of the responsibility for the League was unofficially carried by Lloyd. After a year of working for Pratt, she announced her intention of quitting to join the Marines. At Pratt's request, the League offered her a $35 per month (35%) raise. She joined the marines anyway.

For the League, the situation quickly went from weak to bad: 1943 was among the worst years in League experience. Pratt's September 18, 1943 report told the sorry story:

New credit unions organized 16
Liquidations 28
Net loss of credit unions . . . . (12)

Number of new members 31
Non-renewals of membership 38
Net loss of members . . . . (7)
Total decline in dues-paying membership . . . .(19)

For the remaining members, income was down even though total assets remained stable. The dues schedule called for 3.5% of gross income. This schedule was maintained, despite the fact that it was inevitably producing a substantial decrease in League income, a decrease that the League could ill afford. In fact, the League was fortunately able to resist attempts to further decrease the membership fee schedule.

The April 10 pre-convention meeting of the board included brief discussion of the meaning of "gross income" as applied to dues. It was the first gambit in what eventually became an extended campaign by treasurer Tokay to exclude investment income from the dues base. At the post-convention board meeting, discussion on the meaning of "gross income" was referred to the dues committee for report at the next board meeting.

Dues committee chairman Palmer delayed further discussion of the issue through the war years. In April 1945, he succeeded in winning a resolution defining gross income as including income from loans, investments and capital gains. Palmer's quiet and diplomatic handling of his chairmanship of the dues committee was probably responsible for preventing additional weakening of the League's financial position.

THE WAR YEARS witnessed major difficulties throughout the credit union movement. The Federal Credit Union Section was removed from FCA and placed under the jurisdiction of the Federal Deposit Insurance Corporation (FDIC), the supervisory and insurance agency for banks, by Executive Order 9148, April 27, 1942. Relations between FCA and the credit union movement had been strained; relations between CUNA and FDIC were virtually nonexistent.

FDIC continued FCA's ban against the sale of CUNA Mutual group life-savings insurance policies by federal credit unions. FDIC also refused to support CUNA-sponsored federal legislation or to extend FDIC coverage to credit union share accounts. The Federal Credit Union Section remained the unwanted and unloved stepchild of FDIC until 1948 when it was reconstituted as the Bureau of Federal Credit Unions of the Federal Security Agency.

For Pennsylvania, the nation's leading federal credit union state, this disruption had severe consequences. The Pennsylvania League had always had a close relationship with the

Federal Credit Union Section. Claude Orchard had personally recruited many Pennsylvania leaders including Matt Pottiger. Julia Connor, Milton Rhye, and Jimmy Dacus had
organized many early credit unions, and FCA field staff had
organized a majority of the rest.

The League had always relied heavily on federal organization and support efforts. These were cut off at the very time
that the financially crippled League was cutting back on its
own limited activities. One response was the League's long-
delayed decision to hire a replacement for field assistant
Steinke. In April 1944, H. J. Kirsh joined the League staff,
working out of the Philadelphia office. Supply clerk Cervone
was not replaced. His work was handled on an hourly basis
by a temporary employee while the League waited to determine whether or not to continue supply activities. Lloyd,
who left the League to enlist in the Marines, was replaced by
Florence Jimenez.

The Pennsylvania delegation fought hard at the 1943 CUNA
board meetings in Chicago. The officially sponsored dues resolution called for CUNA dues of 6-cents per credit union member, and a maximum fee of $6,000. As he had at virtually every
CUNA annual meeting, Pratt offered a substitute motion. It
retained the 6-cents per member basis, but maintained the
maximum fee at $5,500. Frank Tokay seconded the Pratt mo-
tion, and Matt Pottiger rose to support it:

> "If you adopt the resolution as proposed by the dues commit-
> tee, which increases the maximum for the larger leagues and
> decreases the per capita dues for the smaller leagues, you are
> passing legislation at this time when both leagues, large and
> small, have the same conditions to face...."

Moore enthusiastically joined in support of the Pennsylvania rebellion:

> "A lot of delegates have told you about the problems of the
> smaller states and I would like to tell you something about
> Pennsylvania.... We have 52% of our credit unions who belong

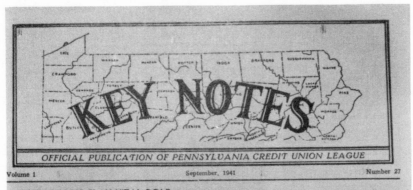

OFFICIAL PUBLICATION OF PENNSYLVANIA CREDIT UNION LEAGUE

Volume 1   September, 1941   Number 27

CREDIT UNIONS PLAY VITAL ROLE IN NATION'S DEFENSE PROGRAM

C. R. Orchard, Director, Credit Union Section, Farm Credit Administration, stresses the opportunity that is given to credit unions to prove their worth, in an article recently published in "Cooperative Saving," in the following words:

"All of us who are in any way connected with the credit union movement in the United States, have watched the growth and spread of the movement with a great deal of satisfaction, and with a sense of pride for having had a part in that remarkable development.

"Upon hearing the news that credit unions were to be given an active and important role in the National Defense Program, I turned my thoughts to the early days of the development of credit unions in this country, and once again I marveled at the progress that has been made in so few short years.

"To me, the announcement that credit unions might qualify as issuing agents in the nationwide sale of U. S. Defense Savings Bonds is another step up the ladder of achievement for credit unions, a natural one for them to take as they become safer and sounder institutions serving many thousands of our people of modest incomes, working people in every walk of life. It is a normal step for them to take as they become more "of age" and reach the maturity of their lives of service to their members. The credit union, we must realize, has become a national institution, a shining example of the beneficence of democratic processes.

"In these days of uncertainty and peril to our Nation, all of us have had one question uppermost in our minds, and that question has been: What can we do to help?" Patriotic credit union members, both as individuals and in their capacities as officers of credit unions, have been asking that question over and over again. To that question the Government has offered an excellent answer by offering them an opportunity to sell Defense Savings Bonds.

"This unusual opportunity is a twofold nature. In the first place, it offers credit unions a chance to take an active part in the Nation's Defense Program, and secondly, makes it possible for them to offer a convenient and easy means for their members and for those in the field of membership to do their bit in aiding the country in times of emergency. This second phase of the opportunity thus offered is, I believe you will agree, the most important, since it goes beyond the credit union itself and applies to the individual working man and woman, especially to the one who feels that his freedom, his aspirations, his standard of living are vitally involved in the world struggle of today and tomorrow.

"Our National Defense effort is a cooperative undertaking on an unprecedented scale. One million of the finest young men in the country have been called to the colors as a part of the great armed forces of the Nation. Hundreds of our factories are devoting the best of their productive powers to the production of the arms so necessary to our common defense. These factories are manned by literally millions of our

(Continued on Page 2)

Installment Credit

In order to promote the national defense and protect the national economy the President of the United States on August 9, 1941, issued Executive Order No. 8843, placing upon the Board of Governors of the Federal Reserve System the responsibility of regulating the extension of consumer instalment credit. The Order recognizes the importance of instalment credit in relation to consumer demand in general and, more specifically, its relation to demand for durable goods manufactured from materials needed for defense. It emphasizes the need for such regulation to promote defense production, to assist in curbing unwarranted price advances and general inflationary tendencies, and to aid in creating a backlog of consumer demand and in restraining the accumulation of a consumer debt structure which might have a repressive effect upon business in the postdefense period.

Under the broad authority delegated in the Executive Order, the Board of Governors of the Federal Reserve System has issued Regulation W, imposing limitations upon the terms under which instalment credit is to be extended. The regulation has been drawn with the aid and advice of representatives of the leading industry, including the Credit Union National Association, which was represented in Washington by William Reid, President, and Tom Doig, Assistant Managing Director. In this conference full consideration was given to the problems and practices of credit unions.

(Continued on Page 3)

World War II brought a rapidly changing credit and regulatory environment. The League newsletter became a vital link in disseminating information to the credit unions during the war era.

to the League and the reason we do not have more is because we have such a high scale. And if we go back with an additional increased dues schedule, we are liable to lose some more of our members.

"We have no objection to helping and we want to help but let me remind you that in some of our counties, we have more potential members than you have in two or three of the states and we would like to bring the credit union movement to those people first of all."

The situation grew worse. CUNA leaders argued that many leagues, including Pennsylvania, had lost managing directors and only CUNA could continue to provide strong leadership. Only a strong national organization could lead the post-war recovery of the movement, they claimed, and CUNA needed to resist all attempts to weaken it.

To the Pennsylvania delegation, the view was reversed. They felt that they had lost their managing director in part because of the excessive fees levied by CUNA. As Moore tried to explain to the CUNA board:

"Now under conditions as they exist today in Pennsylvania, we have been compelled to engage a part-time managing director. The alternate was to have a full-time managing director and that would mean we would have to leave one of our field men go and put on a clerk. Well we cannot continue to service Pennsylvania if we have to curtail the services of our personnel."

CUNA and the Pennsylvania League were facing identical crises. Both had high turnover of personnel; both did make some staff cuts in concession to financial difficulty; both experienced sharp differences of opinions among their directors. Faced with wartime federal restrictions on transportation, neither was able to hold full membership meetings. CUNA had suspended meetings of its national board of directors; the Pennsylvania League had suspended its annual meetings. Under wartime procedures, CUNA was being governed by its executive committee and the League by its board of directors.

As the war continued, the financial distress of the League intensified. The 1944 budget proposed at the January board meeting anticipated membership fee income of $12,800, down by almost 50% from its pre-war levels. This figure was based not on hard data or even on survey information; it was simply a "conservative guess" provided by treasurer Tokay. The League had $5,000 cash on hand and was willing to incur a deficit of $2,000. Including deficit spending, the League would have operating funds of $19,800 for 1944. Of this total, $6,000 was owed to CUNA for annual membership dues.

Pratt explained the situation in futile complaint to the 1944 national board meeting in Madison:

> "Now may I talk about Pennsylvania for a minute, because I think our problem in Pennsylvania may be comparable to the problem of many other leagues, both large and small. Our collections two years ago were $26,000 and $21,000 last year and it won't be more than $16,000 this year. We will pay or be able to pay maybe not all of our $6,000 for this year, as some of it we may have to pay after January 1 in order to have a little cash in the bank. That leaves us $13,000 to operate the league...."

To save money, the League had still not replaced its managing director; *Key Notes* published only five issues; directors met on an abbreviated schedule, and only in Harrisburg, where meeting costs were lowest. A major cost-cutting measure came as a result of compliance with federal regulations. There were no annual meetings held in 1944 and 1945.

Member credit unions were urged to lower or eliminate dividends for the duration. Most credit unions were forced to lower dividends because of their own rapidly dropping income. Government reports showed that credit union loan balances were dropping more rapidly under Regulation W than those of either the banks or the personal finance companies. According to an article in *Key Notes* (reprinted from *Connecticut Credit Union News*), that was because credit unions, through a mistaken patriotic impulse, were setting even stricter standards than those required by the regulation. Since their own income was keyed to member credit union income, the leagues tried to discourage such behavior.

With stressed credit unions and leagues seeking every possible way to economize, substantial anger developed towards CUNA's failure to lower its sights. Much of this anger was directed at the Filene Memorial Fund which was virtually forced to suspend activities. It also brought near warfare within the ranks of CUNA itself. The problem at CUNA was taking shape along lines all too familiar in the Keystone State. "Much of the dissention occurred between the big, wealthier leagues, and the small, poorer ones. The stronger state leagues which had large memberships continued to resent supplying so much of CUNA's budget through the assessment of membership dues."[6]

CUNA faced unique problems from its affiliates. CUNA Supply Cooperative found it virtually impossible to maintain staff and inventory: not only were its employees joining the armed forces, but rationing made it difficult to obtain materials. CUNA Mutual experienced sharp fluctuations in underwriting; the struggle continued with the national association over control of the company and its substantial financial resources. Varying opinions within CUNA over how best to relate to the affiliates widened the split between the national association and its affiliates and between factions within CUNA itself. Under wartime pressures, disputes that had been building for years finally broke wide open.

Like Connor in Pennsylvania, Bergengren would become a casualty of wartime stresses, strained tempers, anxious egos and changing times. Feuds within the national association leadership finally resulted in the firing of Roy Bergengren as

6. Moody and Fite, *Origins of the Credit Union Movement*, pp. 275-76. The opposition was led by the Michigan Credit Union League which in 1943 paid only $1000.00 of its $5000.00 assessment and threatened to disaffiliate. Only the personal intervention of Bergengren averted an acute crisis in the movement.

CUNA managing director. That action was taken with the explicit consent and passive acquiesence of much of the Pennsylvania credit union movement leadership.

But while Connor left the Pennsylvania League suffering from exhaustion, depression, and frustration, she unquestionably left of her own will and at a time of her own choosing. For many years, it was believed that the same was true of Bergengren. It is now known that such was not the case. Bergengren wanted to retain his post, and gave up his fight only when it became apparent that he did not have enough support at the league level to win his battle with the CUNA executive committee.

CUNA president West called a closed meeting of his executive committee in Kansas City in September 1944. Edward Shanney, president of CUNA Mutual was there; so was Karl Little, president of CUNA Supply. Neither Bergengren nor Doig was invited. West made his case that CUNA was suffering from "discord, confusion, and lack of direction." The leaders of the affiliates joined in the attack.

President West neither appreciated the importance of the credit union philosophy nor understood the essential intellectual and emotional roots of the credit union movement. To West and his followers, credit unions were a form of thrift institution that was a low-cost competitor with banks, savings & loans, and finance companies.

> "I cannot evaluate this enthusiasm business too much because I think you can take this whole group—Tom Doig, Charlie Hyland, Roy Bergengren and all of them—and clear them out of this movement today and bring all new men and your movement will go on just the same and maybe better."

That was the essential issue. West was responding to the same kind of thinking on the national level that had first taken root in Pennsylvania back in 1936. Just as H. Andrew Hanemann had been discarded by Doig, Pratt, Moore and the others because of his weak organizational abilities—and just as Connor has been left without support because of her lack

247

of manipulative political skills—now it was Bergengren's turn. The executive committee supported West and the affiliates. Bergengren was out.

The extensive negotiating that followed clouded the picture seen by most contemporary observers. CUNA had no pension plan; Bergengren had no savings. In an attempt to short-circuit the anticipated outcry by Bergengren's legion of loyal admirers, West offered him a post as promotional advisor and a respectable salary. In return, Bergengren would voluntarily step down. Doig waited in the wings. Bergengren used the delay to seek support among friends in the leagues and in the general cooperative movement. He also considered seeking new employment with the Council for Cooperative Development or some other general cooperative association.

Credit union and league leaders from all over the country tried to defend their pioneer. Louise McCarren (Ohio), Henry Strickler (New Jersey), Bill Cyr (Massachusetts), L.R. [Nick] Nixon (Connecticut) and others organized a resistance effort designed to take the issue to the full board of CUNA. In a letter to Nixon, Bergengren recognized the extent of the real issue at the heart of the dispute:

"I think the real issue is that West is an out and out industrialist. He maintains that the credit union is not cooperative...he accepts the old way of economic control in America as a sort of religion. He refuses to see that we are going into a new world and that it must contain a fairer shake for the average man.... I have faith that we can strive to make a better world after the war, a world which will be just a little reward for the terrible sacrifices we are making in this war. Doc and I are at the poles in our economic thinking...."

In the same February 14, 1944 letter, Bergengren was equally perceptive in his realization that he could not count on the Pennsylvania League for support:

"I spent fifteen days at Bill Pratt's request awhile back in Pennsylvania, attended eleven chapter meetings, helped organize some credit unions and, when I got through, Bill thanked me very profusely for what he called a very great service to the Pennsylvania credit union movement. And yet Bill is probably against me."

Bergengren's close associate and longtime friend Agnes Gartland also understood what was happening and where the support was coming from. In a February 25 letter to Nick [Nixon] and Leo [Maynard?] she wrote:

"There is no doubt in my mind that Pratt is [former CUNA president William] Reid's choice to succeed RFB when the permanent appointment is made. He killed organization work in his own league by nagging Julia Connor until she got out, and the league has made no progress since. He tried to kill all organization of credit unions by his [dues] motion which came within a hair of passing the 1943 annual meeting in Chicago. He certainly lacks all the vision and inspirational leadership and ingenuity in accomplishing what looks impossible, which qualities the boss possesses to such an extraordinary degree.... The 'big business' complex will stifle the credit union movement, disguise its consumer credit function, alienate all liberal elements...and deny to us our rightful participation as a stabilizing force in the progress of the people's revolution already under way. We must retain liberal leadership—that's what the fight has been all along in the National Board."

That was what the fight had been all about in Pennsylvania, too. And it had reached the same conclusion. Pratt may also have believed that he was in line for Bergengren's job; there is no direct evidence about that. But the rest of the Pennsylvania national delegates moved swiftly to defend the CUNA executive committee's action. Pottiger wrote that:

"The action of the Executive Committee in removing Mr. Bergengren from the position of Managing Director of CUNA meets with my approval. As I stated at the meeting in New York City in March, the committee merely took the action that should have been taken by the National Board way back in 1939."

Pratt himself wrote simply that the "five national directors of Pennsylvania ... are in accord with actions taken by the national executive committee." At their April 22, 1945 meeting, the Pennsylvania League board of directors voted that they "do hereby endorse the action taken by the executive committee of CUNA in making the necessary changes in administrative positions...."

In May 1945, CUNA's executive committee officially dismissed Bergengren as managing director. They hired him as promotional advisor, and hired Doig to lead CUNA. Many expected that Doig, aging and in poor health, would hold the position only temporarily. With opposition to him sharply divided, with increasing friction between CUNA and CUNA Mutual, and in the absence of futher decisive direction by the executive committee, Doig would remain chief executive officer of CUNA for a decade. If Pratt had anticipated moving to Madison as Bergengren's successor, his hopes were denied.

"Roy F. Bergengren Retires," announced a story in the April-June *Key Notes*. The story gave no indication of the violence behind the events. And while news and rumors of the full story were slowly percolating throughout the credit union movement, League members who wanted to know more about the events in Kansas City and Madison would learn nothing from such official League sources as *Key Notes*. Publicly, the League would say only that "on May 1, our managing director of the Credit Union National Association, retired at age sixty-five. Mr. Bergengren has been associated with the Credit Union movement since 1921 when he was employed by Edward A. Filene to organize credit unions throughout the nation."

As events at the national level stabilized, the Pennsylvania League began preparations for its post-war reconstruction. On May 10, 1945, in a meeting at the Hotel Loraine in Madison, Wisconsin, the executive committee voted that Pratt should become full-time managing director of the League. His salary was more than double that paid to Julia Connor, and scheduled to increase 18.5% for 1947.[7]

In anticipation of post-war expansion, the League acquired a new location as well. The cramped single-room office at 1504 Race Street would no longer be adequate. More spacious quarters were needed. The new office would be at 112 South 52nd Street. It was still a single room, but included a second desk, additional files, and a large closet to house inventories of supplies.

The war was over. It was time to rebuild.

7. In this as in many other matters, the executive committee acted on behalf of the full board under wartime authority. All actions taken by the executive committee under its wartime authority were later affirmed by the full board of directors.

CHAPTER

IX

Reconstruction and Renewal

"But the things that seemed so important at the time, don't seem so important after a few years. We used to get quite excited about issues that came up. And in a year or so we'd forget all about them. And that is good. Some controversies we caried on for years. But most of the big issues were fought out and then forgotten."

Joseph Moore

THE ELEVENTH ANNUAL MEETING (1946) of the Pennsylvania Credit Union League was the first post-war meeting of the League, the first annual meeting since April 1943. It was held at an appropriate setting, the Sterling Hotel in Wilkes-Barre. The Sterling was owned by A. J. Sordoni, the state senator and chairman of the senate banking committee who, in 1933, had played a critical role in passing the Pennsylvania Credit Union Law. Now his hotel was the scene as the Pennsylvania credit union movement convened to begin repairing the damages of the war years and set about rebuilding for the post-war era.

Sordoni was introduced to the group by Rudy Goetz. We have no record of his comments to the assembled delegates and guests. That is unfortunate; Sordoni had worked closely with Bergengren and the others to help pass the legislation, organized an early credit union, and had an extended meeting with Claude Orchard during the early days of the Federal Credit Union Section's activities. His employees had founded one of the first state-chartered credit unions in Pennsylvania. There was some early confusion about who was qualified to be seated with the board at this meeting. Directors were elected at the annual meetings, but there had been none for three years. The terms of all members had actually expired. To further complicate the situation, several newcomers had been accepted by the board as directors—representatives of their districts—during the war. They included Lee DeVoe, A. W. Lawry, and T. W. McGrath. Another newcomer, J. J. Girvan, while not yet a director, had been elected president of the Philadelphia Chapter. As a close friend and associate of

Pratt, he had assumed an important behind-the-scenes role in League activities.[1]

The terms of all directors had technically expired. No elections had been held since the 1943 annual meeting. The first order of business at the 1946 meeting, therefore, was electing directors.

First, by unanimous vote it was determined to retain existing district boundaries and the numerical representation of each on the board. The delegates then voted in an uncontested election to elect one director from each district to a two-year term, with the additional directors from Districts 3 and 6 each elected to one-year terms.[2]

There had also been a change in the increasingly important position of League counsel. George Neal resigned early in November 1945; his resignation was accepted by the executive committee at their January 12-13, 1946 meeting. There followed an extensive debate over the selection of a successor. Neal recommended Floyd Tompkins but League president E. A. Thompson argued for appointment of Thomas Lee, a member of the state legislature who had just been selected by Thompson's Philadelphia Teachers Credit Union to replace Neal. After a day's delay and over the specifically recorded objections of president Thompson, Tompkins won the appointment and the $500 annual retainer.

The League membership fee continued at its wartime level, 3.5% of gross income. That decision came over the objections of treasurer Tokay and a new delegate from the Atlantic Employees FCU in Philadelphia, William M. Noble. They objected to continuing $1000 maximum, arguing that since the

1. Jim Girvan later became active in the international credit union movement. Early in the twentieth century, Sir Horace Plunkett, a pioneering Irish cooperator, had helped introduce Pennsylvania Governor Gifford Pinchot to the credit union concept. During the 1960s, Jim Girvan returned the favor, journeying to Ireland where he undertook extensive organizational activities on behalf of the Irish credit union movement. He is still revered there for his pioneering activities.
2. The post-war board of directors was therefore constituted as follows (following an uncontested election). Elected to two-year terms: District 1,

percentage basis had been reduced during the war, so too should be maximum.

Now, for the first time, managing director Pratt opposed a request for dues reduction. From the perspective of a person who had decided to seek full-time responsibility of League managing director, he realized that wartime ravages could not be repaired by continuing the financially restricting policies of the past. He had decided to seek the full-time responsibility as League managing director and had no desire to continue the financially restricting policies of the past. He argued that credit unions paying at the maximum level were already receiving a special privilege. That level, argued Pratt, should not be reduced. His argument carried the day, and the $1000 maximum was retained.

The League, through CUNA, now took a major step along the road to professionalism. It acknowledged its increasing reliance on and responsibility to professional staff with the creation of a pension plan. When Roy Bergengren was fired by CUNA, the national association had no pension plan. The job of promotional advisor at a salary of $5000.00 was seen by the CUNA executive committee as a way of providing him a pension. Even that appointment and its salary were opposed by some members of the CUNA leadership. They acknowledged that Bergengren had done great things for the credit union movement, but they argued that he had already been well paid for it.

The Pennsylvania League's national directors were among the opponents of any "excessive" pension for Roy Bergengren and his close associate from the early days of the national crusade, Earl Rentfo, who had voluntarily joined

L. F. Hardman; District 2, Lee DeVoe; District 3, Frank Tokay; District 4, Matt Pottiger; District 5, H. Van Brookhoven; District 6, E. A. Thompson; District 7, Mark Raymond; District 8, Walter W. Anderson. Elected to one-year terms: District 3, Joseph A. Moore, G. A. Palmer, Jr., A. R. Thompson, R. F. Goetz, E. D. Klaus, A. William Lawry; District 6, Norman Long, T.W. McGrath, W. W. Pratt.

him in retirement.[3] As the CUNA board worked to find some equitable arrangement, the Pennsylvania League passed a resolution:

> "RESOLVED. That in the absence of a retirement plan, no payment shall be made by CUNA or its affiliates to any employee due to disability, retirement or inactive employment in excess of one hundred fifty dollars ($150) per month, and upon establishment of a retirement plan future payments shall be in conformity therewith."

As a national director and chairman of a special CUNA committee, of which Matt Pottiger was a member, Pratt led efforts to create a CUNA retirement savings plan that would cover both national association and league employees. Pratt agreed to resign from DuPont-Grasselli and accept full-time employment with the League only after the CUNA pension structure was in place. Field assistants Lloyd Sigafoo and Howard Kirsh were included in the pension plan by action of the League executive committee at the May 10, 1946 meeting. Assistant secretary Florence Jimenez was not included; she resigned shortly thereafter.

At the post-convention session of the board of directors, Joseph Moore was elected to succeed E. A. Thompson as president of the League. T. Walter McGrath was elected vice president, and Tokay and Pottiger were reelected treasurer and secretary. William Lawry was elected as an additional member of the executive committee. Moore, Pottiger, Pratt and Tokay were also elected as national directors. Palmer, the

---

3. The Pennsylvania leaders continued their objections to pensions for Bergengren and Rentfro through 1948 (when CUNA finally voted to provide financial support). Jealousy over Bergengren's salary as managing director is evident in their opposition. E. A. Thompson argued "How can you go back into your respective districts....and tell your constituents that they have got to pay more dues and then at the same time justify the expenditure of $2,500 per year additional as a pension to Roy F. Bergengren?" Joe Moore added: "We recognize Mr. Bergengren's contribution and we also believe that he was well paid for such contribution and...we think that this proposal is both unfair and unjust." The motion providing the pension passed.

fifth national director, resigned, apparently because the League had refused to pay expenses for a fifth director to attend CUNA board meetings. Rudy Goetz was elected to complete Palmer's term.

The process and negotiations leading to selection of Pratt as full-time managing director were initiated at this April meeting of the board. It was officially completed at the May 10 meeting of the executive committee in Madison. Subsequently Pratt resigned as both a league director and a national director of CUNA. He retained his position as a vice president of CUNA Mutual Insurance. Noble was selected to succeed Pratt as a director from District 6; Rudy Goetz, alternate national director, succeeded Pratt on the board of CUNA; Lawry became alternate national director.

With that action, the League's post-war restructuring was complete. The team that would lead the Pennsylvania credit union movement through its next period was firmly in place.

WHEN OFFICE ASSISTANT Jimenez resigned shortly before the 1947 annual meeting in Bethlehem, the personnel committee recommended that the League "employ some experienced credit union people, as finances permit, to take over some of the details in the office now performed by the executive director." Pratt later opened negotiations with Lucy Smith of the Roller-Smith Credit Union in Bethlehem to join the League as replacement for Jimenez.

Smith had first met Pratt, Moore, and many of the other League leaders at the January 18, 1947, executive committee meeting. She was there as a member of the local committee on arrangements for the 1947 annual meeting, at the request of Lehigh Valley Chapter representative Josephine Sakovics. When Moore insisted that she take care of some paper work and bring him refreshments, Smith stormed out in a flash of temper.

A few months later, badly in need of skillful administrative assistance in the Philadelphia office, Pratt offered the job to

Smith, over the objections of Moore who had then become League president. The appointment proved to be one of Pratt's most important decisions and the start of a long-term professional relationship.

Smith still vividly remembers her first day of work in October 1948. Having driven from her home in Bethlehem, she arrived before Pratt. When he finally came in, he showed her the office, piles of to-be-filed materials, a stack of to-be-typed letters, and the phone. "When people call, try to answer their questions," he instructed her. "If you can't answer them, leave a note for Howard [Kirsh]. Take care of the rest of this stuff. I'll be back in a couple of weeks."

"He then put on his hat and walked out the door," recalls Smith.

Smith gradually assumed a role that was becoming part of the credit union tradition. Just as Bergengren had benefitted from the executive abilities of Agnes Gartland and Tom Doig had enjoyed the support of Dora Maxwell, Pratt would come to rely on the skills, loyalty and dedicated work of Smith for the remainder of his career with the League.

As its activities increased, the League became increasingly dissatisfied with its new 52nd Street office. Smith describes it as "dingy and crowded." Pratt, Kirsh, and supply clerk Mario Cervone, who had rejoined the League after the War, as well as Smith all worked in the single room—plus a large supply closet. The room was furnished with two desks. Three walls were lined with file cabinets.

Smith recalls that most of the files consisted of piles of paper stacked on top of the cabinets rather than orderly collections of organized folders inside them. "The work was always way behind," she recalls. "We spent all of our time putting out fires. We never had the chance to plan ahead."

Kirsh usually worked in the evenings; Cervone worked several afternoons each week, sometimes assisted after school by Billy Pratt, son of the managing director. Pratt, occasionally accompanied by Jim Girvan, came to the office on a totally unpredictable schedule. In addition to her responsibilities for typing and filing correspondence, Smith became the bookkeeper for the League, unofficial treasurer of Philadelphia Chapter Credit Union, and bookkeeper-billing agent for the supply services. Pratt was out of the office, often for weeks at a time, and Smith was the main resource for information and administration. Field Assistant Kirsh was available for some technical assistance, but even his expertise was far from comprehensive.

Dissatisfaction with the 52nd Street office mounted. There were disputes with the landlord, who refused requests to redecorate and improve the facilities and demanded not only a $10/month (18%) increase, but a five-year lease. Pratt reported that better space would be available shortly at the new headquarters of Philadelphia Teachers Credit Union, and he was empowered by the League board to open negotiations. In April the League voted to move its headquarters to the Cherry Street building owned by Philadelphia Teachers. Even as the files were being packed for the move, however, Pratt was suggesting that relocation to Harrisburg might be in the League's best longterm interests.

Pratt recognized the value in moving the League back to Harrisburg because of increasing involvement with legislative activities and frequent conferences with the state Banking Department executives. Too, Pratt was traveling extensively throughout the state. By shifting the base from Philadelphia to Harrisburg, he would be more centrally located and thus less isolated from Pittsburgh and Erie. Both his office and home would be more conveniently in reach of credit unions throughout the state.

At the time, the League was showing little interest in state legislation. Few Pennsylvania credit unions were state chartered. Banking Secretary O. B. Lippman remained a strong opponent to the credit union system and a formidable roadblock to any group seeking a state charter.

Most of the League's legislative interest was directed at the federal government, and even that was limited. During the war years, only one congressional action, Public Law 574 of the 79th Congress in 1946, held any importance for credit unions. Most of its provisions were technical, affecting involuntary liquidation procedures, penalties for excessive interest charges, rights of spouses as joint tenants, bonding, and the legal definition of "passbook."

The wartime relocation of supervisory authority of federal credit unions had been moved by executive order to the Federal Deposit Insurance Corporation in 1942. The Reorganization Plan of 1947 made that change permanent, resulting in complaints from CUNA and the League, as well as from FDIC itself.

In June 1948, Public Law No. 813 of the 80th Congress transferred responsibility for federal credit unions to a new Credit Union Bureau of the Federal Security Agency in the Social Security Administration. This change was a major improvement for the credit union movement in general, a critical victory for federal credit unions in particular. Yet the Pennsylvania League had provided no active support and took no official cognizance of this important measure.

In Harrisburg, the League's legislative efforts were less successful. Pratt had sought but failed to amend the state law to allow community charters. These efforts were closely monitored by Philadelphia Teachers Credit Union, always one of the more active credit unions on the Pennsylvania legislative front. At this time, the credit union was (in vain) seeking permission to expand and offer credit union service to teachers throughout Montgomery County and in other Eastern Pennsylvania counties as well.

The League had more success implementing internal changes. Managing director Pratt won a change of title to "executive director" at the 1947 post-convention meeting of the board. DeVoe was elected to membership on the executive committee at the same meeting. The continuing feud with CUNA found voice in a board resolution that "payment of CUNA dues should be postponed until the executive committee deems payment warranted."

Pennsylvania's inability to pay its dues started the national

rumor mill running at full tilt. In an October letter to Gartland, Bergengren—still resentful of Pratt's opposition to him
as CUNA managing director two years before—commented on
the Pennsylvania situation: "I have returned much encouraged about the future of CUNA. They told me that the Pennsylvania League is so hard up for money that Pratt came to see
Dutch [CUNA President Gurden Farr] about getting the payment of national dues postponed; that guy is definitely on his
way out."

To the contrary, Pratt's position with the Pennsylvania
League was secure. And under his increasingly capable leadership, the Pennsylvania League was about to enter a period
of active growth and vitality. The payment of 1947 CUNA dues
was postponed for two reasons. One was the dispute over
Filene House and CUNA's continued loyalty to the Madison
location.[4]

Second was the lack of League cash flow. The budget was
in balance; there was no real shortage of funds. Like much of
the business world at the time, and certainly all of the credit
union movement in those days, League management was not
sophisticated in its use of accounting techniques or bookkeeping procedures. Pratt was adamantly opposed to using short-
term bank loans. Postponing the payment of CUNA dues
improved the cash flow, facilitated continued payment of
League salaries, and provided funds to pay increased rent for
the new office space.

Real and serious financial difficulties appeared to be just
around the corner. Executive director Pratt frequently found

4. With the end of the war making necessary materials and workers available, eventual construction of the new Filene Memorial Building as a new
CUNA headquarters was once again a current issue. Even while the flames
of war burned abroad, the Pennsylvania League had passed a fiery resolution demanding that CUNA reconsider the Madison location. Joe Moore had
opposed Madison back in the 1930s, and he carried his opposition into the
1940s. He was continuously supported by the Pennsylvania League. CUNA
board minutes record objections to construction of the Filene Memorial
and demands that CUNA remove to a "more convenient location—preferably
adjacent to Washington D.C." as late as December 1947: "Voted, to receive
and table resolution from Pennsylvania."

it necessary to request a few of the larger and wealthier credit unions to pre-pay their dues to keep cash flows current. The actual number of Pennsylvania credit unions had decreased during the war years. League affiliations had also dropped slightly. Only rapidly growing membership in existing credit unions and increasing credit union income, which generated increased dues without a change in dues schedule, kept the League solvent.

The financial picture would soon improve as an expanding Pennsylvania credit union movement made it possible to increase field staff. Towards the end of the decade and in the early 1950s, credit union organization in Pennsylvania showed new energy. League income increased dramatically, but executive director Pratt would always remember the lean war years. Even as he executed the board's order to withhold CUNA dues, one can readily imagine that he planned to protect the League from having such financial pressure exerted by its own members. He implemented a policy calling for the League to gradually build up an operating reserve equal to a full year's budget. That policy remains in effect, one of many valuable legacies of Pratt's leadership. Never again would the financial survival of the League be threatened.

Ironically, even as Pratt was abandoning his long-term devotion to the lowest possible League membership fee—a position which had significantly contributed to Connor's decision to leave—a group of newer directors adopted the same priority. This group would force Pratt to live with the $1000 per year maximum long after he believed it should be abandoned. The same group would continually insist on reexamining both the budget and the membership fee schedule with an eye towards limiting League activities and keeping fees as low as possible.

The clash over priorities eventually took the form of a dispute involving League personnel policies. Before World War II, League salaries had been low enough and working conditions harsh enough that there was little conflict between volunteers and professionals. Discussions at the September

1947 board meeting in McKeesport make it evident, however, that this comfortable relationship was ending.

E. A. Thompson's personnel committee proposed an extended resolution covering vacation, sick leave, salaries, pension contributions, and other personnel matters. Under it, office and clerical salaries would be $120 - $200 per month. Field representative salaries were set at $200 - $350 per month. The executive director's salary was limited to a maximum of $10,000. The resolution directed the board to set up health insurance and pension plans for all employees.

The resolution went to great lengths to clarify the relationship between the board, the executive director, and "subordinate employees." It empowered to board to define new positions and set minimum requirements, but made hiring and retention of staff the exclusive responsibility of the executive director. It further specified that "All subordinate employees of the League shall be responsible to, and shall be instructed by, the executive director in the performance of their duties as such employees."

Debate over the resolution was heated and extended. Director Goetz demanded that he specifically be recorded as opposing its salary schedule. Other directors opposed the maximum set for the executive director. When the provisions were finally adopted, it was "with the understanding that they are subject to review and revision as circumstances may require."

Board concern with League staff was a new development. It indicated the growing size of the budget and especially the growing salary of the executive director, now suddenly subject to jealousy and ambition. League professional staff, like credit union treasurers and professional managers, had traditionally enjoyed a close relationship with their board members and other volunteer leaders.

That closeness had died at the national level with the forced departure of Bergengren; now it was showing signs of strain at the League level in Pennsylvania.

Personnel difficulties would present major difficulties at the League into the 1960s. Salaries typically remained low; work-

Board of Directors, Pennsylvania Credit Union League, holds its reorganization meeting in Philadelphia, in April, 1948.

ing conditions were harsh. Occasional conflicts between Pratt and individual board members found employees caught by conflicting direction. Through it all, some truly dedicated credit union professionals, Lucy Smith, Michael Judge, Al Sippel, James Findlay, Dom Servillo, Gladys Krout and Geraldine Livingston continued to give the Pratt, the League and the credit union movement their loyal and committed service.

Pratt never hid his lack of respect or personal affection for League staff. Throughout his career, he felt and often stated that all League staff and employees could easily be replaced. Not surprisingly, the league was continually plagued by an extraordinarily high rate of employee and staff turnover. League supervisory staff were forced to invest excessive time training new employees. The League was able to attract devoted staff loyalty only from a few rare and remarkable individuals.

266

. . . And the Board meets in Harrisburg in February, 1956.

Pratt was especially hard on clerical workers and other office employees. Not only was he a harsh taskmaster; they also had to tolerate his Brittany Spaniels which often had free run of the office (after the League moved to Harrisburg, Lucy Smith also occasionally brought her own dog down from her upstairs apartment). For office staff especially, the Pennsylvania League was neither an easy nor particularly pleasant place to work. Few employees stayed with the League for more than a year.

The cost of such harsh treatment of personnel, especially in lost energy, productivity, and efficiency was high. We can trace the origins of this continuing problem, and the friction it generated between Pratt and his directors, to the board's handling of the personnel issue at McKeesport in 1947.

Yet Pratt and the Pennsylvania League acquired an enviable reputation for training credit union movement execu-

267

tives. Five of Pratt's staff—an assistant managing director, two directors of education, and two field representatives—became managing directors of other state Leagues.[5] Many of Pratt's staff left the League but took other jobs in the movement; several other Pennsylvania staffers were subsequently hired by CUNA or CUNA affiliates. So while the executive turnover was unusually high, so too were the achievements of survivors of the Pennsylvania League.

The board of directors took another action at McKeesport that had longterm implications. Pratt, like Copley and Connor before him, had discovered that credit union chapters had extraordinary potential to contribute to the credit union movement, but rarely contributed even to their own survival. He therefore requested that the board take the initiative in making the League itself more responsible for chapter activities.

The resulting bylaws amendment was simple. It did little more than force chapter bylaws to conform to League policy and require the chapters to file annual reports with the League. But it was the first acknowledgment since the first days of the League when the chapters had each elected a director of a formal relationship between the chapters and the League. In future years, that relationship would become closer, and the Pennsylvania credit union movement would prove the beneficiary.

IN LATE 1948, CUNA Mutual finally won approval to sell its life savings insurance to federal credit unions. State insurance commissions had denied CUNA Mutual permission to sell its policies to their credit unions unless it met extensive qualifications. CUNA Mutual did qualify in many

5. William C. Smith (12/8/52 - 7/6/57) became managing director of the Alabama Credit Union League; Fred A. Stahl (9/1/53 - 3/9/56) became managing director in Minnesota; William H. Hensell (3/16/55 - 12/31/60) became managing director in Montana; John A Bickel (6/1/57 - 4/15/59) moved from the Pennsylvania League to CUNA, and later became managing director in Connecticut; William F. Martin (1/1/59 - 6/30/78) became managing director in Massachusetts.

states, but felt that there were not enough state credit unions in Pennsylvania to justify the difficulties. Additionally, first FCA then FDIC had denied permission to CUNA Mutual to offer the program to federally chartered credit unions. Effectively, CUNA Mutual was barred from operating in Pennsylvania.

Faced with a possible congressional override of its ruling, FDIC, as one of its last actions while responsible for federal credit unions, reversed this position. In 1948 it became possible for Pennsylvania's federal credit unions to participate in CUNA Mutual's life-savings program. This program provided life insurance in an amount equal to the member's shareholdings in the participating credit union.

For credit unions participating in the full CUNA Mutual program, this meant that a borrowing member would automatically receive loan protection (credit life) insurance to the amount of loans outstanding and life savings insurance to the full amount of shareholdings, both to specified maximums.

Directors and officers of credit unions and of the League could avoid financial liability for their organizations. Through its insurance policies, participating credit unions would be completely compensated by CUNA Mutual in case of the death of a borrowing member (but not in case of simple nonpayment). Far from sharing liability for other members' debts, a fully-insured credit union member received additional life insurance in proportion to invested savings.

This was still before the days of share insurance. While bank savings accounts were insured against bank failure by FDIC, this same agency, now the supervisory agency responsible for Federal credit unions, refused to consider extending its coverage to credit union share accounts. CUNA itself, remembering the original concept of credit union members' shared liability for their collective financial security and reluctant to incur additional federal regulatory control, refused to push the issue.

Over the next decade, the question of share insurance for federal credit unions would become a volatile controversial issue within the movement. At one point, enforcement and administration of share insurance policies became the focus of a lawsuit brought by the Pennsylvania League against federal supervisors and their agency.

The full insurance concept proved popular in the Commonwealth. In this post-war period of rapid growth, both new credit unions and League affiliations began to increase rapidly. So too did credit union membership. The growth spurt paused during the Korean War, but on a percentage basis, the late 1940s and early 1950s generated growth and expansion at rates that were historically unprecedented and would never be duplicated.

The spontaneous growth proved a financial boon both to the League and to its member credit unions. While CUNA was faced with continual crises and disputes about dues and was nearly torn apart by increasing battles between the leadership of the national association and its affiliates, Pratt led the League through a period of prosperity and smooth internal relationships.

The western part of the state led by Moore was able to work in well-established ways with the East. Pratt headed the eastern caucus, well supported by Jim Girvan. There were some early indications of possible power conflicts in the East, but generally the board seemed willing to cooperate with Pratt and to support fully all his activities and programs. Matt Pottiger, the longtime leader of the central section, welcomed the support of Dominic Servillo, a director from the north central district (District 7) elected to the board in 1948. Under Pottiger's leadership, the central region continued to support Pratt as it had for the entire preceding decade.

The board of directors chose these calm times of international peace and domestic prosperity to follow through on growing member demands that it expand and reorganize. Behind those seemingly reasonable demands lay a struggle for control of the board itself. With little warning, the League was plunged into one of its worst episodes of internal upheaval.

270

The collection of confrontations that shattered the unity of the board was complex. Internal board politics were always laden with intrigue. Even in the calmest times, there were tests of will between regions, between big and small credit unions, between personalities. Occasionally disputes involving national issues pitted members of the Pennsylvania delegation to CUNA against each other and were fought out on the League level. On other occasions there were battles involving particularly strong leaders and their individual, personal ambitions. The 1948 dispute and redistricting debate—which would remain unresolved until 1951—involved all of these facets.

At CUNA board meetings, Pottiger usually cooperated with his fellow national directors from Pennsylvania. Occasionally he could show a stubborn streak of independence. He was the single most experienced credit union person on the League board; his work with Harrisburg Postal Employees Credit Union went back to the earliest days of the Pennsylvania movement. He had been managing director, editor of *Key Notes*, and League secretary as well as a national director for more than a decade. But the unwritten rule was that the vice president came from Philadelphia or Pittsburgh, the two cities always alternating. The vice president was then elected president.

Pottiger had watched newcomers from Pittsburgh and from Philadelphia advance past him to higher League office. The "country boys," credit union leaders from Central Pennsylvania, were confined to the other offices. Pottiger and Tokay retained their respective posts as secretary and treasurer.

Pottiger was tired of taking notes. He wanted to move up the table. He had also tired of taking his orders from Joe Moore, and of Pratt's and Moore's continued opposition to construction of Filene House in Madison.

At the 1948 meeting of the national board, Moore suggested that CUNA Supply be placed in temporary quarters, rather than support a new building for the national association. As previously mentioned, Pottiger generally went along with his Pennsylvania colleagues. But not this time. As Pennsylvania's delegate to CUNA Supply, Pottiger rebelled and seconded a motion from the floor that the executive committee proceed immediately "to obtain definite plans, exactly as to the method of procedure, building costs, the style, and be prepared to show those to us for action at our next meeting."

To Pratt, Moore, and Tokay who had fought construction of the new headquarters in Madison at every possible turn, Pottiger's action was pure treason. But the motion carried. This was an important indication that the solidarity of League leadership was weakening.

Pratt and Moore had cooperated closely throughout most of League history. There had been little reason for conflict. They had been united in their pragmatic approach to credit union programs, League activities, and in their desire to keep costs as low as possible.

Since his promotion to executive director and full time management, Pratt was changing. His statewide view and increased exposure to the goals and values of the credit union movement provided Pratt with a broader perspective. Pratt also had new ambitions. He had been mentioned as a possible successor to Bergengren in 1946. He had hopes of achieving the presidency of CUNA Mutual. Failing that, with Tom Doig's health visibly worsening Pratt saw himself as a leading contender for the leadership of CUNA. Pratt was encouraged by Pottiger's rebellion. The executive director saw it as his opportunity to weaken Moore's hold on the board.

At the 1948 Baltimore meeting of the Eastern District of CUNA, the split between Moore and the Pratt faction took on dramatic proportions. Pottiger recalled the events in an interview 15 years after the event:

> "Joe came in and said, 'You guys [Pottiger and Ed Thompson] have got to put my hat in the ring for the district vice presidency.' Well, when you tell a couple of Pennsylvania Dutchmen they've got to do something and you don't give them a good reason why they just don't do it—you know. So ... this

made Joe hopping mad. They voted about six times because there was a tie and nobody got selected."

The January 1948 executive committee meeting acknowledged credit union demands for redistricting, noting that "consideration should be given to the plan for redistricting the state to provide 10 districts instead of 8, and 18 directors instead of 17." Other than the official acknowledgement, no action was taken. The topic was again side-stepped at the April 9 pre-convention meeting of the board where it was voted:

> "That the Executive Director's suggestions relative to Redistricting the State and Director Representation, as well as the resolution relative to election of directors, be referred to the bylaws committee for study and report to the September 1948 directors meeting."

Pratt's plan, referred to in the board's resolution, would have sharply cut Moore's authority by the simple device of dividing Allegheny County into two districts. Only one of them, Pittsburgh itself, would have remained in the control of Moore. As president of the League and as head of the Pittsburgh area delegation, Moore fought back with all of his considerable abilities. First, he cancelled the September 1948 meeting of the directors. Then he refused to convene the board at all before the annual meeting in Pittsburgh.

The 1949 League annual meeting was in Pittsburgh. But even on his home ground, Moore was unable to prevent the board from redistricting itself. The general membership was loudly and clearly demanding reform. The population of "country boy" credit unions was growing, and they wanted more representation. At the pre-convention meeting of the board of directors, the first board meeting held in a year, an appropriate bylaw amendment was approved for presentation to the annual meeting:

> "Persuant to Section 2, Article V of the By-laws the Western division of the State shall be comprised of Districts 1 to 5 inclusive, and the Eastern division of the State shall be com-

prised of Districts 6 to 10 inclusive, and the several districts shall be comprised as follows:

"District 1—Shall be comprised of the Counties of Erie, Crawford, Mercer, and Venango.

"District 2—Shall be comprised of the Counties of Lawrence, Beaver and Butler.

"District 3—Shall be comprised of the County of Allegheny, with the exception of the McKeesport, Industrial and Allegheny-Kiski Chapter areas.

"District 4—Shall be comprised of the McKeesport, Industrial and Allegheny-Kiski Chapter areas of Allegheny County and the Counties of Washington, Greene, Fayette, Westmoreland, Armstrong, Indiana, Cambria and Somerset.

"District 5—Shall be comprised of the Counties of Clarion, Forest, Warren, McKean, Potter, Clinton, Cameron, Elk, Jefferson, Clearfield and Center.

"District 6—Shall be comprised of the Counties of Delaware, Philadelphia, Montgomery and Bucks.

"District 7—Shall be comprised of the Counties of Lehigh, Northampton, Carbon, Monroe and Pike.

"District 8—Shall be comprised of the Counties of Blair, Bedford, Huntingdon, Fulton, Franklin, Adams, York, Cumberland, Perry, Juniata, Mifflin and Dauphin.

"District 9—Shall be comprised of the Counties of Schuylkill, Berks, Lebanon, Lancaster and Chester.

"District 10—Shall be comprised of the Counties of Union, Snyder, Northumberland, Montour, Columbia, Luzerne, Lackawanna, Wyoming, Sullivan, Lycoming, Tioga, Bradford, Susquehanna and Wayne."

With the task of re-drawing district boundaries completed, the convention approved the redistribution of directors in accordance with the new district boundaries: Districts 1, 2. 4. 7. 8. 9. and 10 each received one seat; District 3 (Pittsburgh) received five seats; District 4 (Allegheny County) received three seats; District 6 (Philadelphia) received four seats. In addition, two directors would be elected "at large," one each from among candidates from the eastern and western divisions.

Directors to fill the new seats would be elected at special meetings held within their districts. The at-large directors would be elected at the annual meeting. District election meetings would be supervised by a member of the board from a different district. Nominees would be from credit unions in the district; only credit unions with current dues paid as of March 1 would be eligible to vote or to nominate candidates. Seconds for nominations would be permitted but not required. No voting by proxy would be allowed. Each credit union would be allowed two votes, but no representative could cast more than one vote. Newly elected directors would be seated at the first meeting of the League board subsequent to the election.

The new plan was approved with only minor debate from the floor. The final element, a plan for apportioning the new seats between one-year and two-year terms, was also approved.

In the furor over redistricting, another resolution was given only passing attention. Yet in the long run, this simpleresolution would become one of Pennsylvania's major contributions to the credit union movement.

> "CREDIT UNION MEMBERSHIP—RESOLVED that this meeting go on record as recommending amending the credit union laws to provide for continued extension of full membership privileges to members who leave the field of membership."

Thus was born the "once-a-member, always-a-member" concept of credit union membership. It would be actively pursued by Pratt, Noble, and other Pennsylvania directors at both the national and state levels. Eventually identified with Pratt, it originated with a resolution presented by Vernor Porath. Porath was subsequently elected director from District 1 (Erie) in 1950.

The delegates to the annual meeting may have thought that the redistricting war was over; the directors knew that it was not. There was still a little matter of payment and punishment.

Moore refused to convene the post-convention meeting. In his place, past president Palmer acted as temporary chairman. Pottiger acted as temporary secretary. When vice president Lawry, from Pittsburgh, was elected League president, Palmer handed over the gavel.

Then Pratt's close associate Girvan was nominated for vice president. Pottiger was also nominated, but Girvan won the balloting. When Pottiger was routinely nominated as secretary, however, Noble was also nominated and went on to win the election.[6] In the balloting for national director, Pottiger lost his seat on the CUNA board to Lawry, and Girvan was selected alternate.

And so it was established: you may not demand action without justification from a "Pennsylvania Dutchman." Neither can you expect rebellion without retribution from a "Pittsburgh Irishman."

A year later, in 1950, Moore had won his hard fought CUNA Eastern District vice presidency, the seat once held by Pratt. At that year's annual meeting, Pottiger won a contested election with Girvan for the League vice presidency. Moore, having taken appropriate disciplinary action and having demonstrated that his power was still intact, was ready to forgive, forget, and restore the expected succession. The "country boys" had won a major victory. At the 1951 annual meeting, after 15 years as an officer of the board, Pottiger was elected to the League presidency.

In the interim, Lawry's record as president proved to be unusual and remarkable. He had assumed the presidency of

6. Pottiger was the last League Secretary with direct personal responsibility for the minutes. Lucy Smith prepared them briefly, then the League hired a stenotypist, and in the early 1950s began using a wire recorder. The system of electronic recording of verbatim proceedings from which minutes are later prepared is still in use by the League.

Floyd Tompkins' service as League counsel spanned its strongest growth period from the mid-40s to the late 70s.

a League that was sharply divided by regional and personal jealousies. Board meetings were bitter and contentious. At the end of Lawry's two one-year terms as president, Pottiger inherited a League and board where peaceful relationship had resumed and the League was prepared to face a whole new set of challenges.

Unexpected aid in facing the new decade came from League counsel. Floyd Tompkins, in assuming the post in early 1946, had immediately taken a much more active role in League affairs than had his predecessor. Neal had reported to Pratt, who included a section on legal affairs as part of the report of the managing director. Tompkins presented his own reports, both to the board and to the membership at the annual meeting.

While his reports covered a range of technical and complex subjects, Tompkins usually managed to make his early reports brief and interesting. Tompkins' recommendations ranged from adding sections to the *Information Manual* to proposing

277

bylaws amendments and suggesting legislative activity. The thrust of his suggestions was consistently towards expanding activities of the League and of credit unions. Always he worked to protect the interests of the board and of the League and was deeply concerned with the future, growth, and development of the Pennsylvania credit union movement itself.

By the early 1950s, many other changes were occurring. Pratt had begun to realize that while the Pennsylvania credit union movement was growing under his leadership, it was not expanding nearly as rapidly as other states. In 1943, Pennsylvania ranked fourth with 638 credit unions. By 1954, the Commonwealth could count 862 credit unions, but it now ranked eighth—trailing behind Illinois, Quebec, California, Ontario, New York, Texas, and Ohio. In the same 11 years, California had organized 639 new credit unions and Illinois had started 573 new groups; Pennsylvania had chartered only 224.

Through the late 1940s and early 1950s, the Pennsylvania board of directors remained unwilling to commit increased finances to League activities. Credit union growth meant that substantial League expansion could have come with a minor increase in dues. Such extended activities could have increased the field staff, accelerated credit union organization, and paid for itself within a brief period of time. But such an approach was not acceptable to conservative League leaders in those years.

The League's national directors even continued to oppose expanding CUNA's Organization and Contact Department, arguing that the leagues should be responsible for such efforts, possibly assisted by CUNA Mutual field staff as necessary. Pennsylvania's two-person (and briefly one-person) field staff was not sufficient to support the kind of exponential growth that was happening in other states.

The Bureau of Federal Credit Unions (BFCU) no longer accepted any responsibility for organization work. Quite the contrary. Faced with restrictive budgets and a congressional directive that BFCU move towards making itself financially self-supporting, Orchard was forced to increase examination fees just to maintain mandated supervisory services.

In several states, these examination fee increases led to credit unions abandoning federal charters and reorganizing under state charter. Because of the limitations of the state law, that shift did not occur in Pennsylvania. Even in the Keystone State, increased federal examination fees led to new League interest in the state credit union law. That federal examination fee increase and the likelihood that further increases would follow doubtlessly contributed to Pratt's interest in moving the League to Harrisburg and stepping up involvement in state legislative activities.

Pratt still was philosophically opposed to expanding the League organization work. He relied heavily on volunteer organizers, primarily League directors and chapter leaders, supported by two field agents.[7] He even cut support for *Key Notes*, the League's effective, respected, and popular magazine. Its frequency of publication declined gradually during the war and it was allowed to die shortly thereafter. *Key Notes* published only five issues in 1944, three issues in 1945, and two in 1946. Publication was then suspended, and not resumed until 1951 when former editor Pottiger acceded to the League presidency.

This meant that during those years, the League had lost one of its most important services to the membership. A second

---

7. At the April 1949 post-convention meeting of the board of directors, newly-elected President Lawry asked that each chapter take "definite action to develop a volunteer organizers committee and appointed the following chairman [sic]. Mr. Frank Tokay, Industrial and Allegheny-Kiski Chapter; Mr. R. Goetz, McKeesport Chapter; Mr. J. J. Girvan, Mr. E. A. Thompson, Mr. J. A. Moore, Mr. A. R. Thompson, Pittsburgh Chapter; Mr. L. F. Hardman, Erie Chapter; Mr. D. Servillo, Luzerne; Mr. W. W. Anderson, Bradford; Mr. M. A. Pottiger, Harrisburg; Mr. N. R. Long, Lehigh; Mr. H. Van Brookhoven, Lancaster; Mr. J. LeVan, Reading; Mr. L. DeVoe, Midwest Chapter." The concept of volunteer organizers was one of Bergengren's pet ideals. He had learned after extended experience that its success was limited. Connor had attempted to use the chapter structure to facilitate her organization work throughout Pennsylvania, but found it more difficult to keep chapters active than to organize credit unions. Pratt was about the make the same discovery as his predecessors.

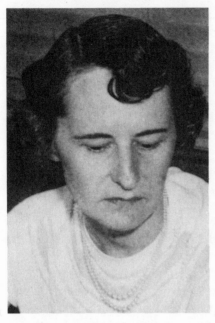

Lucy Smith, assistant to William Pratt, handled extensive administrative responsibilities at League headquarters for more than 30 years.

major service, publication of the *League Information Manual*, also suffered from neglect. The board's Information Manual Committee, chaired by Art Thompson, routinely reported requests by League members for additional material offset by lack of time or staff to keep up with the task. At the September 1946 board meeting, chairman Art Thompson "questioned the need for continuing the committee." The committee was directed, however, to "continue to work with the managing director in the preparation of material for the manual."

S EVERAL OF THE changes that had come with the new decade made the League's return to Harrisburg virtually inevitable. One was the redistricting approved at the 1949 annual meeting. Under the old scheme, the League's Philadelphia location had been acceptable because of Pittsburgh's control of the board. With the new balance between the sections, it became more desirable to base the League in a more neutral and central location.

280

*Bill Lawry served as president
of the Pennsylvania Credit
Union League, 1949–1951.*

Second, counsel Tompkins had made Pratt more legislatively aware and sophisticated than he had been earlier. As various disadvantages of Federal charters became more apparent, improvement of the Pennsylvania Credit Union Law became more important.

Finally, the Pennsylvania Credit Union League was growing into a mature trade association. In Pennsylvania, most of the important trade and professional associations are based in Harrisburg, and Pratt wanted to place the League in this company. What was good enough for the Pennsylvania Bankers Association would be appropriate for the League. Pratt had made similar arguments for years at CUNA, maintaining that the national association should relocate from Madison to Washington, D.C. Now he was prepared to put those ideas into practice for the Pennsylvania League, to bring it back to Harrisburg.

At their October 1949 meeting, the directors formally voted their "desire and intent to locate our League office in Harrisburg." They authorized the executive committee and Pottiger to "act in regard to the decision on the securing of the League office facilities, and related personnel problems."

When an objection was raised, suggesting that a bylaws amendment would be needed before the League could purchase real property, Counsel Tompkins supplied the necessary language. A bylaws amendment permitting the League to purchase property was immediately adopted, "subject to rejection by the credit union membership within sixty days." A later bylaws amendment was required to enable the corporation to use a mail ballot to approve a "change in office of registration." This was provided by counsel at the February 1950 meeting of the board of directors.

Financially, the League was in outstanding condition. Fiscal year 1949 ended with a $9,353.33 surplus for deposit in an operating reserve account. The League had finally emerged from the financial crisis that started early in the war years.

Financing the purchase of a new headquarters building was still a challenge. Pratt and several directors devised a plan involving prepayment of credit union membership fees. Under the terms of the plan, member credit unions would make a major contribution to the building fund. They would then be repaid over a ten-to-fifteen year period through a reduction in their dues. Essentially, this was a plan whereby the League would be borrowing money for the building purchase from their own members instead of from a bank. Director Dom Servillo moved adoption of this plan with repayment over fifteen years.

At the 1950 annual meeting[8] in Reading, Director R. Goetz

8. The directors elected at district meetings and their initial terms of office were as follows: District 1, V. Porath (1 year); District 2, L. DeVoe (2 years); District 3, G. A. Palmer, J. A. Moore, A. W. Lawry (2 years), A. R. Thompson, E. J. Jones (1 year); District 4, R. Goetz, F. Tokay (2 years), R. Lawley (1 year); District 5, J. E. Springer (1 year); District 6, J. J. Girvan, Wm. M. Noble (2 years), E. A. Thompson, F. Harris (1 year); District 7, N. R. Long (1 year); District 8, M. A. Pottiger (2 years); District 9, J. Levan, (1 Year); District 10, D. Servillo (2 years).

introduced the topic of the new building and the proposed plan for its purchase. The full plan required all credit unions to pay one full year's dues in advance, and have it refunded over the next fifteen years at 6.67% per year. Suspicious members immediately suspected that the plan would shortly be offset by a dues increase, but president Lawry assured them that this was not the case. The plan was finally passed by the annual meeting.[9]

Almost ten years later Pratt would describe the working of the plan for a colleague in California:

"The development of the fund was accomplished by an almost universal acceptance upon the part of the credit unions, providing for their payment of one full year's membership fee in advance, which was to be refunded to the credit unions over the next 15 years by their automatic deduction from fee payments during those years of 1/15 of the sum advanced....

"We were able to accumulate almost $60,000 by this process during the next two years, when we had to discontinue the prepaid dues system because the Legal Department of the Federal Bureau ruled against a request by another league that they be permitted to raise building funds in the same manner.

"The funds raised by this program were insufficient to pay for the cost of the building plus renovations, therefore we borrowed $20,000 from CUNA Mutual and used additional funds of our own to complete the purchase.

"Since 1951 we have written down the cost on the basis of the contribution credits taken by the credit unions, and will most likely write off the prepaid dues balance during 1961 by suggesting to the credit unions that they may take credit for any balance on their books against their 1961 payment."

9. The directors had also voted that all funds held by the League could be used by the building fund. On motion of E. A. Thompson, the League's Education and Legislation Fund was exempted from this provision because "this fund had been raised to be used specifically for educational purposes, and it was a moral contract with the people who contributed the money to maintain its liquidity."

Pennsylvania League Executive Director Bill Pratt (at center, rear) joins other credit union and political leaders in the White House oval office as President Harry S. Truman signs a Credit Union Day proclamation.

The first site favored for possible purchase was a large private mansion at 1711 North Front Street, Harrisburg. The building had a general similarity to CUNA's original headquarters in Madison. It included more space than would be needed by the League in the foreseeable future, thereby providing a source of rental income.

On June 10, 1950 the executive committee toured various possible locations, then voted "that the President and Secretary be authorized to secure an option with intent to buy on the property situated at 1711 North Front St." Plans to purchase 1711 North Front were later abandoned without official explanation.

Two building sites, one at 2709 North Front Street and one on Third Street south of Market Street, near the railroad, were later considered as possible locations for new construction. The League initiated procedures to purchase the 2709 North Front site in February 1951, and even applied for the required federal wartime construction permits. Plans were under way to select an architect when snags were encountered. At the executive committee meeting, Pottiger reported that there would be lengthy and expensive delays in obtaining construction materials. He argued that in the present economy, renovation of an existing building might be the best course "if the proposition were sufficiently attractive."

Two months later, in April 1951, a "sufficiently attractive" proposition had been found. As Managing Director Michael Judge recalls hearing from Pratt, a deposit had already been made on the building lot when Pratt discovered a private residence for sale at 4309 North Front Street in Harrisburg. It was located on a well-traveled street in a residential section that was still convenient to the capitol district, "in an area that is becoming the preferred location of various state associations maintaining the head office in Harrisburg." It was on a beautiful site, overlooking the Susquehanna River.

Most important, the price was right. Its owners were no longer interested in maintaining the large, somewhat old-fashioned building. Like the property at 1711 North Front, the

On a 1952 trip to Harrisburg, CUNA's former Managing Director Roy Bergengren visits with Pennsylvania Executive Director William Pratt.

building was larger than current needs, with space on the second and third floors that could be converted to rental apartments. The Victorian exterior was virtually identical to that of CUNA's first headquarters building in Madison. Without consulting the board, Pratt went ahead and made a bid for the building. ("Bill did those kinds of things," recalls Judge.) The League took possession of 4309 North Front on August 1, 1951.

It was the beginning of a new era. There had been several changes in the League leadership. Director and former League president E. A. Thompson retired at the 1951 annual meeting. Pottiger's hard won election as president marked the final end of the inter-sectional feud that had almost shattered the board of directors a few years before. It also meant that J. J. Girvan joined T. Walter McGrath as vice presidents who had not moved up to the League presidency.

Other wounds were also gradually healing. Roy Bergengren, promoting his newly published *Crusade*, toured

Pennsylvania with Pratt. The two did not become fast friends, but each gained new respect for the other. The bitterness of previous years was softened. In the interim Pratt had started to acquire his new, broader vision of credit union affairs.

The perspective from 4309 North Front Street provided broader views and more sweeping panoramas. Bergengren had also mellowed. The intrigues and ploys at CUNA's Madison headquarters were less significant and enduring than they had seemed at close range. The two pioneers realized during their time together that their love and dedication to the credit union movement were far more important than political issues.

X

On the March

"The meetings were tops.... We drove from Harrisburg to Reading, had a big and enthusiastic meeting, and drove to Philadelphia.... What most impressed me was the active Chapter leadership everywhere. It was an altogether satisfactory experience. The Pennsylvania League is on the march."

Roy F. Bergengren, 10/20/52

THE LEAGUE'S MOVE of its headquarters to Harrisburg conveniently marks the start of a new and productive era in its activities. Its senior leadership had seen it through a series of crises. Several had worked for the League when it had fewer than 100 members and most of those had been credit unions with well under $100,000 in assets. They remembered when fewer than half of the credit unions in the state were affiliated with the League. They remembered an era when the League budget totaled $5000.00 and income was not sufficient to pay postage through the end of the year.

The second major phase of the League's development was dominated by financial problems. Every expense was challenged and, if possible, eliminated. Every effort to add new programs or new services for members was denied. Every request from CUNA to secure its own financial strength through increasing dues was resisted. Every attempt by CUNA to increase services—and the dues to pay for them—was thwarted whenever possible.

League services were kept to the barest minimum. League field staff worked long hard hours at pay that hovered near the poverty level. Little time was devoted to planning League programs or activities. Virtually all efforts were dedicated to assuring bare survival. All energies of the directors were directed not at expanding the credit union movement throughout the state, but toward protecting the structure and functions of the League itself.

In 1951 League director Art Thompson took on himself the responsibility of reviving *Key Notes*, the official League publication, which had ceased publication five years before. It was a modest restart. The new *Key Notes* was no longer the polished publication printed on slick paper that it had once been. It was now typewritten and mimeographed. But by January 1953 it was again being typeset and by September 1954 it had resumed its professional appearance.

By then it had already recorded several major events, including the tragic and sudden death of League president Lee DeVoe. A native of DuBois, DeVoe had been an engineer for the Aliquippa & Southern Railroad, and treasurer of its credit union. He had been elected to the League board of directors from District 2 in 1944 and had succeeded Pottiger in the presidency April 18, 1953. DeVoe was in New York City with Pratt to meet with officials of BFCU when he was stricken with a heart attack and died in his hotel room. He was succeeded by William Noble.

Noble, a leader of the giant Atlantic Employees Federal-Credit Union from its creation in 1936, had been its president since 1942. He had been a League director since 1946 and chaired numerous League committees, including the dues committee. An alternate national director, he had been League secretary since 1951. Noble was also active with other thrift institutions; he was a trustee of the Atlantic Employees Retirement System and a director of Union Federal Savings & Loan Association of Camden, New Jersey.

Noble was primarily interested in credit union education. He led the League (and later CUNA as well) in creating management seminars, officers' forums, and other educational activites. As a result of his interest, educational programs became a long-term high priority League activity. He is credited with initiating the League Management Conference and the Credit Union Institute at Penn State University, both of which started in 1955.

Noble was succeeded as president by Art Thompson in April 1955. A participant in the 1936 reorganization of the League, Thompson brought many years of League experience to the top office. As a longtime member of the board, Thompson was always aware of the importance of social activities and political relationships to the League. Yet despite his base in Pittsburgh, he was closer to Pratt than to Moore.

Almost 30 years later, Thompson reminisced about his years with the credit union movement.

> "Over the years, I guess I was more or less always an outsider, the way it was operating. I watched the power struggles— maybe was part of some of them. Because in the position that I was in, there was no use being a rebel where it didn't accomplish anything....
>
> "It seemed to me that money, as of itself, in itself, always has been and always will be a source of power. That for the common person to get together and have a common interest for their individual power—whatever way they could use it—not for themselves, but for what good they could do—would be through the use of money.
>
> "You have to have money to handle anything. And I thought the credit union represented a means by which there was a setting to bind people together—to bind people together for their own benefit and the benefit of other individuals.
>
> I envisioned an organization, nationwide, with the money factor tying you and me together, as individuals, for the common cause, common good. Not for you to borrow my money, or me to lend you my money and not knowing any more about me than I knew about John Doe has the bank account next to me in my bank."

Art Thompson continued to edit *Key Notes* while he served the League as president. He also edited the booklets for the annual meetings, including the extensive "Twentieth Anniversary" booklet for the 1956 meeting.

Art Thompson had been more involved in internal promotional activities. It fell to Thompson as editor of *Key Notes* to try to explain to the membership the new graduated fee schedule adopted at the 1953 annual meeting. This change in the membership fee structure, the first since World War II, was designed to increase League income, reduce the dues payment for most member credit unions, and increase the

293

The League directors and their guests gather each year to celebrate successful conclusion of the annual meeting. This photo was taken at the 1953 banquet.

payments by larger and wealthier credit unions.

Compared with the traditional dues system, the new structure was so confusing that many credit unions did not know if their dues had been increased or lowered. Some credit unions erroneously feared that their dues had been increased to 5% of gross income, the maximum still permitted by the bylaws.

The need to increase League income was occasioned in part by CUNA's demand for sharply increased dues from its member leagues. Pennsylvania's CUNA dues went to $11,000 in 1952, and to $15,000 for 1953. Other increasing expenses faced by the League included salaries, hiring additional field staff, and the resumption of the publication of *Key Notes*.

The new schedule had been passed only after extended

negotiation and acrimonious debate. At their September 13, 1952 meeting, the directors had recognized that the need for changing the dues schedule was inescapable. They also recognized that the greater burden for producing increased income would fall on the larger credit unions, those paying dues at or near the maximum. Accordingly, at the suggestion of Noble, the directors invited those credit unions paying $750 per year or more to send representatives to a meeting in Harrisburg to help the directors work out an equitable way of handling the problem.

Forty people representing 22 credit unions attended the meeting. Discussion was lively. Executive Director Pratt justified the need for more income. The member credit unions responded in a way that should have been familiar to Pratt. A few years earlier he would have been leading the charge as several delegates argued that the League should be decreasing, not increasing its activities. They demanded that every effort should be made to lower dues.

When one delegate suggested immediate removal of the maximum, another countered that he knew of five credit unions that would immediately disaffiliate if that were done. Representatives also demanded to know what steps were being taken to persuade currently unaffiliated credit unions (now only 16%) to join the League.

Finally a consensus resolution emerged. It was formally adopted by the board of directors at their meeting in Philadelphia one week later for subsequent presentation to the next annual meeting. It is especially notable as it marks the first use of the modern, step-type dues schedule:

> "Present schedule of 3.5% of gross income to remain until $1000 is attained. At this stage apply the following formula
> "3.5% of Gross Income up to $30,000
> 3% of Gross Income $30,000 to $40,000
> 2% of Gross Income $40,000 to $50,000
> 1% of Gross Income $50,000 to $100,000
> 0.5% of Gross Income over $100,000
> "However, the increase each year is not to exceed 20% of the

previous year's dues; i.e., 1st year $1000, 2nd year $1200, 3rd year
$1440, 4th year $1728, 5th year $2173, 6th year $2500."

There was some discussion on the possibility of linking
voting representation to the amount of dues paid. Such a
proposal was totally antithetical to the credit union philosophy, yet apparently the meeting entertained the idea. While
no action was taken, the group was left with the suggestion
that it give "further thought to this principle."

The board of directors approved the dues schedule created
at the special committee meeting, and presented it to the 1953
annual meeting in Scranton. This meeting marked Pratt's
tenth anniversary of assuming executive responsibility for
the League, a fact of which he noted in his report.

The annual meeting opened with a silent tribute to Julia D.
Connor, Pratt's predecessor as managing director who had
died shortly before. Work on amending the bylaws to alter the
dues schedule was the first substantial order of business. The
board submitted an amendment eliminating both the minimum ($5.00) and maximum ($1,000) absolute limits, substitut-
ing unrestricted full discretionary authority for the annual
meeting to alter dues requirements. The amendment passed.

While the amendment generated little discussion and no
controversy or opposition, it was actually a critical action.
Henceforth all dues resolutions would require action by the
League members as represented at the annual meeting. This
restructuring, part of the compromise by which the dues
increase gained acceptance, eventually proved more important to the League's future than the specifics of the new dues
resolution itself.

The proposed new dues schedule was presented by dues
committee Chairman Noble to the annual meeting. He made
an impassioned speech which nicely presented the decade's
new goals. He described the special meeting in Harrisburg
and the needs of the League:

"The increasing volume of business, the increase in credit
unions, the need for follow-up of prospects, as a result of radio

and magazine advertising (which should increase as the months pass) will no doubt create a need for additional personnel in the field and office, and the increase in the amount of dues paid by the League to the National Association, are all matters that affect the League budget."

After a brief discussion and with only minor dissent, the recommended dues schedule was adopted. In subsequent years this schedule would occasion frequent attacks, especially by delegates from smaller credit unions who felt that they carried an unfair share of the League's financial burden. It would also be slightly modified on several occasions, primarily at the insistence of Treasurer Frank Tokay and delegates from the larger credit unions who successfully demanded that the maximum dues restriction be maintained at low levels. The basic structure of the League dues schedule, however, remained unchanged until 1965 when the fee basis was changed to exclude investment income.

DURING THE EARLY 1950s, Pratt other Pennsylvania credit union movement leaders from the prewar era, acquired a new, more mature approach to League activities. They grew less determined that their exclusive priority should be holding back League operations and keeping down its budget. Gradually they grew in awareness that the League was a financially secure, firmly established trade association.

As League leaders gained a sense of security and self-assurance, they began to turn their attention away from the internal political workings of the League, and towards expanding the effectiveness of the organized credit union movement. Pratt and the directors were increasingly interested in organizing credit unions, seeking favorable legislation, and spreading the word about credit unions through "education and public relations." Pratt's report to the CUNA executive committee at their November 15, 1952 meeting in Chicago demonstrates his new priorities and broadened perspective.

297

"In a little report I wrote, I tried to develop a program starting nationally and working down through the leagues and through the chapters and through the league operations with the individual credit unions and talking to the representatives at home. In trying to develop this in our own league, we ran into the problem that it leaves many of our persons, even league directors, with the idea that they don't know what to say to the local congressman or representative, or Senator, or whoever he may be getting acquainted with. So the general thought in here was to try to develop a political action program and train our own people to develop a friendship and contact so that they will be familiar with the credit union movement and in that way, you could lay the groundwork for Hubert Rhodes, or any of us who have to do the direct contacting of the congressmen and legislature at the time we have a bill to present...."

Pratt had also developed a new interest in the Pennsylvania Credit Union Act and the state legislature. After a decade of neglect during which unfriendly amendments had eroded the law, the League began a decade of work seeking to protect and improve it. This work would culminate in the complete recodification of the Pennsylvania Credit Union Act which would be signed into law by Governor Lawrence September 20, 1961.

"So far as our own league is concerned, at the present time, every Representative and State Senator and every congressman is getting a letter from the league office with some literature. From there on, there is a program to reach in every other district or precinct a credit union person from a league level down to see them. We hope in that way to get a personal acquaintance with everyone, and in some cases by more than one credit union person and so when we call or write him, or see him in the course of his public functions, we will say here is a credit union, look it over and give us a break on it if you think it is all right. It is a very hard job for one person to do and a difficult job for one person to do in the Congress and they need a backing of a regular system of contacts, at least in our opinion, in our state."

Pratt's attitudes and priorities had clearly changed markedly in the years since he and Joe Moore had supported the firing of Roy Bergengren as CUNA managing director. In the interim Pratt and Bergengren had learned more of each other. Pratt had acquired an increased understanding of the credit union ideals. And Bergengren had acquired growing appreciation of Pratt's pragmatism.

Bergengren had been invited to address the 1950 League annual meeting, but had declined with sincere regret. Writing to Agnes Gartland he commented, "I was sorry to be obliged to pass it up as I would have liked to take another look at the Pennsylvania League." Gartland's reply noted the real importance of that invitation. "It is too bad you had to pass up Pennsylvania," she wrote, "but significant that they should invite you." A rapprochement was underway.

Bergengren did accept an invitation to attend an October 1951 banquet in Harrisburg, but then was forced by ill health to cancel. In June 1952 promotional work for *Crusade* took him into the state for a series of meetings and a week-long tour of the Commonwealth, accompanied by the Pennsylvania executive director.

By mid-1953, Bergengren had become almost a supporter of Pratt. He was well aware of the power of his old adversary. "Bill Pratt is out for some scalps, as they defeated him again for President of CUNA Mutual," wrote Bergengren to Gartland. "I am sorry.... I spent most of a week with him in the fall, attending 5 Credit Union Day meetings and there is much to be said in his favor. I have never liked him particularly well but he has done infinitely more for the credit union movement than Lash has done. This selection of Lash will probably make Pratt Tom's [Tom Doig] enemy for life and that won't help Tom any."[1] Pratt may have forgiven Doig

1. Harry C. Lash was selected for potential nomination as a possible successor to J. Deane Gannon as chief of BFCU when Gannon was offered the CUNA managing director post. Bergengren's comment suggests that Pratt saw himself as a possible candidate to head BFCU, or at least that Pratt was actively mentioned by the grapevine as a candidate for the federal post. In any case, Gannon chose to stay at BFCU and the issue became moot.

after finally winning the CUNA Mutual presidency the following year.

By October 1953 Bergengren had a whole new attitude towards Pratt and the Pennsylvania League. As the leaves fell, so did the old bitterness (editorial comments are in brackets):

> "I visited the Pennsylvania League office at Harrisburg which is much like the original Raiffeisen House, only better. It is a splendid office and the building includes 6 apartments [actually, only 4].... Bill has a secretary—one Ruth [he meant Lucy] Smith—of middle age who seemed to do everything and his field men are good men, up on their toes and producing. Sigafoo has been quite ill and Bill is carrying him along until he gets better. The overall picture was fine. Bill is a hard driver but all his staff is very loyal and I only wish some of the Managing Directors, in States like Iowa, Minnesota and Wisconsin, had only a small part of his industry and enthusiasm. We got well acquainted. He will never be popular but I learned a lot of things which I will talk over with you some time. I came away with new respect for him."

The best news was Bergengren's evaluation of the Pennsylvania League itself. CUNA's former managing director was not easily fooled. He remembered well the early days in Pennsylvania and the difficulties he had in trying to find enthusiastic, hard-working local leadership. "What most impressed me was the active chapter leadership everywhere. It was an altogether satisfactory experience. The Pennsylvania League is on the march very definitely.... What I liked best was the obvious interest and enthusiasm." It was Bergengren's last trip to Pennsylvania. He died at his home in Montpelier, Vermont, on November 11, 1955.

In 1955, and during his campaign to succeed Doig as CUNA managing director, Pratt had his national delegates submit a resolution asking the CUNA executive committee to take official action naming Bergengren as "Father of the Credit Union Movement." The resolution was referred to the planning committee and dropped because the title had already been "reserved in perpetuity" to Edward Filene. The significance of the resolution is that it indicates the change in attitude and perspective which had taken place in Pennsylvania.

There were more substantial indications of such continuing changes. One was an increasingly assertive effort in the area of education and public relations. As Pratt became more involved in CUNA public relations activities, he became more interested in involving the League in more extensive communications programs. The national association's leaders became skillful at gaining the cooperation of their occasionally obstreperous colleagues from Pennsylvania.

As the result of one such carefully planned effort, Pratt's general opposition to public relations programs underwent a dramatic change. His support of the CUNA film production *King's X* was unprecedented and enthusiastic, especially in light of the Pennsylvania League's tradition of excessive budget consciousness and opposition to all but the most tangible and demonstrably necessary activities.

Pratt was appointed chairman of CUNA's film committee and served as technical director on location in Hollywood during production. The Pennsylvania League donated $3000 for the film's special financing fund "with no concern about getting any free copies." Further, the League was willing to loan CUNA $25,000—without interest—to help finance this or other films. The League's only interest, the minutes report, was "to get the film to more people as fast as possible, and will be unselfish if that can be done by reducing the price of the film."

The money came from a specially raised league "Education Fund" which was restricted to education uses. Many directors resented the existence of a fund which could not be tapped for other needs. Members often sought to use it for other purposes. Director E. A. Thompson, a professional educator, defended the fund against questionable uses, including an attempt to use it to help finance the purchase and renovation of the new headquarters building in Harrisburg. On that occasion, E. A. Thompson took his defense of the Education

Fund to the floor of the convention where the directors' plan was overruled.

Doig was rapidly losing his own control of CUNA and CUNA Mutual. His illness made it virtually impossible for him to function. The executive committee removed him in 1955. He died less than a year later. Pratt was frequently mentioned as a likely successor, just as he had been mentioned as a possible successor to Bergengren.

Pratt himself wanted the job. Pennsylvania, he told his assistant Lucy Smith, could easily replace him as executive director. His wife Dorothy was somewhat worried. She told Smith that she did not want to move to Madison and wished that Bill would be satisfied with his work in Pennsylvania. But then, as Pratt told Smith, Dottie had originally opposed the move from Philadelphia to Harrisburg. Knowledgeable observers knew that Pratt's appointment to the CUNA managing director slot was unlikely. "He was just too controversial," say several of his contemporaries. Instead, H. B. Yates, former CUNA president, was elected by the board as a stop-gap successor. Even the mild-mannered, diplomatic Yates proved too controversial, however, and he was unable to control escalating difficulties in Madison. The appointment initiated bitter confrontations in the feud between CUNA and CUNA Mutual. Pratt's presidency of the insurance affiliate had been an advantage in his quest for the CUNA leadership. Once the feud broke out, there was no longer any possibility that CUNA would select a CUNA Mutual leader for managing director.[2]

While he was a candidate for national leadership and as president of CUNA Mutual, Pratt learned much about the his-

2. The offer went to J. Deane Gannon who had succeeded Claude Orchard as director of BFCU, but he was unable to negotiate a satisfactory contract. H. Vance Austin, manager of the Colorado Rural Electric Association, finally accepted the position as head of CUNA and CUNA Supply Cooperative. CUNA Mutual refused to accept him and appointed Charles Eikel as its chief executive officer. The split in management fueled conflicts between the organizations and relationships continued to degenerate. CUNA Mutual would spend most of the rest of the decade trying to resolve growing friction between it and the rest of the credit union movement.

tory and philosophy of the credit union movement. He acquired new ways of looking at the mission of credit unions, and at the task facing the Pennsylvania League.

When the League set up its new Harrisburg offices on March 1, 1952, the staff had consisted of: Pratt, executive director; Smith, office assistant; Joseph Van Jura (Eastern District), Lloyd G. Sigafoo (Western District), and Clayton Borrows (Central District), field assistants; and two clerical employees, one full-time, one part-time. Floyd W. Tompkins was League counsel.

By 1956, and the "20th anniversary" annual meeting in Pittsburgh, that staff had been augmented by William C. Smith (no relation to Lucy Smith) who had been hired as a field representative but had already been promoted to assistant to the executive director. Lucy Smith had been promoted to office manager and Gladys Krout hired as office assistant. Fred Stahl had been hired as director of education in 1953 but had just left to take over as managing director in Minnesota. All three of the field representatives had been replaced, and three additional field representatives had been hired. The new field force included: William F. Gardner (later director of field services), James Whitby, William H. Hensell, Marlin J. Dean, Ralph W. Quigg, and Michael J. Judge (later managing director). The clerical staff also had been expanded considerably.

League president during this rapid expansion were Art Thompson (1955-57) and Norman Long (1957-59). Long was a director from District 7, elected to the board at the 1946 annual meeting, during the post-war reorganization. His highest priority was organizing new credit unions. In his first message in *Key Notes* he sounded the theme for his administration: "The permanence of the credit union movement is possible only by the constant addition of new credit unions." He devoted much of his time as League president to organizational efforts.

James Girvan was elected to succeed Norman Long at the 1959 annual meeting in Pittsburgh. Girvan was a close friend

When the League opened its new offices at 4309 North Front Street in Harrisburg, they hoped to have a permanent solution to the growing need for office space.

and associate of Pratt. The two had worked closely together while the League was based in Philadelphia, and Girvan had supplied much technical guidance to his inexperienced and technically unsophisticated associate. Lucy Smith remembers that Girvan provided extensive support and leadership to the League during those early years of Pratt's term as executive director.

304

A second solution to increased space needs was found with the expansion completed in July 1961. This included a rear extension as well as conversion of the second floor from apartments to offices.

Girvan, treasurer of the Philadelphia Railway Express FCU, former president of the Philadelphia Chapter (1946-50), and treasurer of the Knights of Columbus FCU since 1955, had been a League director since 1947. He had served as League vice president for a year during the disruptive reorganization of the early 1950s, emerging from that period as a national director. At the time of his election to the League presidency, he

305

was first chairman of the national directors for CUNA District 10 (replacing the former "Eastern District") and an active candidate for the presidency of CUNA. With Girvan's national perspective, he was an active and enthusiastic supporter of Pratt's expansion plans.

While the League programs were expanding, the executive director was just as careful of expenditures as he had been in the early days. League staff were under orders to always drive on the inside lane when rounding a curve (to save mileage). And Judge remembers being denied compensation for a 5-cent toll at the Clarks Ferry Bridge north of Harrisburg because he could have crossed the river at a free bridge further north.

League staff were proving to be highly productive. The organization of new credit unions and rate of affiliation increased dramatically. By the 1956 annual meeting, there were 909 credit unions in Pennsylvania; 803 (88%) of them were members of the League. Equivalent figures for January 1, 1955 were 726 members and 112 non-member credit unions (for a total of 838). The period had seen an increase of 71 credit unions and an addition of 77 new League members.

To handle its new size and complexity, it was increasingly important that the movement seek skilled and experienced professional help. Management of the national association had been quick to recognize that need. In 1957 they brought in a team of management consultants to help them restructure the organization. They also brought in a group of experienced League leaders for consultation, including both Bill Smith and Bill Pratt from Pennsylvania. Thus both were in Madison when the latest feud between CUNA and CUNA Mutual reached crisis proportions.

The management consultants found that CUNA department heads had little ability, training, or experience. Subsequently many of those department heads resigned. They included W. B. Tenney of the education department, Clifford Skorstad of organization, Marion Gregory of public relations and C. Gail Keeton of legal and legislative affairs. They blamed CUNA managing director Herbert Yates and assistant Orrin Shipe for mismanagement, then accepted appointments offered by CUNA Mutual. The dispute escalated until CUNA Mutual managing director Charles Eikel signed an eviction order demanding that CUNA vacate Filene House (or pay rent to the insurance affiliate).

For Pennsylvania's leadership, the situation was a delicate one. Pratt was on the board of CUNA Mutual; Joe Moore was a vice president of CUNA; Matt Pottiger was on the board of CUNA Supply. Moore's detailed "Report of the National Directors" at the following annual meeting tells much about the board's view of these events. He reported only that the consultants had offered useful insights to improving CUNA's performance. The mass resignations, he said, came about because "some of our employees took exception to what management deemed necessary to accomplish these ends and left our employ."[3]

The intimate familiarity of Moore, Pratt, Pottiger and the other national directors with the affairs of the national association and their ability to keep the League's board fully informed had one critical and immediate impact on the Pennsylvania League. They had seen at first hand the results of amateurism in Madison, and began work to develop more professional direction for the Pennsylvania movement.

As one result of the crisis in Madison, the Pennsylvania League acquired a new awareness of education, legislative affairs, public relations and other, similar activities. New, more professional staffing was needed. In 1956 the League's education committee was doing nothing more than reporting on Penn State's credit union school ("co-sponsored" by the League), and the public relations committee's main activity was distributing CUNA publications to state libraries.

The League had only recently recognized an obligation to

3. Joe Moore took advantage of the CUNA / CUNA Mutual dispute over Filene House to once again make a familiar suggestion: "I personally have always felt that Washington, D.C., was the logical place for CUNA headquarters."

307

provided the state's credit union movement with public relations activities. The first indication of League interest in public relations is a note in the minutes of the April 9, 1948 meeting of the board of directors. After some discussion it was moved, seconded, and voted that: "a committee on public relations be appointed, which committee shall study the questions discussed and bring a report to the September 1948 directors meeting on various phases of the Public Relations Program." Unfortunately, this was the period when Moore refused to call meetings of the board, and the September meeting never convened. There is no record that the committee was appointed. The 1949 activities of the education committee are of much interest to those tracing the involvement of the League in public relations activities. Chairman Frank Tokay recommended to the pre-convention (1949) session of the directors:

> "First, that the board sponsor spot announcements on the radio, stating that New York State had made records and adopted this method of information to the public in their State.
>
> "Second, that we sponsor an essay contest, the title be "Credit Unions in our Economic Life," that the essay be not more than 750 words and that prizes be: 1st $150, 2nd $100 and 3rd $50 and a $25 award in each chapter area."

The board of directors was suffering from a confusion that continues to plague the communications field; they had difficulty distinguishing between public relations, public information and education.

Their confusion was understandable. Public relations-information-education work was new both to CUNA and to the League. Neither CUNA nor the League understood what they were about. Even at the national level, public relations and information activities were informal at best, non-existent at worst.

In Pennsylvania, Pratt and the directors had no experience and little interest in such intangible programs. By the end of

Lee DeVoe served as president of the Pennsylvania Credit Union League, 1953–1954.

that decade, much of the confusion remained but it had been directed along much more sophisticated channels. This redirection was partly due to CUNA and the creation of its POP program.

The POP program began when CUNA President Gurden Farr proclaimed October 21, 1948 as International Credit Union Day. Under instructions of the CUNA executive committee, Farr used the occasion to stimulate fund-raising activities at the leagues and chapters. Much to everyone's amazement, the events won extensive newspaper publicity and stimulated numerous inquiries about credit unions.

The executive committee followed up on this success by establishing a more formal public relations department in 1952. While staffed and directed by CUNA, it was financed largely by CUNA Mutual and CUNA Supply which viewed the program as a natural extension of their own advertising activities. Charles Eikel Jr. became CUNA's first director of public relations. Within a few years, he built an effective advertising and public communications operation.

POP—for *P*ublic Relations, *O*rganization and *P*ublicity, was financed by contributions from credit unions and leagues. (The Pennsylvania goal for 1951 was $2000.) Its primary intention was to finance radio programs and other promotional efforts, informing and teaching people about the credit union movement. It had the secondary effect of demonstrating the effect of a good advertising program to the various leagues and their leaders. As the program made its impact felt through increased inquiries and requests for organizational assistance, Pratt gained a new appreciation for the power of the media.[4]

The goals of the POP Program included:

"To build the good will of the general public.

"To get the understanding and cooperation of business men, labor unions, government officials, religious leaders and farm groups.

"To double the number of new credit unions each year.

"To give every credit union the benefits of membership in the League and the Credit Union National Association.

"To tell people what credit unions are and what they do.

"To show you (and every one of our 5,000,000 members!) the way to a fuller and a richer life through your credit union.

4. In one way the POP Program caused major problems of its own. Gabriel Heatter, a popular radio newscaster, was hired to narrate promotional credit union messages as part of a weekly nationwide syndication (over the Mutual Broadcasting System). The conservative, anti-union Heatter proved a controversial choice. The Reading Chapter raised serious objections to continued credit union sponsorship of his program. The cost of $591,800 for the first year, financed largely by CUNA Mutual, also proved objectionable to many. The Pennsylvania League wrote Tom Doig to register its objections and to request that the program be discontinued, but Doig chose to continue the broadcasts. Perhaps CUNA would have done better to contract with their Canadian announcer to also handle the United States program. He was a young actor named Lorne Greene who would later become the star of *Bonanza* and Alpo dog food commercials.

"To supply your credit union with the materials and information it needs to give you maximum service.

"To help your credit union more fully serve your community through co-operative savings and credit."

Pratt recognized the value of such programs, and the Pennsylvania League's 1952 contribution to the POP Program was $2630.60, more than 10% of the total raised nationally. Pennsylvania would repeat this heavy support of CUNA promotional programs by providing 10% of National Advertising Program (NAP) funds throughout the 1970s and into the 1980s. But that support was not always given cheerfully.

By 1953 the League was chafing under this added burden from CUNA. At their September meeting, the directors formally went on record as "opposed to the current method of raising funds for the POP Program." They argued that the fund should simply be part of the regular CUNA budget. There is no indication in the CUNA records that the Pennsylvania POP Program proposal was ever brought to their attention.

By 1955, CUNA was actively seeking to stimulate its leagues to more advanced public relations activities. The national association, even with financial help from the affiliates, could not afford to maintain extensive campaigns on its own. So under the direction of J. Orrin Shipe, a former editor of *The Bridge*, CUNA set up a department which produced extensive promotional and advertising materials for use by the leagues and by individual credit unions.

CUNA's public relations, advertising, and promotional activities were even more successful than the national association realized. Without being sure just how to do it, or even what it was, the leagues recognized that public relations and advertising were potentially important to the credit union movement.

In Pennsylvania, public relations and education became important topics at meetings. William Smith, Pratt's assistant executive director, had responsibility for the League programs. Smith had joined the League as a field representative in January 1953. A graduate of Carnegie Tech, he had been a director of the Rieco Greensburg Credit Union. Skilled in handling philosophical concepts as well as practical problems, Smith added a new dimension to the League staff. Pratt soon learned to value his judgment highly. But final approval of all publications and full control of all expenditures remained the exclusive responsibility of the executive director. Pratt also remained much more concerned with legislative relations than with a broad-based communications program.

The League's public relations committee reflected Pratt's priorities. It too remained far more concerned with legislators than the general public. The major 1955 public relations event was a "Legislative Dinner," along the lines first suggested by Pratt two years earlier. The education committee was largely moribund. Its activities were largely confined to distributing copies of *A Study of Thrift and Credit* and *A Poor Man's Prayer* to schools throughout the state. While this year witnessed the beginning of the Credit Union Institute at Penn State, that was not the result of education committee efforts. The education committee was concentrating its work on providing programs for chapter meetings.

The first Pennsylvania Credit Union Institute was held August 1955 at Penn State University. Initiative for the program came largely from the School of Business Administration. University Staff for the credit union program included Joseph F. Bradley, associate professor of finance; T. Reed Ferguson, administrative head, State College Center; and Ossian R. MacKenzie, dean of the College of Business Administration. League staff participating in the project included Pratt and Fred A. Stahl, the League's director of education.

Stahl had joined the league in 1953 as a field representative. He was brought to the home office a year later with the title "director of education." His primary duties were "conducting information sessions at Chapters, District and Chapter Work Shops and other conferences within the League." Stahl was a graduate of the University of Chicago, a one-time law student, and a former steelworker and autoworker. He had

The first class of the Penn State University Credit Union Institute gathered on August 8, 1955. Its 46 students were destined for key roles as credit union volunteers or professionals.*

organized the Flint [Michigan] Buick Employees FCU and served as its treasurer. He had also been secretary of the Flint Chapter of Credit Unions and a director of the Michigan Credit Union League. He stayed with the Pennsylvania League only three years, resigning in 1956 to become managing director of the Minnesota Credit Union League.

Among the students at the Credit Union School's first session were several important leaders of the Pennsylvania

---

*Front row, left to right: Bill Hensell, Ralph Quigg, Josephine Sakovics, Vivian Lansdale, Dolores Kalina, Marie Kraybill, Vern Porath, Florence Edminston, Josephine Oberleitner, Sidney Stahl, Art Burton. Second row, left to right: Earl Radtke, Jim Witsell, Jim White, Ed Gilbert, Ben Shapiro, Clarence Brown, Larry Mellas, Jim Whitby, George Oberleitner, Al Vash, Andy Wehmeyer, Fannie Bable, Anne Doodan. Third row, left to right: Art Thompson, Ralph Miles, Bob Jennereth, Bill Smith, Lee Stratton, George De Homsan, Marlin Dean, Joe Matisko, Don Wheeler, Wendell King, Bill Gardner, Domenic Emanuele. Fourth row, left to right: Ed Miscovich, Professor Joe Bradley (instructor), Charles Howard, League Education Director Fred Stahl (instructor), Tom Walsh, Paul Wersing, Anna Jane Hawkins, Janet Mitchell, Helen Rentschler, Mike Judge, Leo Wenitt, Marty Stern, Clayton Burrows, Al Mariani.

credit union movement. The 46 students included Josephine Sakovics, Verner Porath, Art Thompson, Joseph Matisko, Patricia Doyle, Hugh Kelleher and Josephine Frazier—all current or future directors of the league. A newly-appointed League field representative also attended the sessions, future managing director Michael J. Judge.

Judge first learned of credit unions from League director Dom Servillo. Then' newly married, Judge needed a loan to set up housekeeping. The banks turned him down; the interest demanded by loan companies was excessive. Servillo suggested that Judge try the credit union. The employees' credit union operated at noon from a cafeteria table. It loaned Judge not only the $600 he needed, but the $1.00 initiation fee and $5.00 for his first share purchase as well. He still recalls that day and the devotion and admiration it gave him for the credit union.

When Hazard-Okonite closed its Wilkes-Barre operations, Judge was worried about his ability to repay the credit union loan. Again Servillo came to the rescue, suggesting that he apply to the League to be a field representative.

Judge wrote to Bill Pratt and received an answer from Lucy Smith setting up an interview. He returned from the interview uncertain of his success, but he eventually received a letter from Pratt offering him the job. Lucy Smith's recollections help fill in the blanks. She remembers that Bill Smith was impressed with the applicant from Wilkes-Barre. "It was Bill Smith who got Mike Judge that job," she says.[5]

THROUGH THE EARLY 1950s CUNA and the League faced two major legislative issues. Most critical was an attack on the tax-exempt status of credit unions led by various private groups that opposed cooperatives in general

---

5. There is an interesting coincidental footnote to all of this. Before joining Hazard-Okonite, Judge had been employed on a construction gang with the A. J. Sordoni Company, owned by the same A. J. Sordoni who had chaired the Pennsylvania Senate Committee on Banking in 1933 and had helped pass the Pennsylvania Credit Union Law.

and tax-exempt cooperatives in particular. Simultaneously, many state and local governments looked at credit unions as potential sources of additional tax income.

Attempts to repeal the tax exemption of federal credit unions were made in 1951 and 1953. This campaign may have been related to the general "red scare" of McCarthyism that swept the nation during and after the Korean confrontation. In any case, the two bills attacking the tax-exempt status of federal credit unions introduced in the 82nd Congress were not successful.

On the state level, Pennsylvania credit unions were faced with an unusual and serious legislative threat in 1953. Senate Bill 414 proposed the formation of a "consumer credit board" with jurisdiction over credit unions. While the proposed board would have included a representative of the League, other members would have been selected by such hostile groups as the Pennsylvania Bankers Association, the Consumer Finance Association, and the Pennsylvania Pawnbrokers Association. The League actively opposed the legislation, both directly and by soliciting letters to the legislature from credit union members. The bill was defeated.

CUNA's main interest lay with a bill that would have set up central credit unions in which other credit unions would purchase shares. The same CUNA-sponsored legislation introduced by Rep. Wright Patman of Texas would have permitted federal credit unions to make loans to officers and committee members.

The creation of central credit unions was included in Bergengren's original draft of a federal credit union law. It had been excised by amendment. The same banking powers who had originally eliminated the central bank concept continued to oppose it. Without a central credit union, the movement invested its reserves and surplus funds through banks and savings and loan associations. The creation of central credit unions would have encouraged a form of disintermediation from those banks. The central credit unions would reinvest credit union funds themselves. While potentially important

315

Bill Noble served as president of the Pennsylvania Credit Union League, 1954–1957.

to the Pennsylvania credit union movement which was already large enough to have supported its own central credit union, the federal proposal attracted little interest in the state.

Four separate bills providing federal insurance of members' shareholdings were submitted to the same Congress. None were approved.[6] The question of insured shareholding accounts was an important and divisive issue. Philosophically, it was a modern restatement of the old battle between limited and unlimited liability for credit union shareholders. Just as Raiffeisen and Wolff had opposed limited liability, CUNA opposed federal share insurance.

6. One of these would have provided insurance by the Federal Deposit Insurance Corporation; two called for insurance through the Federal Savings and Loan Insurance Corporation; the fourth, HR 430 introduced by Congressman Eberharter, called for the creation of a special fund to be administered by the director of the Bureau of Federal Credit Unions. This fourth is of special interest since it embodied the approach which eventually became law. These proposals were actively opposed by CUNA, but attracted substantial support throughout the grassroots credit union movement.

Norm Long served as president of the Pennsylvania Credit Union League, 1957–1959.

CUNA's opposition was also based on more pragmatic concerns. Its leaders recognized that with federal insurance came federal fees and federal supervision. League Counsel Floyd Tompkins, familiar with the experiences of savings as loan associations with federal insurance as a director of Colonial Savings and Loan Association, preached that federal share insurance should be avoided rather than subject the credit union movement to additional bureaucratic requirements.

CUNA also feared that a federal credit union share insurance program would increase the distance between the federal credit unions and the state-chartered credit unions. The national leaders feared that such an innovation would almost certainly further split the organized credit union. The creation of a new "American Association of Federal Credit Unions" to serve federal charters exclusively (and protect them from the undue influence of foreign credit unions that were members of CUNA International) did nothing to quiet this fear.

In Pennsylvania, the vast majority of credit unions carried federal charters, and support for federal share insurance ran high. This was one of few issues which split the Pennsylvania leadership from the national leadership. It was an issue on which Pratt chose to keep a low profile. Moore went further. While concurring in CUNA's opposition to existing proposals, he presented a League resolution calling on CUNA to develop its own "acceptable" form of federal share insurance. The bill suggested by Moore would have provided for voluntary participation by state chartered credit unions and premium rates held to low limits.

By 1955, Pennsylvania was willing to go on record as favoring federally supported share insurance. The League's approach called for credit unions to create a special fund, "preferable outside the Bureau." The fund would be supplemented by federal aid if assistance were needed. A lengthy special report listed 16 detailed provisions that the League felt should be included in such legislation. CUNA continued to oppose all federal share insurance, and many years would pass before share insurance became an established part of the credit union movement.

As an alternative to federal insurance, many credit union leaders favored the stabilization approach. The full concept stretched over several levels. The first of these was implemented by the Pennsylvania League in 1961 when the board empowered Pratt to hire three technical assistance specialists. These "trouble shooters" were to be specially trained to work with credit unions in difficulty, moving in to help them avoid liquidations. They would be skilled in obtaining help from various sources in the expectation that such credit unions could be saved "by expert advice, know-how, and such help as technical assistants can render."

Many members favored League creation of a special stabilization fund as a second line of defense. As with share insurance, many other credit union leaders saw the creation of a stabilization fund as unnecessary interference in credit union affairs. Such a fund would function as a "lender of last resort," making emergency funds available to any member credit unions facing financial distress.

318

*Jim Girvan served as president
of the Pennsylvania Credit
Union League, 1959–1961.*

The issue was divisive, causing dissent among the CUNA directors just as it was doing at the League level. The board itself was sharply divided on the question of the need for a League stabilization fund (and the rules for maintaining it). While the question was often raised at annual meetings, the board was so divided that no decisive action could be taken. Executive Director Pratt opposed the concept. The decision to create the technical assistance team (following a CUNA model) was at least partially an attempt to defuse demands for creation of a stabilization fund.

At the 1961 annual meeting, the Naval Supply Depot Mechanicsburg FCU brought a resolution angrily stating that the technical assistance and service program was no substitute for stabilization and demanding that the "League board be directed to present a workable financial stabilization plan for member credit unions for implementation upon approval by the 1962 convention." The resolutions committee recommended that this resolution not be adopted, but in an unusual procedure, the resolution was passed.

319

The following year, as ordered, the board presented a stabilization plan to the membership. In a series of parliamentary
maneuvers choreographed by Floyd Tompkins, creation of
the stabilization fund was couched in a bylaws amendment
offered by a credit union delegate from the floor. Lacking
board support, such an amendment required support of three-
fourths of the present and voting delegates, and the affirma-
tive response of a majority of the membership to a mail ballot.
Amidst noisy controversy, Parliamentarian Tompkins ruled
that the bylaws mandated that the three-fourths was based on
the maximum number of delegates present, two per registered credit union. His precaution incited substantial personal antagonism and insistence that Counsel no longer serve
as parliamentarian. The furor was unnecessary. In the balloting, 322 delegates voted for the fund and 291 voted against.
Lacking the three-fourths majority, the stabilization fund was
defeated.

In another important but unrelated development at the
same annual meeting, a resolution from the floor called on the
board to prepare a special resolution "requesting both United
States senators from Pennsylvania to use their influence to
bring the Truth-In-Lending Bill out of committee for action." This was the beginning of the League's long and dedicated commitment to Truth-In-Lending legislation.

THROUGH THE LATE 1950s and early 1960s, the single greatest challenge facing Pratt and the Pennsylvania League was the need to build a cohesive and
skilled professional staff. Finding a director for the League's
education programs proved to be difficult. After Fred Stahl
left in 1956, the job was held by J. Edward Reiter, on a temporary basis by field representative Joe Shanosky, by William F.
Martin, and Joseph Corasanti before field representative John
Edinger took over in the mid 1960s.

By 1965, League staff consisted of 40 full-time people including the executive director (Pratt), the assistant executive director (Judge), director of field services (William Gardner,

This rare, early 1960s group portrait of the League's senior staff shows Lucy Smith, Bill Pratt, and Mike Judge, seated. Bill Gardner and John Edinger stand behind them.

later James Findlay), director of education (Edinger), director of office services (Lucy Smith), three assistants to the director of office services, 10 field representatives and 29 typists, stenographers and other clerical staff. Two additional field representative positions had been approved but not yet filled.

Personnel problems continued to plague the League. In 1951 Art Thompson had been ordered to study the staffing and personnel activities at the Philadelphia office. His report was critical of Pratt, observing that the League staff (then five full-time people) was functioning without supervision and "making work." He concluded, however, that the League was getting its money's worth.

At the February directors meeting, Pratt took issue with the report's neutral conclusion. In a ringing defense of his staff, he told the directors: "you have been getting much more than your dollars' worth. These people are doing much more than you should expect from the average employee." He ended with an impassioned plea for more staff. The response from Moore was that Pratt had been empowered to hire as many people as he needed. Pratt acknowledged that, but pointed out that the directors had not provided the budget for additional staff. The exchange even left Secretary Noble confused:

> "SECRETARY'S NOTE: For the purpose of the record—Mr. Thompson's services were not terminated nor was any action taken with regard to the extension of his activities. Furthermore, the question as to whether or not the Executive Director has the authority to hire additional office personnel was not resolved."

The dispute soon resolved itself in favor of the executive director as the board began a general practice of appropriating whatever budget was required to pay League staff as hired by Pratt. But the conflict first seen here, a jealous confrontation between professional League staff and the volunteer leadership would continue to cause strife.

Thompson's personnel audit of the League office was the

The staff of the Pennsylvania Credit Union League were able to gather in the front lobby of their office building complex in this mid-1950s photograph.

first such review ordered by the directors. It was not the last. Comprehensive reviews would later be undertaken by committees of the directors and by professional consultants. Such reviews were evidence both of real problems in the personnel area, and of problems generated by the conflicting viewpoints of volunteer and professional leadership.

High staff turnover remained a critical problem at the League throughout the years of Pratt's leadership. As the staff grew in size and complexity, the problem became more severe. League central office staff and employees typically left after short stays. Exceptions include Judge and Findlay, both former field representatives; Lucy Smith; Gladys Krout; Geraldine Livingston; Agnes Beistline and Jane Wagner.

While more of the field representatives stayed longer, they too experienced a high turnover rate. Among the field representatives serving the League during 1960-65 were such individuals as: Dom Servillo (who resigned from the board of directors when joining the professional staff); James Whitby, William Hensell, Marlin Dean, Paul Demmer (later a League director), John Bickel, Joseph Shanosky, James Andrian, Richard Dodge, Edwin Yeager, Harry Latimer, Albert Sippel, Allen Schminkey, James Reber, Donald Septer, Carmine Dorazio, Edwin Mailander, William Thomas, Edward Colgan (later a League director), and Larry Bittle. While several did stay with the League, most served only briefly before moving to other positions within the movement or leaving credit union work.

Pratt was a demanding boss. Working conditions, especially for clerical staff, were restrictive and difficult. Orders were often contradictory and confusing. Expectations were frequently unrealistic. Between the 1951 move to Harrisburg and June 30, 1956, the League employed 23 different clerical workers to hold only a handful of available positions in the Harrisburg office. These personnel problems continued through the 1960s. Few clerical workers stayed as long as a year.

The rapidly growing League staff meant that the once spacious Harrisburg offices were becoming crowded. In 1960, the League began planning to expand the space available by moving into the second floor of the headquarters complex and adding a new section to the rear of the building. This meant that two of the rental units would be lost, but the appearance of the front of the building as seen from Front Street was preserved.

Thus even as the headquarters unit was expanded to house an expanded staff and new technology, the tie to the older days of the League and to Raiffeisen House in Madison was retained. In a way it was symbolic of what was rapidly becoming the main mission of the Pennsylvania credit union movement. Increasingly the League was concerned about keeping the movement true to the old philosophy and concept of credit unions, while equipping its rapidly growing list of members to handle the changing financial needs and requirements of the new era.

Financing the new addition was no problem. The League had built a sizable reserve fund. It was one of Pratt's proudest accomplishments. As he reported in a letter to a California colleague:

> "Last week ground was broken for a $100,000 addition to our present building, the entire cost being payable out of our surplus account which has been increased each year by the surplus of membership fees over actual expenses. The reason we have sufficient surplus for the building addition, which represents about 35% of our operating reserve, is because our 1948 presentation as to the membership fee schedule provided income in excess of needs for the specific purpose of endeavoring to create an operating reserve by annual additions until such reserve would equal the most recent year's expenses.
>
> "The reason behind such a proposal was caused by the experience of the world war II period were in our annual expenses, which seriously retarded our operations and that the development of such an operating reserve would provided funds for use during any future periods and because of business or other conditions beyond the control of the credit unions, their income on which our dues are computed would be materially reduced."

Pratt had apparently forgotten that the financial crisis of the World War II era was caused in part by the dues reductions of the preceding four years—reductions which he had sponsored as a director and had won over the objections of the then League management.

A gala open house in the addition was held July 29, 1961. Credit union volunteers and professionals from throughout the state came to inspect the new facilities. It had been almost

325

exactly ten years since the League had moved into the two front rooms on the first floor of 4309 North Front Street. Within a few years, League offices would completely fill the basement and first two floors of the expanded complex.

By 1983 a third floor was added to accommodate expanded League activities. The architectural integrity of the Victorian exterior was still retained intact, vividly symbolizing the credit union movement's dedication to its original principles. It was an era of exciting and dynamic growth. The future looked even better.

XI

The Sixties

"The ultimate goal of the credit union movement is
that each man should be the master of his economic
situation rather than its servant. It is where economics and democracy come together that the credit
union can exist; it is to keep these two together that
the credit union does exist."

John McCullough

P UBLICATION of *Key Notes* was suspended from May
through September 1965. When the magazine resumed
publication in October, there were a few subtle
changes. The name William W. Pratt did not appear any-
where in the issue. The page-two masthead listed Michael J.
Judge as acting executive director. Also gone from the official
staff list was the name Lucy Smith; Gladys F. Krout was
identified as director of office services.

There was no other indication of the difficult decision
which had faced the board of directors during the months that
the magazine was silent. It had been a hectic time. During
that period Pratt had been appointed as director of research
and development with an office of his own, and League president Benjamin F. Summers had been reelected to an unusual
third term.[1]

On July 12, the League had released a brief announcement
to its members:

"Mr. B. Frank Summers, President of the Pennsylvania Credit
Union League, today announced the elevation of Mr. William
W. Pratt from the position of Executive Director of the
League to the newly created post of Director of Research and
Development, effective September 1, 1965....

"In order to carry on the work effectively, the Research and
Development headquarters will be established at a new location, to be announced at a later date.

1. Summers was the only League president after Joe Moore to serve so long.
In order for him to have a third term the directors passed and members
ratified a special amendment to the bylaws removing the two-term restriction on the president, a restriction originally imposed at the same time as
the similar amendment to the Constitution of the United States. Attempts
to restrict League presidents to three years failed twice to pass the board.

"Mr. Michael J. Judge, Assistant Executive Director for the past three years, has been appointed Acting Executive Director, effective September 1, 1965."

References to Pratt's "elevation" fooled no one. Pratt had been relieved of leadership of the League and removed from League headquarters.

Public recognition by the League that the change had actually occurred came with a page one photo in the November 1965 *Key Notes*. The picture of the annual Credit Union Day proclamation ceremony featured Governor William Scranton and acting executive director Judge along with Summers, Steven Pirk of the Bureau of Federal Credit Unions, and James Robb, director of the Consumer Credit Bureau of the Pennsylvania Department of Banking.

The League announced formal completion of the transition to the press March 1, 1966:

"Mr. B. Frank Summers, President of the Pennsylvania Credit Union League announced at the Quarterly Meeting of the League board of Directors on February 25-26, 1966, in Harrisburg, the appointment of Mr. Michael J. Judge as Managing Director of the League, effective February 26, 1966.

"Mr. Judge has been serving as Acting Managing Director of the League since September 1, 1965 and as Assistant Executive Director for three years prior to September 1, 1965."

In the absence of more extensive official information, rumors of a coup and of forced removal swept the Pennsylvania credit union movement. To this day, half-remembered stories and half-believed rumors still surround discussions of the last days of the Pratt administration and the beginning of Judge's stewardship. They are the legacy, not of cabals and star chamber politics, but of ill-considered secrecy—a simple lack of effective communication.

Pratt's health had been gradually declining for years. He was a victim of diabetes, a debilitating disease requiring careful medical treatment and constant attention to diet. Caught up in the strenuous social and physical demands of credit union life, Pratt provided neither. His self-treatment with insulin was irregular. He ate out often and without proper attention to nutritional composition. Worst of all, credit union people constantly insisted that he join them in a drink —and he all too rarely refused.

Aware of the problems, Pratt had been thinking of retirement for years. To some extent, he had even planned for it and structured League management accordingly. The directors were also well aware of Pratt's physical problems. They had watched his health deteriorate and had seen him face increasing difficulties fulfilling his role. Those who had known him for a long time were especially aware of the change, and especially upset by it.

The change in leadership was the result of long and careful deliberation by the board. The eventual inevitability of a change in League management was clear at least five years before it actually occurred. When the transition finally came, it was the result not of immediate crisis but of long maneuvering and planning. In fact, board leaders devoted extensive energy to questions of League management throughout the first half of the 1960s.

Leadership of the board was divided. The board was in the midst of its most critical power struggle in ten years. Leo L. Gleese was president of the League in 1961 when the likely need for action by the board first surfaced. He was a newcomer, elected in 1955 from District 5. An engineer with Struthers Wells Company, he was a charter member and president of Struthers Warren FCU. His most active work as a director had been as a volunteer organizer of credit unions. Holding the board together was an almost impossible task for him.

Gleese had won the vice-presidency in 1960 by one vote in a contest with Joseph Matisko. Jim Girvan had been reelected as president only after a hard campaign against Michael Casper. B. Frank Summers had been elected secretary by a one-vote margin over Regis Lawley. Even seats on the execu-

*Michael J. Judge has served as
managing director and
president (the board of directors
changed the title in 1978) of the
Pennsylvania Credit Union
League since 1965.*

tive committee had been contested. In a unique procedure,
the board had voted to limit the committee to eight seats, then
elected Joe Moore, Bill Lawry, and Josephine Sakovics to the
vacancies. John T. Taurish was denied a seat in the process.
Bill Noble and Jim Girvan were elected national directors;
Lee Sell, C. S. (Tiny) Cowan and John McCullough were the
unsuccessful candidates.

Among the questions splitting the board were disputes involving increasing the maximum membership fee, staffing
and management of the League, the stabilization fund issue
and the perennial question of redistricting. Member credit
unions had again grown insistent in voicing their dissatisfaction with the existing districts and representation. The annual meetings were receiving growing numbers of
increasingly strident resolutions calling for changes in the
distribution of seats on the board. The latter had just been
resolved by a tenuous compromise at the pre-convention
meeting of the board.

That compromise took the form of a group of bylaws amendments, drafted barely in time to defuse a near revolt of the delegates at the Philadelphia annual meeting. The changes included: retention of the existing districts on a one-year basis but increasing representation from districts 1 and 9 by assigning the two at-large directors to their own home districts; eliminating future at-large election of directors; and reassignment of seats to districts every two years in the future.

The League was understaffed and somewhat demoralized. *Key Notes* appeared irregularly, and not at all between May and November 1961. Pratt's report at the 1962 annual meeting mentioned his difficulties in obtaining applicants for League positions.

It was a time when the Pennsylvania movement was expanding dramatically, but the League could not claim credit for the rapid growth of the era. Expansion came in spite of League inaction. Worse, it severely strained League capabilities to provide the most basic and essential services.

An early indication of the changing relationship between Pratt and the board of directors came at the August 1960 board meeting in Harrisburg when Pratt requested creation of several staff positions. He asked for an assistant executive director, a special assistant for technical assistance, a director of public relations and publications, a replacement for the director of education (then vacant) and a "writing assistant" for education materials. Under established precedent and procedures, Pratt was already empowered to make such appointments. While he had often consulted with board leaders before taking action, he had never before formally requested their approval. Apparently he sensed a new need for caution and bureaucratic prudence.

Pratt had brought Judge in from the field in January 1960 to be director of special services. He was assigned a variety of tasks including public relations, legislative relations, and rewriting the League *Information Manual*. He also continued to help out in the field as needed. In retrospect, it seems clear

333

that Pratt was preparing Judge eventually to assume full management responsibility.

Following the August 1960 meeting of the board, Pratt began the process of promoting Judge from director of special services to assistant executive director (effective December 13, 1961). He polled the League executive committee in October, seeking their reactions to the prospective appointment. Their responses indicate that they understood that Pratt was grooming Judge as his eventual successor.[2]

Judge was deeply involved in the recodification of the state credit union law. He carried much of the responsibility for legislative relations during the campaign. As he later recalled:

> "It was a thrill, watching that whole process—making the contacts—getting sponsors on the legislation....
>
> "I have always contended since that point in time that it's almost best to send someone down there who doesn't know his way around because there are no inhibitions and they find their way into areas that people in the know wouldn't even venture into. I went into the highest offices not knowing any different. But I think as a result that it paid dividends....
>
> "I became very familiar with the process at that point.... watching that whole process, working it out of the committee, seeing the debate when it got stuck over in the Senate...."

Judge proved instrumental in helping to free the recodification from the Senate log jam, winning support of the Republican and Democratic caucuses. He then helped it move through the House of Representatives late in the 1961 session.[3]

2. President Gleese was enthusiastic: "Bill, I am glad you have confidence in Mike, rather than considering going 'outside.' I trust this action will lighten your load considerably." Frank Tokay and Jim Girvan thought the idea "OK." Bill Noble responded with his "heartiest endorsement."
3. One major provision of the bill brought mortgages under the "loan" provisions of the law, rather than the "investments" provisions. This meant that mortgages would have to be supported by reserves. As a result of the recodification, Philadelphia Teachers Credit Union disaffiliated, claiming that the bill was not in the best interests of the credit union movement. Philadelphia Teachers later reaffiliated.

Leo Gleese served as president of the Pennsylvania Credit Union League, 1961–1963.

"I remember how excited you get watching legislation being processed. It was getting near the end of the session when our bill was being called up.... I got so mixed up, I thought our bill went down to defeat. I got real discouraged. Then it dawned on me that I was looking at it wrong. I remember rushing out and calling Bill Pratt and telling him 'We got it through! Now we have to get the governor to sign it.' "

Judge's work on the recodification legislation later proved to be a valuable part of his education.

Pratt kept his assistant informed about board priorities, including executive session activities, CUNA and CUNA Mutual events and issues, and other peripheral aspects of League and credit union affairs.

While League staff were working on recodification, a board committee was progressing with the stabilization issue. The 1961 annual meeting had passed a resolution over board objections demanding that the board submit a stabilization program to the members in 1962. At the August 1961 meeting Joe

335

Moore presented a committee report recommending that the League set up their own fund and not participate in the CUNA stabilization program. The committee's program called for the transfer of $25,000 from the League's general reserves to a "stabilization services reserve." It set aside 2.5% of annual League income from dues as a regular contribution to the stabilization fund. And it created a special committee to control the fund as a virtually autonomous function of the League. While that plan was defeated on the floor (as hoped and expected by some members of the board),[4] it established the basis for a future stabilization program. Merely presenting the plan satisfied member demands, at least for the moment.

With stabilization and redistricting issues defused, the board was able to reunify itself in 1962. At the post-convention meeting in Philadelphia, Leo Gleese was elected president, B. F. Summers vice-president, Josephine Sakovics secretary, and Frank Tokay, treasurer, all without opposition. All other elections, including seats on the executive committee and national board, were similarly filled without rancor. The increasingly serious question of what to do about League management was not so easily resolved.

It was a united board that turned its attention to continuing personnel management problems. Their growing concern was reflected in their September 1962 decision to form

4. The board did not approve changes in the bylaws needed to implement the plan. Since the needed amendments were then submitted by member credit unions from the floor, they required the vote of three-fourths of the delegates "present and voting." Floyd Tompkins ruled that the phrase meant "twice the number of credit unions registered for the meeting" since each credit union was entitled to two votes. Far fewer were actually present on the floor, and the resolution had no chance of gaining the required support of three-fourths of them. It received a majority vote but failed to meet the 3/4 requirement as defined by Tompkins. At the subsequent request of the board and of Summers, a supporter of stabilization, Pratt hired an outside parliamentarian, W. H. Clay Keen, the following year. Keen was not familiar with League practices however and caused almost as many problems as his appointment had resolved. Tompkins returned as parliamentarian at the 1968 annual meeting.

a personnel committee as a special subcommittee of the executive committee. Vice president Summers, a professional personnel manager, was appointed to chair the group. Its other members were Bill Lawry, Frank Tokay and Bill Noble. This was a dramatic change. Personnel matters had always—by explicit, reiterated policy statement—been the exclusive concern of the executive director. Even in the face of staff complaints to board members, that policy had been rigidly maintained. Now the board was preparing to intervene.

Given its concern over such internal matters, it would have been understandable if the League had not had time or energy to devote to external concerns. Yet throughout this period, the League and cuna continued a cogent and active campaign in support of Truth-in-Lending legislation. Convinced that such legislation was not only in its own best interests but that helping the public improve its understanding of credit lay at the heart of the credit union philosophy, the credit union movement became the only component of the thrift industry to support consumer demands for Truth-in-Lending. John McCullough reported for the public relations-legislative education committee at the 1963 annual meeting:

> "The Credit Union Movement, both State and National, is expending all efforts to have the Truth-In-Lending bills passed. These bills have been introduced in both houses of the U. S. Congress and also in the Pennsylvania Senate. The Pennsylvania Credit Union League is supporting these bills and has sent notices to all credit unions urging them to write to their representatives in Harrisburg and Washington."

He requested that those credit unions who had not yet written letters, to please do so and send carbon copies of the letters to the League office.

Summers' attention was now focussed on League personnel. His committee was at work surveying League staff with an eye towards formulating job descriptions, classifications, wage guidelines and performance checks. Staff management

337

was no longer an exclusive concern of Pratt's. The board, through Summers and his personnel committee, was directly involved in all personnel decision-making.

John McCullough, then a member of Summers' personnel committee, remembers that there were many troublesome problems involving Pratt's relationship with League staff. "There were no job evaluation criteria, no standards. If Pratt was in a good mood, he'd give an employee a raise. We had to do something about that."

League activities were clearly suffering. Publication of *Key Notes*, now edited by Pratt, had become erratic. Pratt found it necessary to apologize for that as well as delays in issuing updates for the *League Information Manual*, the directory, and other publications. Creation of the stabilization fund, the board's top priority project, was removed from League management and handled directly by a committee of the board with some assistance from League staff. Pratt's long-term objection to stabilization programs was now totally ignored.

The fully developed stabilization plan deviated only in minor details from the one rejected by the membership a year earlier. For one, the executive director, while still projected as a member of the stabilization committee, was now denied a vote. For another, the full plan included provisions for removal of committee members and other such specialized contingencies. These changes reflected board concerns about Pratt's ability to conduct business.

While the initial funding level in the final plan was $25,000 as it had been in the original, continuing funding was left to the discretion of a three-fourths majority of the members of the board in properly convened regular or special meeting. The 2.5% annual contribution had been abandoned.

The function of the stabilization fund had also been subtly altered. It was originally conceived as a means of protecting credit unions in trouble, and of helping them to avoid possible liquidation. While that primary purpose was maintained, under the altered proposal, the stabilization fund had become a surrogate form of share insurance. A secondary function

B. F. Summers served as president of the Pennsylvania Credit Union League, 1963–1966.

was to "control losses of credit unions as a result of liquidation, and the desired objective is to make possible the payment of up to but not in excess of 100% of the members' net investment in the liquidating credit union."

The enabling resolution also mandated that the stabilization fund "is not intended or to be construed or identified as an insurance or guarantee of the shares of members in their credit unions." Judge remembers that the phrase was inserted to provide specific legal protection and be certain "that neither the League nor its service corportion would be construed as an insurance or guarantee and thus expose the assets of the League." The provision also satisfied those who objected to share insurance on philosophical grounds. That camp included Pratt. "Bill Pratt vigorously objected to it," recalls Judge. Had he still been completely healthy and still in control of the Pennsylvania credit union movement, Pratt presumably would have blocked the creation of the stabilization fund as constituted in 1963.

Pratt's opposition was based on the premise that a League-financed stabilization fund could well prove to be a false promise to credit union members, that if a particularly large credit union had serious difficulties, the League would not be able to meet its implied obligations. He thought that if the League were to have such a fund, it should have sufficient capital in it to be able to weather either collapse of a major credit union or a general economic collapse like the Great Depression where many credit unions would simultaneously be experiencing major difficulties. Federal share insurance could provide such guarantees. A League-financed stabilization fund could not.

Leadership of the League had functionally passed from the executive director to the League president, from Pratt to Summers. The long-term work of Floyd Tompkins to isolate League leadership from the general membership through elaborate bylaw amendment and other procedural requirements, efforts intended to benefit the executive director, now worked to aid Summers in his attempts to wrest control from Pratt.

Under Summers' leadership, other critical changes in established League policy continued to pass over the objections of the weakened executive director. The 1964 dues schedule lowered the base fee, kept the maximum fee at $2073, but added a provision discounting 10% of the membership fee "if paid before March 1, 1964." Since dues had to be paid before March 31 for credit unions wishing to vote at the meeting, this was effectively a camouflaged 10% across-the-board reduction in the dues schedule. More specifically, it was a 10% reduction for those paying the maximum.

While a stronger Pratt might have entertained fee reductions, he probably would not have allowed it to extend to credit unions paying the maximum fee. Yet when the dues committee of the board proposed the 10% early payment discount at their February 15, 1963 meeting in Harrisburg, he voiced no objection. Neither did any member of the board. Clearly, the shift in power to the Summers-led group of new leaders was now recognized by all concerned.

Pratt did object vociferously to suggestions that income on investments not be included in the membership fee calculation. He had, in fact, been fighting Treasurer Tokay's attempts to redefine gross income to exclude investment income for more than a decade. Even in his weakened state he resented and resisted this additional attempt by the wealthy big-city credit unions to lower their own contributions to the support of the League.

Tokay's own credit union had substantial income from investments. He typically based his request to exclude investment income on the claim that such investments were only a trivial part of credit union income and "the total fee paid on investment income was $41,020 or slightly less than 10% of total income." Pratt objected that "the majority of the credit unions making such investments now have the benefit of reduced League fee rate [either because they pay the maximum or through the 10% early payment discount]." Pratt succeeded in defeating the measure.

In 1964, the finance and budget committee again recommended a reduction in the fee schedule.[5] But Pratt again succeeded in postponing consideration of changing the fee basis to eliminate investment income. That recommendation was resubmitted by the finance and budget committee at the April 1965 meeting. The recommended dues schedule was otherwise unaltered. This time a dispirited Pratt made no objection. The measure was adopted.[6]

5. The new schedule: "3% of gross income up to $40,000; 2% of $40,000 - $50,000; 1% of $50,000 - $100,000; 0.5% over $100,000; maximum of $2,073; discount of 10% if paid by March 1, 1965.
6. It was implemented through a Tompkins-designed amendment procedure that bypassed the annual meeting completely. The change was implemented through resolution by a member credit union (PACEDOC) to the board, and approved as a bylaw amendment by three-fourths of the board. It was then submitted to the membership for ratification by mail ballot. Under provisions originally designed by A. R. Thompson, ratification could only be denied if two-thirds of the members actually cast negative ballots. In the future, excluding investment income from membership fee calculations would cause substantial problems for the League. The change was repealed in 1982, ironically through an updated version of the identical procedure.

At the 1965 post-convention meeting, Summers was elected president and McCullough was elected vice president, both with no opposition. Josephine Sakovics was elected secretary over the weak opposition of Joe Matisko, who was absent from the meeting due to illness. All other elected positions were filled without opposition. The stabilization issue had been settled; dues had been decreased; the personnel committee had assumed control of League management. The issues that had divided the directors in 1960 had been resolved. The bitter schism of 1961 was healing. Only one major action remained to be taken.

President Summers was a management professional, the personnel director of the Pittsburgh Tube Company, a position he had held since 1945. He had been a League director since 1954. He had been secretary and president of his Beaver Valley Chapter, as well as secretary and vice president of the League. As president, Summers moved quickly to bring professional management practices to the Pennsylvania Credit Union League.

Among his first actions was to persuade Pratt to appoint John Edinger to replace Anthony Novitsky as education director, and Robert Ewing as the League's first director of public relations and publications.

Edinger had been a field representative for five years. While he eventually proved adequate in his new post, he had no real preparation or training for it. Ewing was a former secretary and president of the Babcock and Wilcox Employees FCU. A worker in the Tubular Products Division, Ewing was a department representative to the company public relations and publications staff and a good friend of Summers'. Unfortunately that background proved inadequate; Ewing was discharged by the League less than one year later.

One other individual who joined the staff that year stayed much longer. Carmine Dorazio was appointed as a field representative the same day that a Ewing joined the League. He joined Albert Sippel who had become a field representative in 1961. Later in 1963 they were joined by Edwin Mailander.

These three were starting long and distinguished careers as field representatives.[7]

As Pratt's physical condition continued to deteriorate, Summers' determination to take action became stronger. To that end he called a special meeting of his personnel committee for September 21, 1963, in the League office. While no copies of the minutes of that meeting seem to have survived, its repercussions as well as the results of subsequent consultations with the executive director are evident in Pratt's report to the February 1964 meeting of the board. Pratt suggested to the board that the technical assistants no longer report to him, but be placed under the management of the director of field services. Further, as the minutes report, "Mr. Pratt suggested that since his retirement must be anticipated, serious consideration should be given to [several areas] related to directorship responsibility."[8]

Most of these "suggestions" were accepted with alacrity. At their 1965 pre-convention meeting the board shifted responsibility of technical assistance from the executive director to field services and recommended that Judge be promoted from "assistant to the executive director" to "assistant executive director."

League President Summers was under fire from several directors and many delegates for an apparent conflict of interest. They criticized him for staying on as chairman of the personnel committee while serving as League president. Summers felt it necessary to defend himself to the annual meeting. He argued that having been charged with preparing a personnel policy manual, he "felt he would be remiss if he

7. Sippel retired in 1983. Dorazio died in October of that same year. His funeral was held on International Credit Union Day.
8. Pratt went on to recommend a new management structure wherein he maintained "overall direction" for the League, but a "managing director," reporting to him, would "supervise all staff and oversee all operations, and perhaps directly supervise public relations." He also requested appointment of a staff manager and increased responsibility for the office manager." It seems evident that while Pratt was speaking of "retirement," he was thinking rather of decreased responsibility but continued active leadership of the movement.

did not remain on the committee until the project was completed." He advised the group that the manual was near completion and continued his report:

> "Executive director is Bill Pratt who is top man. Mike Judge has been named assistant managing [executive] director who will supervise Bill Gardner, director of field services; John Edinger, director of education; and the director of public relations and Lucy Smith, director of office services, and that these lines of organization be maintained."

The problems at the League continued. George Shelly, an experienced newspaper reporter and editor, was hired July 13, 1964 as public relations director. He tendered his resignation to Pratt less than two weeks later. *Key Notes* continued its erratic publication schedule. The publications committee continued to issue periodic apologies.

At the January 29, 1965, meeting, the board began to prepare for final action. A previously contested and postponed bylaws amendment eliminating the two-term restriction on the League president passed without official comment. A three-term restriction was defeated. The new bylaw was designed to allow Summers to continue as president, providing continuity during a transition of League management. It also, in effect, shifted power from the executive director to the League president.

In recognition that the League presidency was assuming new importance and that sitting table officers might have a long wait for the presidency to open, the board had already created a second vice presidency.

To provide justification by an outside expert for changes the board would soon be making, the personnel consulting firm of Don Latella and Associates was retained to survey League operations.[9] Their disinterested recommendations, it

9. The Latella firm was also retained by Pittsburgh Tube Company where they reported to Summers. Bids were not sought from other consultants. While Judge says that it has always been his understanding that the report strongly recommended that Pratt be replaced, no copy of the report seems

was hoped, would defuse any objections from members to changes in League management.

While Pratt chose not to retire, he knew that he could not continue to carry executive management responsibilities much longer. His "Executive Director's Report" to the 1965 annual meeting was a valedictory address. He opened his comments by noting that 1965 "would be the twenty-second time he had the pleasure of presenting an annual report since he became executive director of the League." He went on to lecture the board and the annual meeting, explaining that "the objective of credit unions is promoting thrift, granting loans, constant enrollment of members ... and increasing the value of savings in share accounts." The League's task, he reminded his audience, is "service through education."

His report included a statistical summary of progress made during the previous five years. He closed his report with a reminder that the credit union's purpose is to promote thrift and to supply credit equitably in true spirit of the Brotherhood of Man.

William Pratt had learned the lesson well. Roy Bergengren would have been proud. These two great credit union pioneers had travelled different paths, but they had reached a similar understanding of the credit union movement. John McCullough recognized that despite significant differences, the two shared common ground. "They were two of a kind, Bergengren and Pratt. They were both emotional men— strong-willed, emotional men."

After the meeting, the board undertook the reorganization as mandated by the new bylaws. Summers was reelected to his third term; McCullough was elected first vice president, Josephine Sakovics was elected second vice president (putting her in line to become the League's first woman president);

---

to have survived. Judge says he was told that Latella recommended that he not be appointed to replace Pratt. They recommended that the board seek a new CEO outside existing staff. If so, that recommendation of the consultant firm was overruled.

Joseph Matisko was elected secretary; and Frank Tokay was elected treasurer.

Pratt's final report as executive director was presented to the July 9 meeting of the board in Camp Hill. To most observers, that seemingly routine meeting appeared special only in that the League discussed a possible contract with Iliff and Sill to launch a pilot billboard advertising program in the Lehigh Valley and Beaver Valley Chapters. Concern with such an extensive program marked a new awareness of the importance of advertising to the future of the League, and a new emphasis on communications.

The following day the executive committee met with the consultants from Latella. They decided to write an end to this extraordinary chapter of League history. Pratt was brought in and informed of his appointment as director of research and development. Mike Judge was appointed acting executive director. The board asked Judge to accept the position immediately. He demurred and requested that the new appointment take effect September 1 instead to allow him some vacation time. The board accepted that condition. Lucy Smith was assigned to work with Pratt in new offices leased for his use. Gladys Krout was promoted to director of office services. Agnes Beistline became Judge's secretary.

Pratt's health had been eroding, gradually, for years. So too had his relations with the board. Most of his friends and close supporters had retired. Their replacements were less awed by Pratt's past contributions to the credit union movement and his influence in Madison than they were intolerant of his growing incapacities and imperious style of management. "Pratt rubbed people the wrong way," recalls McCullough. "He upset league staff, and the directors, and the people in the credit unions. He was a good man in his day. But we needed someone younger, someone more flexible and more responsible."

Pratt had headed League management during its most important period of growth. When he took over, the annual budget was about $10,000; in 1965, League income was nearing

$500,000. He was initially the part-time manager of a staff of five; when he left, League staff included 40 full-time employees. When he took over, there were about 550 credit unions in the state and only a little over half of them were affiliated with the League; at his departure, there were 1284 Pennsylvania credit unions and all but 88 of them were League members. During Pratt's early years, the League supply service was run from a closet by a part-time clerk; in 1965 it was a $34,000-per-year business which had been separately incorporated as a for-profit, wholly-owned subsidiary of the League in January 1965.

His personal and professional accomplishments were remarkable. Pratt was born December 30, 1902, in Philadelphia, the oldest of three children. His father died suddenly in 1916, and Pratt left school to support the family. His first job was as a messenger for Fels Naptha Soap. His second position was on the loading dock of the DuPont Grasselli plant. He had been promotedto traffic manager and transportation supervisor before he left in 1947 to become full-time executive director of the Pennsylvania Credit Union League.

Hundreds of credit union people from all over the nation gathered in Harrisburg on November 17, 1967 at a testimonial dinner in his honor when he retired from League service. A second testimonial dinner was held in Madison, hosted by CUNA and CUNA Mutual.

During his years with the credit union movement, Pratt had been a charter member of Philadelphia DuPont Grasselli Employees FCU and its president 1941-47. He was secretary of the Philadelphia Chapter, 1936-47, and a director of the League, 1937-47. He was a national director of CUNA, 1937-47, vice president, 1938-41, and chairman of the CUNA retirement savings fund board of trustees, 1946-65. He was a director of CUNA Mutual 1935-67; vice president, 1942-1951; and president of the insurance affiliate, 1954-55 and 1961-62. He was a director of CUMIS Insurance Society, 1960-67.

He was a giant of a man whose tremendous drive helped him surmount the odds that were stacked against him person-

Employees of the Pennsylvania Credit Union League, Credit Union Day, 1966.

ally. In turn, he used his energies to help those who were still back where he had started from. He drove himself and others unmercifully. Building the credit union movement was a great and difficult fight. Its pioneers were warriors. In Pennsylvania, Bill Pratt was its champion.

THE CHANGE THAT had occurred went well beyond a change of personnel. Pratt had spent many years asserting the independence and primacy of League management. While he had looked to the directors for some purposes, more typically they had looked to him for guidance. But from late 1962 to July 10, 1965, he gradually surrendered leadership to the directors and especially to President Summers. We need only look at Summers' report to the directors on November 19:

> "This a report of the stewardship of the President's Special Committee during the period of March 8, 1965 to the present. This is the period during which the Consultants were employed and this report will outline their activity and accomplishment. You will recall the reason for employing a

348

management consultant company was to endeavor to eliminate the contention, friction and turnover in the headquarters'
office."

In the five-page report that followed, Summers outlined his
complete redesign of the League in accordance with his management consultants' recommendations. The other directors
gave their approval to the changes.

A second significant indication of the new primacy of the
board was the change from two-year terms for directors to
three-year terms, effective May 21, 1965. The change, like so
many other board actions of this transition period, was accomplished with little board effort and less attention by the
members. It had been effected through bylaws amendment by
the board (October 9, 1964) and submitted to the membership
for ratification by mail.[10]

The assumption of control by the directors might have
been less traumatic for the Pennsylvania credit union
movement had the board itself not undergone its own gradual transformation. The call of the roll at the November 19,
1965 meeting presented few familiar names. While former
presidents Joe Moore, Jim Girvan, Bill Lawry, Leo Gleese,
and Matt Pottiger were all still on the board, Tokay, Moore,
and Pottiger were the only directors who remembered
the early days of the League and their impossible mission.
Once, with Pratt, they had been giants of the movement. Now they, too, were relegated to largely symbolic
functions.

The new directors were impatient newcomers to the movement. This was the time when Lee Sell, Harold Brown, Joseph Matisko, and Mike Casper came on the scene, a group of

10. To qualify for this procedure, amendments had to be proposed by
resolution of a member credit union. The required resolution was provided
by PACEDOC FCU. Other resolutions at the same board meeting provided the
three-year terms for directors (adopted) and eliminated the two-term restriction on the presidency (defeated for lack of three-fourths majority).
The three-term restriction amendment passed at the next meeting of the
directors. This group of amendments mark the assumption of substantially
increased power by the board in its relationships with the professional staff.

young rebels as Pratt and the older generation of directors
doubtlessly perceived them. Judge later described their move
to power:

> "They were wanting to make the challenge. They knew that
> the stronghold was Joe Moore....
>
> "I admired the way they went about it. They were not
> vindictive.... They were doing it quietly, trying to make in-
> roads, I think, on a gentlemanly basis, trying to win their goals
> by proving their point...."

This group emerged through active campaigning in chapters
of the League. They were a new breed who had learned about
the credit union movement by observing it, not by building
it. Like Pratt himself when he first became active in the movement, their interests tended to lie more with personal goals
and the short-term preferences of their own typically large
and wealthy credit unions, rather than the long-term interests
of the League which predominantly comprised smaller organizations.

Over the years through his activities at the national level
and the broadened perspective provided by some of the senior
members of the board such as Palmer and E. A. Thompson,
Pratt had acquired a deep commitment to the philosophy of
the credit union movement. Given time and effective leadership, the new directors might also learn those lessons.

Judge had a hard task ahead of him. He would have to learn
to work with this board of directors. He had not yet had time
to acquire either Pratt's vision or skill. Certainly he did not
have Pratt's influence with the board or at CUNA. Nor did he
have strong and powerful supporters on the board, as Pratt
had in Moore and Girvan.

Judge had been brought into the League in 1955 as a "pros-
pector," a field representative who would work throughout
the state organizing new credit unions. That plan soon
proved less effective than hoped; the travel expenses for one
field representative handling most organizing made it equally
inefficient. Judge did personally organize 44 credit unions,

making him a special member of CUNA's Founders Club.

Judge, a 1944 graduate of Larksville High School and a veteran of service in the U. S. Navy, had studied at Kings College and Wilkes-Barre Business College. He was a one-time construction worker who had left his job with Hazard Okonite and was a door-to-door salesperson for *Encyclopedia Britannica* in the Wilkes-Barre area when he became involved with credit union work.

He met Pratt at a Credit Union Day dinner in Wilkes-Barre before interviewing with Pratt in Harrisburg. "He fascinated me all through my career. That man was truly dedicated to this credit union movement, absolutely dedicated," recalls Judge:

> "I didn't always agree with the man. I walked away shaking my head a lot of times saying, 'What's his motive this time?' But in my opinion he was a great teacher, by making you search your own mind, not by doing for you, but by challenging you at every turn that came about. Sometimes people got frustrated by that whole thing.... Ultimately I knew what his philosophy was, and that was: 'If I tell you, you're never going to depend upon yourself, to find the answer for yourself. The best thing for you to do and the best way you're going to remember is doing it, and looking it up yourself....' If you've challenged something, by your own research, you'll believe in it and then you're worth something! He always liked people who would challenge him.

JUDGE'S YEARS AS a field representative gave him a more intimate knowledge of credit union operations than Pratt had ever known. His travels throughout eastern Pennsylvania, often accompanied by Ralph Quigg, gave him a closer knowledge of credit union people throughout the region than the directors had. Judge also worked with Clayton Borrows and Bill Smith in the western part of the state.

At the time, few Pennsylvania credit unions maintained an office or a full-time staff. Most operated from the home of the

John McCullough served as president of the Pennsylvania Credit Union League, 1966–1968.

treasurer or in borrowed offices of the sponsor. The common bond was strictly observed. Credit unions were informal organizations, and Judge still fondly remembers the hospitality provided him by credit union people and their families. As the new managing director, deprived of structural powers by the board, lacking Pratt's forceful and overbearing presence, Judge would rely on personal contacts and diplomacy with the members to impose, gradually, his own perspective on the movement.

Judge was appointed managing director (the title was changed from executive director at his own request to conform with common usage in other leagues) in February 1966 and McCullough was elected League president in May. McCullough, a District 6 director since 1957, had been first vice president throughout the three years of Summers' administration. He had been on the board of directors of the Philadelphia Chapter since 1956 and chapter president 1963-65. A former Pennsylvania Railroad yardmaster, he was a credit union professional, the full-time treasurer-manager of the Local 169 I.B.T.C.W. & H. of A. FCU.

As League president, McCullough had a reputation for impatience, especially with such formalities as parliamentary procedure, and a desire to cut through to the core of issues. He had a deep and enduring commitment to the credit union philosophy. As chairman of a CUNA International planning committee, McCullough was the author of "Credit Union Philosophy: Some Considerations," a report later excerpted and reprinted by the League as *Philosophy and a Challenge*.

> "The ultimate goal of the credit union movement is that each man should be the master of his economic situation rather than its servant. It is where economics and democracy come together that the credit union can exist; it is to keep these two together that the credit union does exist.
>
> "The democratic nature of the movement must be preserved. It can and should be implemented in such a way that it will achieve economic efficiency. The movement as a whole can and should offer to credit unions and their members all the services they need, including the unique informational service of the credit union and all the collateral services which are usually offered by other financial institutions.
>
> "Our task then is to keep our organized movement both democratic and efficient."

The League now emerged from the painful stresses of the transition period with this renewed commitment to democratic and efficient operations.

As one step towards that end, the League organized its electronic data processing subsidiary, CUEDS Inc., which began operations August 1, 1966. Summers assumed the presidency of the new corporation. Its treasurer was a newly-elected director from Philadelphia, Joseph Hinchey, a former examiner with BFCU and the manager of Bell Telephone Employees FCU. Managing director of the new subsidiary corporation was a director from Harrisburg, William Saltzer who resigned from the League board to accept the new position.

353

The League became extraordinarily active. Gerald Heberling was hired as director of public relations to oversee the League's membership recruitment advertising pilot program devised by Ball Associates, Philadelphia. Heberling had been a newspaper reporter and president of the *Lebanon Daily News* credit union. He was the League's first professional director of public relations. New field representatives joining the League at the same time include William J. Dooner and Kenneth E. Noca, both of whom are still on the staff.

Other indications of new League activity came with the 1967 licensing by the Pennsylvania Insurance Department of CUNA Mutual Insurance Society and its affiliate, CUMIS Insurance Society, Inc.; the 1968 amendment to the Pennsylvania Credit Union Act; and the 1969 amendment to the insurance law to allow direct sale of Life Savings policies in the Commonwealth.[11]

Lee Sell, District 9 director, was the policyowner representative to CUNA Mutual from Pennsylvania. Sell, at the urging of CUNA Mutual, began to press the League to seek licensing and the right to actively solicit insurance sales in the state.

Moore had actively opposed seeking state licensing for CUNA Mutual. He opposed most expansion of CUNA Mutual activities. As a veteran of the CUNA vs. CUNA Mutual wars in Madison, Moore had no desire to see a CUNA Mutual sales staff working in the Commonwealth, forming a new power base and possibly undercutting the work of the League's field staff. Pratt had supported Moore in opposing licensure. He held that offering policies by mail was adequate and that if licensure were actively sought and denied, the Insurance Department might well force CUNA Mutual to cease all solicitation activities in Pennsylvania. The new League leadership was more sympathetic to the goals of CUNA Mutual, and Sell was

11. The policies had been available to all federal credit unions in Pennsylvania—by mail—since Life Savings had been approved by the Credit Union Section of FCA.

Josephine Sakovics served as president of the Pennsylvania Credit Union League, 1968–1970.

an effective lobbyist for the insurance interests. A League-sponsored 1968 amendment to the state Credit Union Act had legislated approval of the insurance programs for state-chartered credit unions. As Judge remembers the unusual sequence of events:

> "We wrote into the state credit union act the provision that the state-chartered credit unions could make available to their members this ... life savings insurance. My interpretation was that even though we were putting it in the state act it was null and void until such time as the insurance law was changed. Well we got the bill through, the governor signed it, and then the Secretary of Banking issued a ruling saying that the legislature had decreed it a proper insurance and the state-chartered credit unions could now have it.
>
> "So it immediately opened up all of the doors of the state-chartered credit unions, and that was another helpful area in bringing about the qualification of CUNA Mutual coverage in the state."

355

By March 1969 the sequence was complete. The insurance companies were fully licensed and their policies were fully approved for sale in Pennsylvania to both state and federal credit unions.[12] As Moore had feared, CUNA Mutual immediately established a full sales force in the state. Their Pennsylvania field staff would soon include Edinger, the former League director of education, and former League field representatives Bill Thomas, Harry Latimer, Ed Yeager, Larry Bittle and others. The Pennsylvania League, once again, was the training ground for the movement.

Frank Tokay, League director and treasurer since the 1936 reorganization, died July 22, 1966. Tokay had been a national director since 1937. He was elected first vice president of the League in May, shortly before his death. His responsibilities as first vice president were assumed by second vice president Josephine Sakovics. Other changes of League officers included the election of District 1 director Harold Brown as treasurer. National director Bill Lawry succeeded Bill Noble as CUNA District 10 vice-president.

Unlike Pratt, Judge was not attempting to run the League by himself but was seeking special expertise and assistance. League staff was changing even more rapidly. In June, Judge brought Frank Wielga of Wilkes-Barre to the League as administrative assistant. Wielga was a Woodrow Wilson scholar at the University of Chicago. While in college, he had been manager and assistant treasurer of the Wilkes-Barre VA Employees FCU. Through League efforts, credit unions had gained the right to participate in the educational loan programs of the Pennsylvania Higher Education Assistance Administration. Under Wielga's aggressive credit union man-

12. Charles F. Eikel Jr., president of CUNA Mutual and CUMIS, later cited the Pennsylvania League, Managing Director Michael J. Judge, and Counsel Floyd Tompkins, "for the role they played in obtaining the legislative amendment ot the insurance law which made approval of Life Savings possible."

agement, his Wilkes-Barre VA Employees FCU was the first
credit union to instituted the PHEAA program.[13]

Wielga and Heberling represented the new breed of
League staff, bringing needed specialized skills to the Penn-
nsylvania credit union movement. To some extent, Edinger
and Findlay had similar credentials, having learned the needs
of the education and field services departments respectively
during their years as field representatives. The gradual building of this staff marks a new professionalism Judge brought
to the League.

Unfortunately these ambitious young staffers did not stay
with the League for long. They had barely begun what could
have been a dynamic and exciting era when erosion set in.
Lacking appreciation of Judge's lengthy training and his support by the League board of directors, Heberling, Edinger
and Wielga sought to expand their roles with the League.
Their hopes were frustrated.

Edinger left in 1968 to join the CUNA Mutual field force. He
was replaced by former school teacher Maurice Roberts.
Wielga left in 1969 to assume a senior staff position with the
Philadelphia City Employees Federal Credit Union. Heberling left in November 1971 and was replaced by his assistant
Doris K. Ellis. Findlay stayed with the League, eventually
becoming assistant managing director.[14]

The League had been plagued by personnel problems since
its inception, but now there were signs of gradual improvement; the revolving door to the clerical positions slowed
under the new management. Stability of the field staff had
improved sharply. Among the new field representative join-

13. Wielga later designed a popular "Credit Union Profile Analysis" form
that was made available through CUNA Supply. It is still in use today. Wielga
is now manager of the Pennsylvania State employees CU. In 1983 he received the William W. Pratt Memorial Award as Credit Union Professional
of the Year.
14. Ellis is currently vice-president, communications. Findlay was vice-
president, special projects when he died in 1982.

ing the League were Al Garttmeier and Paul Sullivan in 1968 and George Shevenock in 1969. Jack P. Barth, current vice president, member services, joined the League as a field representative in 1971.

There were also signs of continuing difficulty; departing staff had complained to Summers who retained his chairmanship of the personnel committee of the board. They had claimed that management was doing no planning, refused to properly delegate duties, and had no long-range goals. The personnel committee held a special meeting on June 28, 1969, to review the situation.

The directors responded with strong support for their managing director.[15] They also moved to implement recommendations of an earlier study by a board committee suggesting substantial increases in League salaries, especially for staff positions. The personnel committee explicitly moved to restate its right to review and evaluate staff performance, functions first assumed during the last years of the Pratt administration.

Leadership of the directors was still with the "city boys," but there were new people seated at the table. Also, the use of "boys" was becoming outdated. Along with Robert Neubaum from District 8, new directors installed at the 1968 annual meeting included Patricia Doyle from District 10 and former president James Girvan, newly reelected to the board he had left two years before. Josephine Sakovics was elected president following the annual meeting, the first and to date only woman to hold that position.

Sakovics was a charter member, treasurer and office manager of the Heights St. Joseph FCU in Miller Heights, a suburb of Bethlehem. President of the Lehigh Valley Chapter and the

15. There is substantial evidence that the problems were caused more by excessive staff ambition and disloyalty than by Judge's inexperience or lack of ability. The personnel committee report concluded that: "We advised Mike that the League board is in full support of him and the job he is doing as managing director. We also advised him that the League directors are interested in helping him and strengthening his position."

League's leading supporter of youth involvement activities, her credit union won a national award from CUNA 1963 recognizing its outstanding promotion of International Credit Union Day. She had been elected to the board in 1959, and served as League secretary from 1961 to 1965.

Sakovics was first vice president when the League received extensive national publicity through the visit of Sister Mary Gabriella, pioneer of the Korean Credit Union Movement. Sister Mary Gabriella, a native of Scranton and first cousin to Scranton's Patricia Doyle, was a Maryknoll missionary and founder of the Korean Cooperative Education Institute. During her visit to the United States, she spoke at International Credit Union Day banquets at the Wyoming Valley, Schuylkill Valley, Scranton, and Philadelphia chapters of the League. She was honored for her work by the Pennsylvania legislature, CUNA, and CUNA Mutual as well as the League. Her visit was a highlight in the history of International Credit Union Week celebrations.

Sakovics and McCullough both had great appreciation and understanding of the importance of publicity and promotional efforts in marketing credit unions. Sakovics' own credit union and chapter were active in youth involvement and International Credit Union Day activities, programs that were expanded by the League during her administration. She and McCullough gave impetus to League publications and public relations activities. They saw to it that these activities were financially well supported during their years as senior League officers. The public relations department had once gone totally unstaffed. After only two years on staff, Heberling had been given additional help. He had hired advertising copywriter Pierre Hill to succeed him as public relations assistant in 1968. When Hill left in 1970, he recruited a former colleague, Doris K. Ellis, to succeed him as public relations assistant.

Heberling initiated a program to refine and stabilize League communications efforts. *Key Notes* became a monthly publication, finally issued more regularly than apologies for its delay or non-appearance. He established a monthly newsletter, *Keystone Extra*, to help credit unions cope with the plethora of regulations and regulatory changes that marked the 1970s.

Heberling also initiated publication of a League *Yearbook* for distribution to the media, to libraries, and to other sources of public information about credit unions. Consisting of statistics and other important credit union data, the *Yearbook* would eventually evolve into an important source of up-to-date information about the credit union movement. Heberling and Ellis would establish a new place for Pennsylvania League publications. *Key Notes*, *Keystone Extra*, and the *Yearbook* all have consistently received first-place awards in various CUNA competitions.

In 1965 Pratt had resisted efforts by the League board to initiate statewide advertising programs.[16] Judge had no such hesitation. He fully backed his public relations staff in their efforts to tell the state about credit unions, especially through radio, television and newspapers.

A 1970 general marketing program designed by League staff working with Robert Charles of Michener Associates, Harrisburg, proved more successful in pilot testing. The "Lucky Shares Spree" materials resulting from that program were adopted by CUNA Supply Cooperative for national use. It was the first seriously encouraging credit union marketing effort by the League, and led to optimistic planning. "We should be looking forward to the day when the League and its member

16. In a June 17 1965 letter to Summers, Pratt told of the experience "of a league which recently completed a six month program at a cost of $15,000." He wrote of negative replies to the direct mail aspects of the campaign, especially from plant managers. "A prize was offered in relation to the person organizing the greatest number of new credit unions. There is a possible winner, an elected league officer who did produce one new credit union. They report that there is a possibility of one more credit union being formed as the result of the campaign." The results from the campaign in Pennsylvania conducted by Iliff & Sill, a Harrisburg agency, were about what Pratt expected. The agency claimed that "while few credit unions were organized as a result of the campaign, the secondary objective of informing residents of Lehigh Valley and Beaver Valley about the credit union movement was attained." The pilot program was a failure and a full statewide campaign along similar lines was never attempted.

Lee Sell served as president of the Pennsylvania Credit Union League, 1970–1972.

Harold Brown served as president of the Pennsylvania Credit Union League, 1972–1974.

361

Sister Mary Gabriella, a Maryknoll missionary from Scranton, pioneered the credit union movement in Korea. She is shown here with Joseph Finn and John McCullough during a visit to Pennsylvania when she addressed the League annual meeting.

credit unions will support mass media advertising on a regular year-round basis" reported the public relations committee to the 1971 annual meeting in Reading, home town of League president Lee Sell.

President Sell was a charter member and the first president of R.S.R. FCU, its treasurer and manager since 1952. He had been a League director since 1957 and a special member of the Founders Club who had organized 16 credit unions. A national director of CUNA, he was also secretary of CUNA Mutual and treasurer of CUMIS Insurance Society.

The 1971 annual meeting was notable in several other respects. One was the first Miss Credit Union of Pennsylvania

Pageant. Cathy McDonald, Miss York Chapter of Credit Unions, was the first winner of what would become a popular
annual event and six years later would become the Credit
Union Youth Ambassador Contest. Another highlight of the
annual meeting was a presentation to I. W. Abel, president of
the United Steel Workers of America, of an original oil painting commissioned by CUNA Mutual and CUMIS Insurance Societies. Labor-related issues had often caused friction in the
credit union movement, especially at Reading meetings.
Third, the annual meeting succeeded in passing a motion
from the floor demanding that the board find an equitable
way of redistricting itself in time for the 1972 meeting.

As the League prepared for the 1972 annual meeting, the
directors faced another major problem. They had improved
working conditions at the League and substantially increased
salaries. The League publications program had expanded
markedly—both in quality of publications and in quantities
of each that were printed and distributed. The stabilization
fund was receiving a small but continuing portion of the
League budget. The League had dramatically expanded its
educational and training offerings as well, especially the
Officers Forums and the Management Conference. This overdue modernization program was expensive. It was becoming
evident that the board had cut the membership fee once too
often. The League was forced to go to the members seeking
an increase in the membership fee.

The dues increase resolution generated much discussion
but little controversy. It passed 104-65, a comfortable, if not
overwhelming, endorsement.[17] The new schedule involved
little change for those credit unions paying maximum fees. In
1970 the maximum had been increased to $2,500 and the dis-
count had been lowered to 5%. As they had demonstrated
before, this board of directors was much more willing to

17. The new membership fee schedule, adopted at the 1972 meeting: 3% of
net income from loans to $40,000; 2.25% of net income from loans $40,000
to $50,000; 1.25% of net income from loans $50,000 to $100,000; 0.5% of net
income from loans over $100,000; Minimum fee, $5.00; maximum fee $2,500;
3% discount if paid before March 1.

*Miss York Chapter of the
League, Cathy McDonald,
becomes the first Miss Credit
Union of Pennsylvania in 1971.*

increase the burden on the smaller credit unions than to increase fees paid by the larger and wealthier organizations.

Proceedings were much more contentious when reappor-
tionment and redistricting of the board were discussed.
After a series of complex, confused resolutions and negative
motions, the recommendations of the board's committee
stood unchanged. There would now be 28 directors drawn
from ten districts. The district lines were changed slightly
to accommodate some shifts in the credit union population.

At the reorganization meeting, Harold Brown was elected
to succeed Lee Sell as president. Brown, League treasurer
from 1966-1970, had been elected first vice president in 1970,
interrupting the normal order of succession. A member of
Standard Stoker Employees FCU since 1941, Brown was manager of P-C Erie FCU, president of Erie Chapter (1945-1949),
and had been a League director since 1957. A founder of the

364

In 1975, the Miss Credit Union Contest became the Credit Union Youth Ambassador Contest. Now open to all members between 18 and 25, it attracts young men as well as young women candidates for the title. With their trophies following the 1977 competition are: Youth Ambassador Michael D. Will of Lancaster Chapter; first alternate Mark O'Brien of Philadelphia Chapter; and second alternate Denise Russell of Pittsburgh Chapter.

365

Erie Credit Union Service Center, Brown was a recipient of the Erie Chapter Appreciation Award.

The other officers elected in 1972, all without opposition, were: Joseph Matisko, first vice president; William Seanor, second vice president; Joseph Finn, secretary; and Michael Casper, treasurer. Election of the at-large members of the executive committee was contested until Noble and Moore withdrew. It marked the first time Moore was not a member of the executive committee since the committee had been formed. On August 3, 1971, Past President Bill Lawry died. It was the first of a series of losses to the movement. Jim Girvan died December 25, 1971. Bill Pratt died April 20, 1972, the day before the opening of the annual meeting. Joe Moore died a few months later, on September 13, 1972, during the Management Conference. In all too real a sense, the old generation of Pennsylvania credit union movement leadership was passing from the scene. The Pennsylvania credit union movement was in the midst of another transition, ending its growth phase and starting a new era with new issues to be confronted by new leadership.

XII

The Modern Era

"Our problem simply stated is this: how do we retain the credit union philosophy while it changes its expression? My own answer is that if we serve the financial needs of our members as our members want them served, we will be acting in the very best tradition and philosophy of our movement."

Josephine Sakovics

T HE FEDERAL TRUTH-IN-LENDING LAW became effective July 1, 1969, successfully concluding an extended legislative campaign by the organized credit union movement, including the Pennsylvania League. It was the first of several major legislative advances. Another law created the National Credit Union Administration (NCUA), a new autonomous agency that replaced the old Bureau of Federal Credit Unions. Other action created the National Credit Union Board and the National Credit Union Share Insurance Fund (NCUSIF).

Pennsylvania credit unions took great pride when President Richard M. Nixon's appointments to the board were announced. Two Pennsylvania directors, Harold Brown and Joseph Hinchey, had actively sought the appointment. After extensive deliberation and balloting, Brown was officially endorsed by the League and CUNA but was not appointed. Hinchey did get the nod from President Nixon. Manager of the Philadelphia City Employees FCU and a director of CUEDS, Inc. Hinchey is currently chairman of the board of Pacul Services, Inc.

U. S. Marine General (ret.) Herman Nickerson Jr. was appointed by Nixon to head NCUA. CUNA and the League had supported J. Deane Gannon, chief of the Bureau of Federal Credit Unions. Gannon was appointed instead to assist Nickerson at NCUA. Nickerson would need the help. His new agency not only retained the supervisory and regulatory functions of BFCU but would have responsibility for the new insurance program as well.

Under the new NCUSIF, credit union member accounts would be insured to a maximum of $20,000. Participation was

369

mandatory for all federal credit unions and optional for state-chartered credit unions. In Pennsylvania that meant that nearly 90% of credit unions in the state would come under the protection—and the requirements—of the share insurance program.

Credit union leaders greeted the new program with mixed emotions. Share insurance was the final and total rejection of the old unlimited-liability concept. Historically, credit union members had relied on their knowledge of each other to maintain financial security. Such great credit union pioneers as Raiffeisen and Wolff had rejected even the limited liability protection offered by incorporation. To people committed to this concept, the introduction of compulsory federal share insurance was one more indication of an unfortunate deterioration of credit union ideals.

The stabilization funds which had become popular a few years earlier had maintained some vestiges of the old concepts. Stabilization was still people helping people—credit unions helping each other. Share insurance was intervention by a government agency. To many leaders, the inevitability of the government regulations that had to come with the share insurance was even more threatening than the loss of movement ideals.

Both CUNA and League leadership had long been ambivalent about share insurance. Many credit union managers, especially those working with large, aggressive, and wealthy urban organizations, saw federal share insurance as a vitally needed component in their activities. Increasingly, this new generation of professional credit union managers saw their institutions as competition for banks and other thrift institutions rather than as unique membership organizations offering their own special services. Without share insurance, they felt weakened in their ability to compete with federally insured institutions such as banks or savings and loan associations.

Share insurance soon proved to be even more of a problem than its opponents had anticipated. Nickerson and NCUA is-

Joseph Hinchey, member of the original National Credit Union Board, is a League director and chairman of the board, Pacul Services, Inc.

sued highly restrictive reserve requirements for insured credit unions. Worse, NCUA set only vague guidelines covering other qualifying criteria, and allowed only a brief time period for credit unions to enter the insurance program.

Without share insurance, federal credit unions would have to liquidate. Furthermore, even state credit unions that did not obtain insurance now that it was available and standard, would be highly suspect in the eyes of their members and the general public. As a result of the new law, Nickerson and NCUA held life-or-death power over all credit unions. Under the law:

> "If the application of a Federal credit union for insurance is rejected, the Administrator shall suspend or revoke its charter unless, within one year after the rejection, the credit union meets the requirements for insurance and becomes an insured credit union."

Considering the harsh inflexibility of the penalties, NCUA proved itself restrictive and intolerant in its interpretations of

371

the law's provisions. To NCUA, its primary responsibility was to establish a secure insurance fund that would be able to keep premiums low by eliminating potentially weak credit unions.

The League objected to NCUA's insistence that credit unions which had not yet built up their regular reserve fund to the required 10% of outstanding loans immediately transfer (as a condition for insurance approval) funds from their special reserve or from reserve for contingencies or from undivided earnings. Some credit unions would be unable to pay dividends. Others, especially those that were overextended on loan or long-term investments, simply could not meet the conditions. The requirements were especially hard on new credit unions that had to transfer more than 10% of gross earnings in a single year to the regular reserve fund.

For credit unions in tenuous financial condition, the NCUA requirements were tantamount to a liquidation order. That was precisely the intent of NCUA. The agency wished to eliminate any credit union likely to face liquidation before federal insurance became effective. To the organized credit union movement, that concept was anathema. Their traditional method of operation was gradually to bring troubled credit unions back to financial health. The movement always sought to avoid liquidation of any credit union than could possibly be salvaged. At no point in credit union history was the difference between the conventional attitude of government and traditional financial institutions—and the credit union movement approach—more dramatically portrayed than in the Pennsylvania League's dispute with NCUA over the new federal share insurance.

The share insurance fight brought the Pennsylvania credit union movement one of its greatest moments of national leadership. While CUNA hesitated and carried on extensive debate over the best course of action, while other leagues voiced their helpless frustration, the Pennsylvania League, behind managing director Mike Judge and president Harold Brown, joined several of its member credit unions and filed a class-action suit against NCUA, Nickerson, and regional administrator Stephen Pirk.

The suit was filed by League counsel Floyd Tompkins of Clark, Ladner, Fortenbaugh & Young. He was assisted by David Jones, a colleague in the firm who was gradually assuming increased responsibility for the League's legal affairs. (By 1971 when the suit was filed, Jones and Tompkins were jointly writing the "Report of Counsel.") For the share insurance suit, they were also assisted by Richard Watt of the same firm. Their initial document concluded that:

> "The Administrator's practice of requiring certain Federal credit unions to agree to make certain periodic payments to regular reserve in excess of the schedule...and of requiring certain Federal credit unions to make lump sum payments to regular reserves as a condition to approval of their application for insurance violates the Federal Credit Union Act as well as his own regulations...."

The League joined with several of its member credit unions[1] in filing suit in the United States District Court, in and for the Eastern District of Pennsylvania [Civil Action 71-2754]. On November 13, 1971 the League obtained a temporary restraining order estopping all actions by NCUA which would lead to credit union liquidations. Specifically, NCUA was restrained from: rejecting any further applications for share insurance filed by any members of the plaintiff class; requiring any member of the plaintiff class to execute addenda (committing them to transfer funds to the regular reserve fund); effectively requiring plaintiffs to liquidate as an alternative to reapplication for share insurance.

Originally the class action was filed on behalf of the 180 credit unions in Pennsylvania that had been rejected for share insurance. In December, as negotiations with NCUA continued

1. Joining with the League were: Zion FCU, Philadelphia; Northampton County Teachers FCU, Easton; G.S.M.I. FCU, Philadelphia; American Bakery Workers FCU, Philadelphia; Deliverance Evangelical FCU, Philadelphia; Turbo Machine Company Employees FCU, Lansdale; Lutheran FCU, Philadelphia; and Spitz Employees FCU, Chadds Ford. A second group of credit unions later agreed to join the suit. They included: Penn Trafford FCU; Mochem FCU; Fraternal Association of Steel Haulers FCU; Fox Grocery FCU; Heylpat FCU; Top Flight FCU; St. Paul's FCU; and Freihofer Employees FCU.

under court supervision, the suit was expanded to include all rejected federal credit unions in the United States.

While the suit was in progress, Congress considered a bill which would allow provisional share insurance for all federal credit unions for a period of two years. This bill was strongly opposed by the National Association of Federal Credit Unions. Most NAFCU members were the larger, wealthier urban federal credit unions. NAFCU agreed with NCUA and sought to minimize share insurance premiums rather than to maximize service to the credit union movement. Ironically, some of the larger NAFCU member federal credit unions subsequently drew extensively on the fund, generating greater expenses than the combined liabilities of the smaller groups NAFCU had sought to exclude.

The provisional share insurance law passed. It provided a two-year grace period during which rejected credit unions could bring themselves within NCUA standards. During the same period, NCUA promulgated a series of regulations providing for notice, hearings, and reviews before suspending or revoking charters because of uninsurability. NCUA also published new regulations covering and clarifying their reserve requirements.

When NCUA finally filed an official answer to the League's complaint, it was able to argue that all demands by the League had been met. As League Counsel reported: "In effect NCUA says—you have gotten what you asked for and the suit should be ended. League counsel substantially agrees."

On January 3, 1972, the Administrator of NCUA issued provisional certificates of insurance to 138 federal credit unions in Pennsylvania that had previously failed to qualify for the program. Without intervention by the Pennsylvania League, these credit unions would have been forced to transfer additional funds to regular reserves immediately, and if unable to do so, would have been forced to liquidate. The League mobilized its field force who worked tirelessly under director of field services Jim Findlay to assist all credit unions with provisional coverage to qualify for permanent share insurance.

Joseph Matisko served as president of the Pennsylvania Credit Union League, 1974–1976.

Only three months later, 16 of those credit unions had fully qualified and received permanent insurance certificates. Five more credit unions had completed restructuring their accounts and reapplied for the insurance. In addition, 25 Pennsylvania credit unions had been sent new applications by NCUA with a request that they resubmit "as the examiner and Regional Office believe that they can qualify for permanent insurance." The other 92 credit unions were receiving assistance and special guidance from the League so that by the expiration of the two-year grace period, they too would be qualified for the program and able to avoid liquidation.

Other direct and indirect results of the suit were many and complex. One credit union that had filed for voluntary liquidation as a result of NCUA orders was able to withdraw its application and return to business. More significantly, NCUA and its administrator learned that the credit union movement would not unquestioningly accept its actions and edicts.

In the "Report of the Managing Director" to the board, April 20, 1972, Judge, with typical generosity, gave special

William Seanor served as president of the Pennsylvania Credit Union League, 1976–1978.

recognition to the legal team which had guided the League through the suit. "We can all be thankful for that great team headed by Floyd W. Tompkins and his colleagues, David M. Jones and Edward C. Toole, Jr."

The Pennsylvania League earned the confidence of its own members that the League would challenge even the federal government when credit union interests were at stake. Similarly, the Pennsylvania League and its managing director earned the respect of other state leagues and of CUNA. That was acknowledged in resolutions from CUNA and the Florida Credit Union League commending Pennsylvania for its leadership, industry, and outstanding effort.

CUNA provided background information and moral support, and along with many state Leagues later made substantial voluntary contributions to help Pennsylvania pay the extensive legal bills incurred in the share insurance dispute.

The successful suit brought honor to the Pennsylvania League and national prominence to Managing Director

Michael Casper served as president (chairman of the board) of the Pennsylvania Credit Union League, 1978–1980.

Judge. Following completion of the legal battle, Judge emerged as the strong and respected leader of the Pennsylvania movement and a successor in his own right to the tradition established by Pratt, Moore, and other national leaders from Pennsylvania. In 1972, he was elected president of the International Association of Managing Directors. In 1974, he was elected chairman of the board of the new United States Central Credit Union. Just as Pottiger, Pratt, Moore, Noble and other Pennsylvania credit union leaders had used national office to strengthen their own positions with the League, so too Judge became a stronger League managing director through this national recognition.

EVEN WHILE THE League was in the midst of its battle with NCUA, it was making major staff changes of its own. Doris Ellis was promoted to director of public relations, replacing Gerry Heberling in December 1971. She had been Heberling's assistant since May 1970. Before that,

377

Joseph Finn served as chairman of the board of the Pennsylvania Credit Union League, 1980–1982.

Ellis had worked with Dun & Bradstreet as a reporter, in the advertising department of Pomeroy's Department store, and as advertising manager for Leinhardt Brothers of Hanover and York. Richard Ebeling was hired to replace her as public relations assistant in January 1972. A former junior high school English teacher, Ebeling had been a communications assistant with Capital Blue Cross in Harrisburg and the owner-editor of *Travel Time*.

With Ebeling taking some of the responsibility for *Key Notes* and other publications, Ellis was freer to concentrate on League participation in the newly endorsed National Advertising Program (NAP). Just as Pennsylvania had shouldered a major part of the financial support for the old "POP" program, so, too, did the League move quickly to the fore in supporting this new advertising activity. The League was already conducting a statewide advertising program on behalf of its credit unions. When CUNA announced its new NAP, the Pennsylvania League quickly cooperated, incorporating its

378

own activities into the CUNA program. Thus was created the State & National Advertising Program (SNAP), and the League continued its tradition of outstanding support for the national advertising program, a tradition dating back to the Pratt years and CUNA's first national advertising efforts.[2]

THE SUDDEN FLASH flooding hit without warning early Thursday, June 22, 1972. The handful of employees who had been able to get through to the League office that morning were sent home shortly after their arrival as reports of collapsing bridges and flooding roads were broadcast by local radio stations. The rain-swollen Susquehanna River and its muddy tributaries were overflowing their banks, spreading destruction and devastation.

This was only the beginning. Hurricane Agnes, the Flood of '72, was to become the worst natural disaster ever to hit the Harrisburg area and much of the rest of the Northeast.

The day after the river crested at more than 33 feet (it floods at 18 feet), managing director Judge secured a pass which allowed him to go into the riverfront section to investigate what damage, if any, the water had done to League headquarters. He recalled hearing that the last major flood in 1936 had left the building untouched and he hoped that history would repeat itself. Instead, his investigation revealed that the entire basement of 4309 North Front had been flooded with water six feet deep. Much of the damage had been caused when the drainage system designed to let water out of the basement backed up and let the flood waters in.

Pacul Supply inventory had filled most of the basement. It was a complete loss. That could be replaced. Gone forever were countless historical records which had been stored in the basement. They included memorabilia and other materi-

2. Among the first Pennsylvania credit unions contributing to NAP were Altoona Sacred Heart FCU, C-B Grove City FCU, McKinney-Scranton FCU, and P.R.R. FCU. League Past President Lee Sell was appointed by CUNA as one of five trustees for the NAP fund.

als dating back to the birth of the credit union movement in Pennsylvania. Caught in the flood, those priceless materials had been turned into soggy pulp.

Some League records had been removed by William Pratt when, as director of research and development, he began work on the history of the Pennsylvania League. At his retirement, some of those records were returned to the League but most were removed to his home. Tragically they were stored in the basement of his home and they too were destroyed by the flood waters. As a result, some episodes and aspects of the history of the Pennsylvania credit union movement had passed beyond retrieval.

When Harrisburg streets were opened once again, those employees that could do so returned to work. People who had been hired to do office work pitched in wholeheartedly in the effort to clear the destruction and debris from the premises. They formed a "bucket brigade" and passed plastic bags, heavy with ruined operations forms, records, and other documents up the stairwell from Pacul Supply to the parking lot at the rear of the building. After five days, they had a pile of slimy, soggy pulp more than 30 feet long, 15 feet wide, and more than nine feet high at its center. Judge, who had long before worked on construction projects, once again found himself digging and shoveling. He remembers those days vividly:

> "We were down, I guess, almost two weeks.... Our supply operation had been totally put out of business. We got completely wiped out there. We took the loss. We had no insurance.[3] We got many offers for assistance, but we never really had to take anyone up on them. The Maryland League offered us the use of their facilities if we had to relocate.
>
> "The best thing is that no credit union people were killed or seriously injured. Fortunately very few credit unions were

3. The Small Business Administration provided low-interest loans to many of the victims of the flood. The League took full advantage of that program and used federal funds to help replace damaged and destroyed equipment and to re-stock the lost inventory.

380

actually hurt. There were a few up in Wilkes-Barre that really got hurt, and several in Johnstown, but only one or two lost records. Most of them got their records out before the flood hit. We were really surprised. We and NCUA got in touch with them as soon as we could, because we were really concerned. But very few of them had any difficulty. They came through it OK.

"The employees were great. They got through here and went out to help Lucy Smith and Gladys Krout and Agnes Beistline. Their homes were hit worse than the League.[4]

Jim Findlay stayed the whole day when the waters were coming up. He made sure that everyone else was OK and that the building was secured. When he closed up, there was no water in the basement at all. It looked like we were going to be Ok. I tried to come in on a boat that Gladys Krout's son had, but they wouldn't let us launch it.

NCUA regional director Joseph Bellenghi and a group of his examiners established a temporary headquarters in Wilkes-Barre to aid credit unions in their salvage operations. They were assisted by a group of volunteers including League directors Joseph Matisko and Patricia Doyle. Philadelphia and Erie chapters sent financial contributions and offered the help of their members to the League and to affected credit unions. In all, it was a remarkable demonstration of the spirit of cooperation and brotherhood that is a basic part of the credit union concept.

THE LEAGUE WAS back to business as usual three weeks after the flood. Carl Rabold, administrative assistant, had left League employment shortly before the waters rose and bookkeeper Phyllis Meeker took early retirement. With the flood long gone, Judge was able to turn his attention to rebuilding his staff.

---

4. Smith, Krout and Beistline suffered extensive losses from flood waters in Harrisburg. In Wilkes-Barre, field representative Jack Barth was completely wiped out.

The flood of 1972, resulting from the rains of Hurricane Agnes, caused great destruction at the League. The entire staff joined in the clean-up.

Gary Keisling was brought in as League accountant, Andrea Bair as executive secretary and Richter L. Voight to fill the new position of technical writer. Voight's primary responsibility was to update and revise the League's *Information Manual*, the vital guide provided to all member credit unions. Previously employed in the Pennsylvania Senate library, he soon became deeply involved in the eventually successful efforts to amend the Pennsylvania Credit Union Act in 1974. His job title was changed to legislative/information specialist, and after passage of the Federal Election Campaign Act Voight helped the League create its political action committee, PACULAC. Jim Findlay was promoted to assistant managing director and field representative Jack Barth was brought to League headquarters to replace Findlay as director of field services. In turn, Barth was replaced in the field by Raymond Gagnon (now deceased), and Charles Gemberling. When Maurice Roberts left the League, Ebeling shifted to education specialist.

PACUL SERVICES, INC., the for-profit corporate affiliate of the Pennsylvania Credit Union League, took its modern form in 1973 through a reorganization which merged three separate special-purpose subsidiaries. Each of the older subsidiary corporations became a division of Pacul Services at that time.

There was nothing conceptually new about the service corporation that was formed in 1973. That it was the responsibility of the organized credit union movement to provide support materials and services to credit unions is an idea dating back to the earliest days of the Credit Union National Extension Bureau founded by Edward Filene and Roy Bergengren in 1921. Even then Filene and Bergengren had realized that such activities would provide credit unions with a low-cost, efficient source of needed goods and services and that it would simultaneously provide the organized credit union movement with an independent source of income. That was especially important to Filene, the financier behind CUNEB.

383

In Pennsylvania, H. Andrew Hanemann's earliest correspondence seeking members for the new League suggested that the organization would become a source for supplies as well as technical assistance. Hanemann was not particularly successful in recruiting members, possibly because the League was not yet equipped to provide much more than booklets with reprints of speeches by Filene and Bergengren. Hanemann had continued to argue that through cooperation in a League, Pennsylvania credit unions would gain improved purchasing power.

Those were simple times, less encumbered than our own with regulations and tax laws. The Pennsylvania League, like many other state leagues and CUNA itself was legally able to provide a full range of services within the single organization. As CUNA Supply Cooperative developed (under the leadership of Pennsylvania voting delegate Mattis Pottiger), the League was able to increase its services to members—and its own income —through supply activities.

The operation was not elaborate. In Philadelphia, Mario Cervone and part-time assistant Willie Pratt (son of managing director William W. Pratt) were able to handle most of the labor. The operation was housed in a closet of the one-room League headquarters. Cervone went into military service for World War II and the supply operation all but closed for the duration. It was handled by one part-time worker and by the League office manager. When Lucy Smith joined the staff, she became the bookkeeper and shipping clerk for Pacul Supply as well as the secretary and entire office staff for the League.

In the late 1950s, CUNA Supply Cooperative decided to formalize its relationships with all of the state league supply operations. As part of this effort, CUNA suggested that the leagues consider separating their supply functions from other activities to protect the nonprofit status of the leagues themselves. In Pennsylvania, that advice was rejected. League leaders felt that such elaborate legal structures were too fancy and unnecessary.

At the time, gross annual sales of supplies amounted to less

384

than $6,000 and produced a profit of $968. "It hardly seems likely to create a problem," wrote League counsel Tompkins to executive director Pratt in March 1959.

CUNA Supply Cooperative lost its tax-exempt status in 1963, leading Pratt to call for a reexamination of the entire issue. It was the time when Pratt was losing his power over the League, and president Summers insisted that he personally would direct the review of supply activities and the relationship of the supply function to other League undertakings.

At the October 1964 meeting of the board, the directors passed a resolution initiating the incorporation of the supply operation. Pacul Supply, Inc. was officially created January 1, 1965.

CUNA Supply immediately adopted the new corporation as its "supply depot" for Pennsylvania. The negotiations were not easy. As always, relationships between the Pennsylvania League and the national association involved jealously guarded prerogatives. There were questions about the League's continued freedom to pursue it own marketing activities and about the extent of League financial responsibility for the affairs of CUNA Supply which was chartered under Wisconsin law as a cooperative corporation. The contract, when finally approved, became the forerunner for the marketing agreements which continue to define the commercial relationship between CUNA and the League.

The relationship between Pacul Supply and CUNA Supply Cooperative proved profitable for both. At the founding of Pacul Supply, Inc., there had been some concern about the financial strength of the new corporation. By 1967 the League's major financial concern about its subsidiary involved appropriate ways to allocate Pacul Supply, Inc. earnings.

Evolution of the second major component of Pacul Services, CUEDS Division, was similar to that of its corporate predecessor in some respects. The League began offering data processing services in 1967. Computer technology was still in its infancy, and few people realized just how important the new technology would eventually become. League leaders did, however, realize that assuming responsibility for credit union records involved potential liabilities far beyond the character and charter of Pacul Supply. Accordingly, they formed a new corporation, CUEDS Inc. Under its own charter, its responsibilities included providing Pennsylvania's credit unions with comprehensive computerized communications. CUEDS thus became responsible for keeping the Pennsylvania credit union movement up-to-date with the technological revolution.

The third arm of Pacul Services was created in 1967 to house the complex operations of the stabilization fund. At the time, the League's board of directors was contemplating purchase of a bank to handle and house the Pennsylvania credit union movement's increasingly complex stabilization operations. This creative and imaginative approach to high finance would, they thought, provide a home for the stabilization fund and for the investment activities of credits unions throughout the state. They formed a corporation under the name Pacul Services, Inc. as a corporate home for the bank and to handle stabilization or other financial services. The directors investigated Dauphin Deposit and Trust Company in Harrisburg and considered possible purchase of Keystone Trust Company and Reading's Knoblauch Bank. Even though the bank purchase never took place, the new corporation assumed responsibility for all League subsidiary activities that were neither supply related nor involved with electronic data processing.

In 1971, League counsel initiated proposals to streamline these different activities. Restructuring, Tompkins argued, would "improve the quality of...services, result in economies in administration, accounting and taxes and provide greater revenue-producing potential...." In March, 1973, the League's three service subsidiaries were merged into one corporation.

Because it had experienced substantial losses, losses that were valuable assets from the viewpoint of taxation, the surviving corporation was CUEDS, Inc., chartered in Delaware.

386

The name of the corporation was changed to Pacul Services, Inc. The old Pacul Services charter was terminated, along with the charter of Pacul Supply, Inc.

A T THE APRIL 1974 reorganization meeting of the board, Joseph Matisko of Edwardsville was elected League president. An officer of his own Hazard Wire Rope Division FCU since 1949 and treasurer of the Triangle Employees Credit Union since 1972, Matisko was a recipient of the National Credit Union Administration's Award of Merit and the CUNA Mutual Insurance Program Award. Other officers elected without opposition included: William Seanor, first vice president; Michael Casper, second vice president; and Joseph D. Finn, treasurer. Robert F. Neubaum was elected secretary in a contest with Anthony Bartock.

The meeting marked a transition for the board as an unusual number of directors were leaving. Two past presidents, John McCullough and William Noble, retired from the board. Both had been powerful and influential leaders. Noble was a 25-year veteran of the board, and he was honored by unprecedented election as "Senior Advisor to the League Board."

One of Noble's primary commitments had been to keeping the Pennsylvania League at the forefront of credit union educational activities, a role he assumed when E. A. Thompson retired. The Credit Union Institute at Penn State University was initiated while Noble was president. He was also the founder of the Management Conference; the first of these popular and productive annual meetings was held during his presidency.[5]

New members of the 1974 board included: Kenneth L. Morrow of New Castle, District 2; James E. Springer of Warren, District 5; Edward A. Colgan, Jr. of Philadelphia (a former League field representative), District 6; Michael J. Symons of

5. In 1983 the Management Conference was split into a Managers Conference and a Presidents Conference.

387

Bethlehem, District 7; Josephine O. Frazier of Camp Hill, District 8; and Carl W. Knowlden of South Williamsport, District 10.

About this time a new name was appearing with increasing frequency in *Key Notes* and other credit union movement publications. Neither a member of the League staff nor a director, James McCormack was the first chairperson of the Pennsylvania League's new Youth Involvement Board (YIB). As such, he was writing for different publications and accepting speaking engagements throughout the state. In 1974 McCormack represented Pennsylvania at the National YIB Conference. In 1975 he was honored as Outstanding Delegate and elected to the national YIB executive committee. He later resigned from the state and national YIB positions to accept employment as a CUNA Mutual field representative in the Pittsburgh area, and was later promoted to a post at the national headquarters in Madison. In May 1981, McCormack was appointed vice president, finance and administration of the Pennsylvania League, a position he currently holds.

At the 1976 reorganization meeting, the board elected William Seanor of Greensburg as the new League president. Seanor had been treasurer of Westmoreland Federal Employees FCU since 1942. He was also a member of Pennsylvania Central FCU and of Pittsburgh Officers FCU. A former letter carrier and civil service examiner, Seanor had retired from the postal service in June 1974 to devote his full-time efforts to his credit union. At the conclusion of his second term as League president, Seanor made a strong but unsuccessful bid for the post of secretary of CUNA.

Other officers elected included: Michael Casper, first vice president; Joseph Finn, second vice president; Robert Neubaum, treasurer; and Robert Hendrickson, secretary. Two new members of the board of directors were seated at the April annual meeting; Kathryn M. Schmidt, Springfield, from District 6 and Raymond R. Barber, Erie, from District 1. Schmidt was loan officer for Philadelphia Telco FCU and a member of four other credit unions. Barber had previously

Robert Neubaum served as chairman of the Board of the Pennsylvania Credit Union League, 1982–1984.

served on the board 1967-1974. He was treasurer-manager of Rubber Employees FCU in Erie and a past president of the Erie Chapter.

One other critical shift in League personnel was also taking place. Floyd Tompkins had served as League counsel since the 1940s. While he and his firm continued to fulfill that function, ever since the share insurance suit he had been sharing League affairs with colleagues. David M. Jones had assisted him in 1971 and 1972; A. D. Kerr and Joseph Duffy in 1973; J. F. McMullen, Jr. in 1974 and 1975. Anthony A. Geyelin[6] and Joseph Duffy shared the responsibility from 1976, but increasingly it was Duffy who assumed primary responsibility. Tompkins was still available for occasional consultation, but by the end of the decade Duffy had taken over responsibility

6. Geyelin later left the firm to become counsel for the Pennsylvania Insurance Department and in October 1983 he was named insurance commissioner.

Joseph Duffy succeeded Floyd Tompkins as League Counsel in the mid-1970s and served until 1983.

for the League's legal affairs. Eventually Duffy's name replaced Tompkins' as League counsel in official publications.

When Pacul Services, Inc. reorganized in April 1976, Harold Brown was elected president of the service corporation; Lee Sell was elected vice president; Joseph Hinchey, secretary; and Charles Hill, treasurer. Brown and Sell were past presidents of the League. Hinchey's career included service as a federal credit union examiner as well as his tenure on the National Credit Union Board.

Pacul Services, Inc. added a new dimension to its activities when it provided a grant to finance the 1976 production of *Credit: The 6% Illusion*, a television program produced by Mark H. Dorfman and WITF-TV. The program was broadcast throughout the state by the Pennsylvania Public Television Network in January 1977. It was later broadcast by public television networks in other states and several other countries as well. A sequel, *Debt: The Grand Disillusion*, and a full-hour combined version of the documentaries were produced and broadcast in 1978. The programs starred Virginia Sassaman and John Lierzaph as a young couple with credit problems. Harrisburg Belco FCU Manager Lonnie Maurer played himself in the popular programs.

In January 1977, the League staff underwent a general reorganization. Gladys Krout retired as director of administrative services and the position was dissolved, its duties delegated to other staff. League assistant managing director James Findlay added the title and duties of assistant general manager of Pacul Services to his other responsibilities. Andrea Bair, formerly League executive secretary, became executive administrative assistant. Other staff changes included the promotion of Geraldine Livingston from group leader to supervisor, support services. Carol DeLuca was named assistant supervisor. Dean Carpenter, former systems analyst for CUEDS Division, became supervisor for the division and Ted Baldwin, former group leader for Pacul Supply, became supervisor for Supply Division. In 1977 Elizabeth Weimer joined the League as communications specialist. Other new staff joining the League included field representatives William Talada (l978), Lanny Horn, and Janet Kubica (1979). Roger Kelley succeeded Voight as legislative/information specialist in June 1979.

Michael Casper was elected League president at the 1978 organizational meeting. Casper first joined the board in 1957. He was treasurer of Doehler-Jarvis Pottstown FCU, a national director of CUNA, and a director of the Montgomery County Chapter which he helped organize. Casper was plant purchasing agent for the Doehler Jarvis Division, National Lead Company, Pottstown. Also elected as board officers at that meeting were: Joseph D. Finn, first vice-president; Robert F. Neubaum, second-vice president; Hugh Kelleher, secretary, and Robert L. Hendrickson, treasurer. Kelleher died suddenly two months later, shortly after helping in Seanor's unsuccessful bid for national office. M. Jane Bunch of Altoona Butterick FCU was elected to fill his seat on the board. Paul J. Rowland of Wilkes-Barre, a 30-year member of Wilkes-Barre Belco FCU, was the only new member of the board seated at the annual meeting.

League President Michael J. Judge was honored in his 25th year with the League, February 18, 1980, at the Hotel Hershey.

At the November 1978 meeting of the board of directors in Hershey, the board approved several bylaws amendments, including one which changed the title of the managing director to president, and the titles of the president, first vice president, and second vice president of the board of directors to chairman, first vice chairman, and second vice chairman. This brought League usage into concert with usage current at CUNA.[7]

The late 1970s were most notable throughout the credit union movement for the legislative battle over share drafts. Share drafts allowed members simple access to their dividend-paying share accounts. Functionally similar to bank checks, these negotiable instruments, new to the credit union

7. The title of the assistant managing director was also changed to vice president of the League. During a subsequent reorganization, department heads Doris Ellis and Jack Barth became vice president, communications and vice president, member services respectively. The title "field representative" was change to " consultant."

movement, were first given legal recognition by NCUA Administrator Nickerson. Subsequent rulings by both federal and state authorities indicated that credit unions could issue and accept share drafts.

Other trade associations sought to have this competitive threat regulated or legislated out of existence and an extended battle ensued. The Independent Bankers Association, the American Bankers Association and other similar groups brought suit against NCUA to stop the program. When enabling legislation was introduced in Congress, these organizations brought forth their considerable legislative experience and contacts. The credit union movement initiated a nationwide grass roots campaign to "Save Our Share Drafts."

The credit union movement won the battle and the uncontested right to use share drafts when President Jimmy Carter signed the appropriate legislation in 1980. Over the course of the legislative campaign, both the Pennsylvania and national legislatures acquired a new respect for the size and organizational ability of the credit union movement. The American Public Relations Society issued its Silver Anvil Award to CUNA for the comprehensive "Save Our Share Drafts" campaign.

The decade of the 1970s was an economically turbulent and troubled era. American consumers learned a whole new vocabulary and acquired new financial sophistication. They became acutely aware—to some extent overly aware—of interest rate differentials and advanced investment instruments. One result was a wave of disintermediation as consumers began removing funds from banks and credit unions, and investing directly in federal notes and other securities.

Banks, credit unions, and other thrift institutions began to compete directly with each other to offer new services and new investment opportunities. Through instruments like share drafts, the credit union movement saw itself competing with banks for a bigger slice of the thrift industry, Through legislation, reports from counsel, and NCUA rulings, the movement gradually broadened the common bond concept and expanded fields of membership.

"Once a member, always a member," long espoused by such Pennsylvania credit union leaders as Verner Porath, Bill Noble, Bill Pratt and others, became policy for federal credit unions in 1968. It was just the first of a long series of actions expanding membership privileges. Later rulings extended membership to all "blood relatives living under the same roof." Most recently, the concept has been broadened by NCUA to qualify the extended family of any credit union member for membership in the same organization.

At the same time, many federal credit unions are seeking conversions to community charters extending to broad geographical areas. Such charters make credit union service available to people who were not previously eligible for credit union membership. The concept behind the community charter dates back to the original credit unions chartered by Raiffeisen, but Pennsylvania state law does not currently permit them. While the original Pennsylvania Credit Union Act did allow community charters, they were written out in an early ammendment. An amendment introduced in 1983 would allow for state chartered community credit unions, but it is being actively contested by other banking and related trade associations.[8]

Recently, NCUA Chairman Edgar Callahan approved the concept of Select Employee Groups (SEG's). These broadly defined charters would allow expansion of existing charters to embrace other small groups that are not necessarily related to them and when misused, dilutes the common bond concept beyond recognition.

As originally structured, the SEG concept would have allowed unrelated groups to combine as a quasi-community, a special-purpose "common bond," and qualify for a federal charter. As applied, however, some larger, wealthy credit

8. The legislation was passed and signed into law by Governor Dick Thornburgh during International Credit Union month of the League's golden anniversary year.

unions have used the new provision to expand, absorbing groups that might well have qualified for their own charters. In many cases, they have even carefully excluded less wealthy groups or segments of their communities—people most in need of credit union service. Like the ideal of "unlimited liability," the "common bond" seems likely to become a victim to expediency and the drive to expand.

At the 1980 reorganization meeting, Joseph D. Finn of Philadelphia was elected chairman of the board. Finn was president of the NADC Federal Credit Union, Warminster (subsequently merged with Ft. Monmoth FCU in New Jersey), president of Fifth and Godfrey FCU, and a past president of the Philadelphia Chapter of the League. Also elected to board office at the meeting were: Robert Neubaum, first vice chairman; Robert Hendrickson, second vice chairman; Paul G. Demmer, treasurer; and Anthony Bartock, secretary.

Newly elected directors installed at the annual meeting included: Raymond Barber, District 1; John Filipiak, District 3; Coy R. Smith, District 8 (installed at the quarterly meeting to complete the unexpired term of M. Jane Bunch)[9]; and David L. Sleppy, District 9. Joseph Hinchey was elected chairman of the board of Pacul Services, Inc. Other Pacul Services officers who were elected included: Charles L. Hill, vice chairman; Kathryn Schmidt, secretary; Michael Symons, treasurer.

Four Pennsylvania credit union veterans, Floyd Tompkins, William Seanor, Dom Servillo, and Michael Judge became charter members of a new organization, the National Association of Retired Credit Union People, in early 1979. With the aging of the American population in general, and with so much dynamism and knowledge, and such a deep commitment to the ideals of the credit union movement among retired credit union leaders in particular, NARCUP promises

9. Bunch, elected to fill the vacancy created by the death of Kelleher, had resigned from the board to accept employment with Data Procession of the South (DPS), the data processing firm for CUEDS.

The second renovation of the League building was completed in 1974 with a major extension of the rear wing which had been added in 1961.

to become a powerful organization, both within the credit union movement and in the larger, external political arena.

The 1981 annual meeting will long be remembered in the Pennsylvania credit union movement for its angry debate over a projected change in the membership dues schedule. Approved by the full board of directors at the February quarterly meeting, the proposal called for a ten-year plan whereby the fee would be paid on the basis of gross income rather than net interest income—a return to the historically traditional basis for the fee. No credit union would pay less than the CUNA dues paid for each by the League; annual increases were limited by a strict formula; the maximum would gradually increase to $7,500 in 1991.

The proposal was overwhelmingly defeated by the delegates in attendance at the 1981 annual meeting. Subsequent revisions of the dues schedule were offered to the delegates at annual meetings in 1982 and 1983. As tempers and rhetoric

As the Pennsylvania credit union movement has grown, so has the League headquarters complex, shown here under renovation during the summer of 1983.

escalated, the membership fee schedule remained unchanged.

The problem had become more acute than the surface issue of the membership fee indicated. Once there had been two issues on which members could exercise frustrations: 1) the districting, apportionment, and election procedures for directors; 2) the membership fee. Once, directors were elected at the annual meeting. This allowed a full range of participation by the membership. Since then, as the foregoing chapters document, the selection of directors has become formalized and complex. Additional changes currently in process and likely to be adopted will make election of directors subject to a mail ballot. While this change will allow greater participation by credit unions in the democratic process, it will make the elections even more distant and aloof than they are now.

Similarly, rules surrounding resolutions and bylaw amendment have become increasingly restrictive over the years. League parliamentarians have traditionally acted to shut off

397

debate and maintain board control of proceedings. Recently the frustration level has risen to heights not seen since the schism of 1950. That anger and frustration took the form of bitter fighting and legal disputes in the Philadelphia Chapter, the creation of a rump organization which provided its own displays at the 1983 annual meeting, and finally exploded onto the floor in angry exchanges of temper and bitterness. The movement has been threatened by such internal dissent in the past; always it has managed to revive the spirit of cooperation in the interests of credit union unity.

In an extraordinary procedure planned to help heal the wounds of that unhappy annual meeting, the board had a special meeting on May 28, 1983. It resulted in terminating the legal services of counsel Joseph H. Duffy and the League's contract with Clark, Ladner, Fortenbaugh & Young, a contract that dated back to the original incorporation of the Pennsylvania Credit Union League. The board directed that an attorney be hired as vice president, legal & government affairs to assume the duties of League counsel.

In 1984 the Pennsylvania Credit Union League celebrates its fiftieth anniversary, yet the divisions which have always been part of the Pennsylvania credit union movement are still present. Small credit unions and large still have different, sometimes conflicting, needs and expectations. There are few rural credit unions and their requirements are rarely recognized by the urban-dominated board. The big and wealthy credit unions, primarily those from the eastern part of the state, still clash with the "country boys" from the balance of the Commonwealth, just as they did in 1936.

Ironically, many of the Pennsylvania credit union movement's most dynamic and influential leaders in recent times have come from among the "country boys." Without the spirit of compromise and understanding that has traditionally been part of the movement's history, many of these leaders would have been denied an opportunity to serve. Without their dedicated efforts, the Pennsylvania credit union movement would have been significantly weaker.

By 1984, the League and Pacul Services employee group had grown to include, from left, seated or kneeling: Betsy Mallison, Kati Shoop, Pauline Umlauf, Sherri Chrisemer, Doris Ellis, Gerry Livingston, Lori Gray, Andrea Bair, James McCormack. First row, standing: Pamela Peck, Roger Kelley, Tami Schmick, Michael Judge, Jack Barth, Susan Downs, Carol Sheetz, Joli Ickes, Ted Baldwin, Robert Besko, Frank Snavely, Elizabeth Weimer, Richard Ebeling. Standing on first step: Karin Guerrini, Carol DeLuca, Pearl Hoffman, Janet Johnson. On top two steps: Susan Gabel, Doris McCormick, Cathy Peters, Eryl Pettit, Pauline Wood, Kathy Nies, Ronald Malatesta, Cathy Miller. Missing from photo are Dean Carpenter, Linda Heberling, Teri Rissel.

Robert Neubaum, active in the Pennsylvania movement since 1934, was elected chairman of the board at the reorganization meeting in 1982. He has been an officer and member of the Harrisburg Postal Employees Credit Union, the Harrisburg Consumers Cooperative FCU and the Pennsylvania Cen-

tral FCU. A director of the League since 1968, Neubaum was awarded the NCUA Award of Merit in 1974, only the second member of a state chartered credit union to be so honored. Other officers elected at the meeting were: Robert Hendrickson first vice chairman; Paul Demmer, second vice chairman; Anthony Bartock, treasurer; and Kenneth L. Morrow, secretary. All table officers were reelected in 1983. New members of the board of directors seated in 1982 and 1983 were Harry Hahn, District 1; John Gulick, District 4; Val McGrogran, District 8; and Donald Graham and Alice Rossell, District 6.

John Gulick was elected to complete the term of Regis Lawley who died in January 1983. Val McGrogan filled the unexpired term of Josephine Frazier, who retired following the 1983 annual meeting.

Throughout this period, League activities continued to expand. The League became increasingly involved in the SNAP advertising program, substantially increasing the direct involvement in individual, interested credit unions. In a directed development, Pacul Services initiated a new advertising and marketing program program to offer member

400

Originating with a four-page mimeographed newsletter back in 1936, the publications program of the Pennsylvania Credit Union League has become a valued function of the Pennsylvania credit union movement.

credit unions individual assistance with their own marketing activites. The League's advertising program continued to attract national attention, winning numerous CUNA "Blockbuster" awards for advertising in all media.

New publications during the last decade include *Keystone Extra*, a short lead-time newsletter issued to provide up-to-date information to Pennsylvania credit unions and *Keystone Stats* which serves a similar but more specialized function, concerning itself with Pennsylvania and national credit union statistics and trends. Like the advertising program, the League's publications and public relations programs became consistent winners of CUNA "PRO" awards for "Best Public Relations Project" and "Best Public Relations Program."

The traditionally extensive League program of educational offerings has been greatly expanded. That program now annually includes: six officers' forums; the marketing institute at Penn State University; conferences for credit union employees, managers, and presidents; a series of special interest seminars; and the recently created credit union attorney's conference. Former league counsel Floyd Tompkins died in

The League's 13 consultants and their supervisor take a brief recess from their 1984 staff conference. From left, they are, front row: George Shevenock; Jack Barth, vice president, Member Services; William Dooner; Lanny Horn; Janet Kubica; William Talada; Al Garttmeier and Kenneth Noca. Rear row: Edwin Mailander; Ronald Schueler; Paul Sullivan; James Ritter; William Harmon and Charles Gemberling.

1983, just months before the first attorney's conference was scheduled to be held. In his honor, that conference was named the Floyd Tompkins Memorial Conference for Credit Union Attorneys.

Several new professional positions have been created as the League staff has expanded its efforts to help credit unions meet the increasingly complex demands of the contemporary thrift environment. New posts include additions to the field staff, an education specialist, a technical information special-

President Lyndon B. Johnson greets League Managing Director Michael Judge in the White House at the signing ceremony for the Credit Union Omnibus Bill, December 13, 1967.

ist, and a director of research and development. The service corporation has added an advertising/marketing specialist and an automated teller machine (ATM) and auditing service.

In 1983 the League completed the latest of its physical expansion programs, adding a third floor to the North Front Street headquarters complex. The expansion had been in planning and development stages for several years. Expansion was required not only to house the growing League staff, but also to house the CUNA Mutual Eastern District headquarters which occupies rented offices in the League building. The plan finally adopted was but the latest of several proposals. One alternate actually adopted by the board but never implemented called for construction of a wing connecting the current headquarters with a neighboring structure also owned by the League and since demolished. The newly expanded complex provides adequate space for existing League, CUNA

403

Credit Union Day at the Ballgame was an annual League tradition in Philadelphia and Pittsburgh in the 1970's.

Mutual, and Pacul Services staff as well as space for eventual future expansion if needed.

Recent appointments to League staff include: field consultants William Harmon and Ronald Schueler; Harmon took over the area served by Carmine Dorazio (deceased) and Schueler succeeds former YIB chairperson Bill Allmann who had stepped in for the accident-disabled Joe Shanosky. Allmann was one of the first credit union leaders to achieve Certified Credit Union Executive status under a new national educational program. He left the field service in 1983 to manage a credit union. Ronald Malatesta, a 20-year veteran with NCUA, remained in Harrisburg as League education specialist when the agency moved its Region II offices to Washington. Other recent appointees are: public relations specialist Mary Mallison; technical information specialist Robert Beskovoyne; and director of research and special projects Theresa A. Rissell.

As a goal for 1984, the League board has approved a credit union needs and attitudes audit which will be conducted by

The directors of the Pennsylvania Credit Union League, 1983–84, include, seated from left: Kenneth L. Morrow, secretary; Anthony E. Bartock, treasurer; Robert L. Hendrickson, first vice chairman; Robert F. Neubaum, chairman of the board; Paul G. Demmer, second vice chairman; Joseph F. Hinchey, chairman, Pacul Services, Inc. First row, standing: Richard J. Ritter; Harry J. Hahn; Charles L. Hill; Val J. McGrogan; Patricia Doyle; John Filipiak; Alice Rossell; Michael W. Schultz; William C. Seanor; Edward A. Colgan. Back row: Donald W. Graham; Paul J. Rowland; Michael Casper; John J. Monico; Coy R. Smith; Raymond R. Barber; Vincent J. Golletti; John W. Gulick; Andrew L. Kulik; David L. Sleppy. Missing from photo: Josephine Sakovics, Michael J. Symons.

Robert Charles Associates. Charles was with Michener Associates when the League completed its first marketing study in 1970. This study will provide direction and guide long-range planning for the League and Pacul Services, Inc. as the

Pennsylvania credit union movement prepares for the twenty-first century.

On the national legislative front, the League helped in the extended battle opposing 10% withholding of interest on behalf of the Internal Revenue Service. This battle was a rare instance in which all American thrift institutions and their diverse trade associations were able to work together. Their cooperation succeded in stimulating the repeal measure and obtaining the reluctant approval of President Ronald Reagan who had originally demanded the withholding requirement. But that uneasy alliance has already collapsed, as credit unions face a heated battle against demands that they be taxed on an equal basis with the privately owned, for-profit thrift institutions. Resisting that effort will require a united credit union movement, dedicated to its historic mission as well as to future needs.

The League's directors and staff, both newcomers and veterans, will have responsibility for guiding and assisting Pennsylvania credit unions through the 1980s and on into the future. December 1984 marks the half-century anniversary of the Pennsylvania Credit Union League. Current leaders of the Pennsylvania credit union movement inherit more than sixty years of state credit union history and over a century of international credit union tradition.

With it they also inherit an opportunity for the future and an obligation to the past.

Postlude

"A credit union exists for the welfare of its members. When it forgets this and becomes a business enterprise, it is doomed to ignominius obscurity.... The chief danger credit unions face is the loss of the cooperative spirit."

Richard Y. Giles
Credit for the Millions

THE PENNSYLVANIA CREDIT UNION movement was created through a remarkable cooperative effort. It required the dedicated work of Roy Bergengren and Agnes Gartland, the financial backing of Edward A. Filene, the untiring efforts of many state and local leaders who were interested in seeing credit unions in the Commonwealth and the support of leaders from agriculture, industry, manufacturing, and organized labor. Long-term economic and political natural enemies accepted a temporary truce to help Pennsylvania start its credit unions. Professional rivals cooperated instead of undercutting each other. National, regional, and local jealousies were temporarily shelved.

Just as the international credit union movement was built on the concept of the common bond, credit union pioneers worked to reach a common goal.

The Pennsylvania credit union movement was built by rank financial amateurs. People like Joe Moore, Matt Pottiger, and Bill Pratt had no knowledge of economics and even less business experience. They learned the hard way. It was hard on them, and hard on the movement. More experienced, more skillful leadership might have built faster and more efficiently. But they would not have created as fascinating a structure. Those early leaders were usually aware of their own limitations. They knew that they lacked education and technical expertise. They trusted in God and in their own common sense. And they were possessed with the zeal of missionaries.

The second generation of leadership was less ignorant but also less in touch with their mission. They responded to different priorities. They were concerned less with the movement and more with their own welfare and the welfare of their credit unions. Gone was the exuberance of the at-large election of directors at the annual meeting. In its place came back-room caucuses, pomp and privilege.

A sense of vital unity still held the alliance intact. Many times the movement seemed to be on the verge of destroying itself. Philosophical differences, personal jealousies, ego conflicts, ethnic and regional differences and country-boy/city-boy feuds all threatened to ambush unity.

The current generation of leaders is different from its predecessors. It is more professional, more educated, more experienced in financial management and more sophisticated in political affairs. In the League and the statewide movement, today's volunteer and professional leaders control a $3 billion institution that is powerful and efficient, but one that still carries extraordinary potential for improving the human condition.

The Pennsylvania credit union movement is at a crossroads. It is internally torn in an institutional identity crisis. It must decide whether to abandon its heritage and become an indistinguishable part of the thrift industry landscape, or to rededicate itself to to the achievement of the movement's basic philosophical goals by adapting its newfound skills to the new technologies in a deregulated environment.

The alternative is for the movement to split. Pennsylvania

League president Judge is one who reluctantly acknowledges the possibility of such a divided future:

> "We will have very large credit unions with many branches, sub-divisions of those credit unions. These could be crossing state lines, certainly crossing district lines. We will have a mishmash of boundaries. And if we want to stick strictly to political areas, it would be difficult to evaluate what is happening in a particular district.
>
> "I think also we're going to have some consolidation of leagues in the future. Maybe fewer leagues, but yet service arms of a regional league or a regional corporate structure, with each league area having its own service arm as part of a regional concept.
>
> "That will happen ultimately because of the economies that will be required. The one major thrust bringing that about, I think, is really within the political structure of our movement. Being able to move the elected leadership to recognize that maybe the loss of a political position is not that bad if it's going to assist the development of the credit unions and services to the members.
>
> "There will always be a group of small credit unions.... the credit union that is relating more specifically and directly to the individual member on a local level. First of all there's too much pride in the individuals who are operating individual credit unions ... the good that they can see that they are doing. They don't want the influence of the large credit unions. As long as that pride is there, it's going to preserve its services. They don't want to deal with the outside service.
>
> "So even though we're going to have a lot of large credit unions, we are still going to have a lot of small credit unions operating throughout the state."

Pennsylvania League chairman of the board Robert Neubaum fears such division. He sadly notes the increasing loss of the credit union movement's unique vocabulary, words that have come from its traditions and help constitute its heritage. "Share drafts" all too easily become "checks." Where the distinction between "shares" and "deposits" or "dividends" and "interest" was once a vital issue (as outlined in the first two chapters of this book), now it is seen as meaningless and increasingly ignored.

The unique credit union vocabulary exists because of the credit union mission. It distinguishes credit union members (owners) from a bank's customers. It represents the credit union promise to bridge the gap between borrower and lender. At stake are individual freedom and cooperative dignity. These are not esoteric, semantic distinctions. They symbolize the heart of the credit union movement. Without them, Edward Filene would never have become interested in credit unions.

Ironically, the common bond has itself become a divisive issue. Under President Reagan's concept of deregulation as administered by Edgar Callahan's administration at NCUA, credit unions are being freed to compete with banks by, in effect, becoming banks. Many welcome the opportunity, seeking only that their neighboring credit unions be prevented from competing with them. The threat is that as some credit unions become larger, more powerful, and indistinguishable from banks, all credit unions will lose the tax exemptions and other privileges historically granted to American cooperatives, concessions that have allowed the cooperative movement to exist. The threat is also that the credit union movement will lose its sense of mission and its philosophy, those intangible but priceless assets that have given the movement its vitality.

Fifty years from now, another historian will write the centennial history of the Pennsylvania credit union movement. It has been my privilege to comment on the work of giants, of Schulze-Delitzsch and Desjardins, of Filene and Bergengren, of Connor, Pratt, Moore, Pottiger, Noble, Lawry, and the others. Someone else will tell the story and evaluate the records of those who sit in the board rooms and conference rooms today and lead the movement on to the new millenium.

A Note on the Sources

THE HARRISBURG FLOOD of 1972 destroyed many of the historical records and much of the memorabilia of the Pennsylvania credit union movement. Among the lost materials are the annual meeting booklets with their reports by officers and committee chairpersons. Also lost were all filed correspondence by William W. Pratt and Julia Connor.

Fortunately the minutes of League annual meetings and open meetings of the board of directors survived. These are securely maintained at League headquarters. Some other records have also survived from the early years of the League, preserved by past president Art Thompson and now retained in the League's reference library.

The papers of William Lawry and Joseph Moore are also now housed by the League. Moore's papers include notes and texts for his frequent speeches, as well as papers relating to his long tenure as a national director. Lawry's papers contain some especially valuable materials relating to the League's service corporation as well as the records of his tenure on the personnel committee.

Other surviving materials kept by the League include clipping files and memorabilia from International Credit Union Day celebrations, and complete runs of League publicatons such as *Key Notes*. The League also maintains files of *Credit Union Magazine* and other CUNA publicatons.

Research for the chapter about the campaign for the Pennsylvania Credit Union Act drew heavily from the papers of Gifford Pinchot housed at the Manuscript Division of the Library of Congress. Pinchot retained the orginals of all correspondence as well as copies of most of his replies. The collection is extensive and well calendared. It proved valuable not only for correspondence from Bergengren and Gartland at CUNEB, but also for correspondence from Filene and other supporters of the legislation. The Pinchot papers also yielded valuable correspondence with Edward Filene, Charles McCarthy, Sir Horace Plunkett, Louis Brandeis and other progressive, cooperative, and credit union leaders.

Many principal sources for this work are housed at the Information Resource Center of the National Credit Union Administration, home of the Bergengren and Filene collections. CUNA also has the minutes of its own executive committee and board of directors and a complete file of *The Bridge*. The papers of John Eidam also yielded some valuable materials. Also housed at the CUNA research libarary are copies of much of the correspondence of Alphonse Desjardins. Since I did not have access to the originals, this material was most useful.

CUNA Mutual Insurance Society files include transcripts of recorded interviews with Mattis Pottiger, Pratt (with Lucy Smith), and Moore. In addition, the author recorded interviews with Art Thompson, Dorothy Pratt, John McCullough, and Michael Judge. These interviews have not been transcribed, although some recorded comments are quoted in the preceding text. Unrecorded interviews were also conducted with Lucy Smith, Louise Herring, Frank Wielga, Bob Neubaum, and other credit union pioneers and leaders.

There are relatively few helpful works specifically on Pennsylvania credit unions. Three particularly useful articles include: "The Credit Union Movement in Pennsylvania," *Pennsylvania Business Conditions* [issued for Management of the Bell Telephone Company of Pennsylvania], (August 1961), pp. 1-2; Joseph F. Bradley and Joseph P. Giusti, "Growth of Credit Unions in Pennsylvania," *Pennsylvania Business Survey* (May 1960), pp. 11-15; and Walter Polner, "Economic Trends for Credit Unions in Pennsylvania" (unpublished paper presented to the 1973 Management Conference, Mount Pocono, Pa., Sept. 7-8, 1973).

The bibliography of published materials on credit unions is more extensive than most people would suspect. Many of these works are promotional in character and have limited historical value. There are, however, several important treatments of credit union history. The most significant is J. Carroll Moody and Gilbert C. Fite, *The Credit Union Movement, Origins and Development, 1850-1970* (Lincoln, University of Nebraska Press, 1971). Other useful works included Richard Y. Giles, *Credit For the Millions; The Story of Credit Unions* (New York, Harper, 1951); and Charles Morrow Wilson, *Common Sense Credit; Credit Unions Come of Age* (New York, Devin-Adair, 1962).

A useful collection of the speeches of Edward Filene including some interesting material on credit unions is *Speaking of Change; A Selection of Speeches and Article by Edward A. Filene* (Former Associates of Edward A. Filene, New York, 1939). A similarly useful source is Edward A. Filene, *Successful Living in this Machine Age* (Simon & Shuster, New York, 1931).Readers interested in a fine biography of Filene should see Gerald Johnson, *A Liberal's Progres* (Coward-McCann, New York, 1948).

Useful works by Roy Bergengren are *Cooperative Banking* (McMillan, New York, 1923) and *I Speak for Joe Doakes* (Harper, New York, 1945). Another important source is Bergengren's autobiographical *Crusade: The Fight for Economic Democracy in North America, 1921-1945* (New York, Exposition, 1952). Bergengren's memory was not a totally reliable historical source, but the work provides invaluable insight in the intense spiritual commitment that is so significant a part of the credit union movement.

Other vital works include: Henry W. Wolff, *People's Banks: A Record of Social and Economic Progress* (London, P. S. King, 1919); Myron T. Herrick, *Rural Credits: Land and Cooperative* (New York, Appleton, 1914); Donald S. Tucker, *The Evolution of People's Banks*, (New York, Columbia University, 1922); Joseph G. Knapp, *The Rise of American Cooperative Enterprise, 1620-1920* (Danville, Ill., Interstate, 1969); and John T. Croteau, *The Economics of the Credit Union* (Detroit, Wayne State University, 1963).

Works on other forms of cooperative credit or other banking reform systems include: Clark Evans, *Financing the Consumer* (Harper, New York, 1930); Maurice Goldman, *You Pay and You Pay* (Howell, Soskin & Co., New

York, 1941); Peter W. Herzog, *The Morris Plan of Industrial Banking* (A. W. Shaw Co., Chicago, 1928); Rolf Nugent, *Consumer Credit and Economic Stability* (Russel Sage Foundation, New York, 1939); R. O. Moen, *Rural Credits in the United States* (no publisher listed, n.p., 1931); and Raymond J. Saulnier, *Industrial Banking Companies and their Credit Practices* (National Bureau of Economic Research, New York, 1940).

Pennsylvania Credit Union League
Board of Directors
1983–84

Robert F. Neubaum—Chairman of the Board
Robert L. Hendrickson—First Vice-Chairman
Paul G. Demmer—Second Vice-Chairman
Anthony E. Bartock—Treasurer
Kenneth L. Morrow—Secretary

NAME	CITY	DISTRICT	LENGTH OF SERVICE		
Michael Casper	Douglassville	9	April	1957–April	1984
Josephine Sakovics*	Bethlehem	7	April	1959–April	1984
William C. Seanor*	Greensburg	4	April	1964–April	1984
Joseph F. Hinckey*	Philadelhia	6	April	1966–April	1984
Anthony E. Bartock*	Uniontown	4	Nov.	1966–April	1984
Patricia Doyle*	Scranton	10	April	1968–April	1984
Robert F. Neubaum	Harrisburg	8	April	1968–April	1984
Charles L. Hill*	Derry	4	April	1969–April	1984
Robert L. Hendrickson*	Coatesville	9	April	1971–April	1984
Paul G. Demmer*	Pittsburgh	3	Sept.	1971–April	1984
Andrew L. Kulik	Philadelphia	6	March	1972–April	1984
Kenneth L. Morrow*	New Castle	2	April	1974–April	1984
Edward A. Colgan*	Philadelphia	6	April	1974–April	1984
Michael J. Symons	Easton	7	April	1974–April	1984
Richard J. Ritter*	Pittsburgh	3	April	1975–April	1984
Michael W. Schultz	Sugar Grove	5	April	1977–April	1984
Paul J. Rowland	Wilkes-Barre	10	April	1978–April	1984
John J. Monico	Luzerne	10	April	1979–April	1984
Coy R. Smith	Altoona	8	March	1980–April	1984
Raymond R. Barber	Erie	1	April	1967–April	1974
			April	1980–April	1984
David L. Sleppy	Laureldale	9	April	1980–April	1984
John Filipiak	Pittsburgh	3	Nov.	1972–April	1977
			April	1980–April	1984
Vincent F. Golletti	Beaver Falls	2	Aug.	1980–April	1984
Harry J. Hahn	Erie	1	April	1982–April	1984
Alice Rossell	Levittown	6	April	1982–April	1984
Donald W. Graham	Feasterville	6	April	1983–April	1984
John W. Gulick	Lower Burrell	4	March	1983–April	1984
Val J. McGrogan	York	8	July	1983–April	1984

*CUNA Director

415

Pennsylvania Credit Union

Term			President
Dec.	1934–July	1936	*H. Andrew Hanemann
July	1936–June	1937	*Howard H. Hook
June	1937–March	1939	"
March	1939–April	1942	*George A. Palmer, Jr.
April	1942–April	1946	*Edmund A. Thompson
April	1946–April	1947	*Joseph A. Moore
April	1947–April	1949	"
April	1949–April	1950	*A. William Lawry
April	1950–April	1951	"
April	1951–April	1953	Mattis A. Pottiger
April	1953–March	1954	*Lee Devoe
March	1954–April	1956	*William M. Noble
April	1956–April	1957	Arthur R. Thompson
April	1957–April	1959	*Norman Long
April	1959–April	1961	*James J. Girvan
April	1961–April	1963	Leo L. Gleese
April	1963–June	1965	*B. Frank Summers
May	1965–April	1966	*B. Frank Summers
April	1966–April	1967	John McCullough
April	1967–April	1968	"
April	1968–April	1970	Josephine Sakovics
April	1970–April	1972	Lee L. Sell
April	1972–April	1974	Harold F. Brown
April	1974–April	1976	Joseph Matisko
April	1976–April	1978	William C. Seanor
April	1978–Jan.	1979	Michael Casper

Chairman of the Board

Jan.	1979–April	1980	Michael Casper
April	1980–April	1982	Joseph D. Finn
April	1982–April	1984	Robert F. Neubaum

*Deceased

416

League Table Officers 1934–1984

Vice President	Secretary	Treasurer
N. Horace Berman	John C. Hoshauer	William R. Koester
D. J. Shannon	Mattis A. Pottiger	*Frank Tokay
Ira W. Kreider	"	"
*Edmund A. Thompson	"	"
*Joseph A. Moore	"	"
T. Walter McGrath	"	"
*A. William Lawry	"	"
*James J. Girvan	*William M. Noble	"
Mattis A. Pottiger	"	"
*Lee Devoe	"	"
*William M. Noble	A. R. Thompson	"
Arthur R. Thompson	*Norman Long	"
*Norman Long	Ray R. Beidler	"
*James J. Girvan	Leo L. Gleese	"
Leo L. Gleese	*B. Frank Summers	"
*B. Frank Summers	Josephine Sakovics	"
John McCullough	Josephine Sakovics	"
John McCullough-First	Joseph Matisko	"
Josephine Sakovics-Second		
*Frank Tokay—First	"	Harold F. Brown
Josephine Sakovics—Second		
Josephine Sakovics—First	"	"
Lee L. Sell—Second		
Lee L.Sell—First	William C. Seanor	"
Josephine Matisko—Second		
Harold F. Brown—First	*George W. Spindler	William C. Seanor
Joseph Matisko—Second		
Joseph Matisko—First	Joseph D. Finn	Michael Casper
William C. Seanor-Second		
William C. Seanor—First	Robert F. Neubaum	Joseph D. Finn
Michael Casper—Second		
Michael Casper-First	Robert L. Hendrickson	Robert F. Neubaum
Joseph D. Finn—Second		
Joseph D. Finn-First	*Hugh E. Kelleher	Robert L. Hendrickson
Robert F. Neubaum—Second	Paul G. Demmer	

Vice-Chairman

Joseph D. Finn-First	Paul G. Demmer	Robert L. Hendrickson
Robert F. Neubaum—Second		
Robert F. Neubaum-First	Anthony E. Bartock	Paul G. Demmer
Robert L. Hendrickson—Second		
Robert L. Hendrickson-First	Kenneth L. Morrow	Anthony E. Bartock
Paul G. Demmer—Second		

Pennsylvania Credit Union League

STAFF

Michael J. Judge, *President*
James J. McCormack, *Vice President, Finance & Administration*
Andrea A. Bair, *Executive Administrative Assistant*
Jack P. Barth, *Vice President, Member Services*
Doris Ellis, *Vice President, Communications*
Frank Capaldo, *Vice President, Legal and Government Affairs*
Richard A. Ebeling, *Education/Training Director*
Roger D. Kelley, *Legislative/Information Specialist*
Tammy M. Youhon, *Technical Information Specialist*
Mary E. Mallison, *Public Relations/Publications Specialist*
Ronald A. Malatesta, *Education Specialist*
Theresa A. Rissell, *Director of Research and Special Projects*
Gerry Livingston, *Supervisor/Support Services*

OFFICE SUPPORT SERVICES

Carol DeLuca, *Group Leader*
Susan Downs, *Clerk*
Susan Gabel, *Clerk*
Kathleen Nies, *Clerk*
Carol Sheetz, *Clerk*
Joli Ickes, *Typist*
Pamela Peck, *Typist*
Lori Gray, *Machine Operator*
Pauline Wood, *Machine Operator*
Doris McCormick, *Building Attendant*
Janet Johnson, *Secretary, Communications*
Kati Shoop, *Secretary, Administrative*
Pauline Umlauf, *Secretary, Member Services*
Cathy Peters, *Senior Accounting Clerk*

FIELD STAFF
Consultants

Paul J. Sullivan
Ronald F. Schueler
James Ritter
Lanny L. Horn
Kenneth E. Noca
William L. Talada
Al J. Garttmeier
William J. Harmon
Edwin F. Mailander
Charles A. Gemberling
George L. Shevenock
William J. Dooner
Janet M. Kubika

Pacul Services, Inc.

STAFF

Michael J. Judge, *President*
Andrea A. Bair, *Executive Administrative Assistant*
James J. McCormack, *Vice President, Finance & Administration*
Jack P. Barth, *Vice President, Member Services*
Doris K. Ellis, *Vice President, Communications*
Pacul Supply Division
Ted Baldwin, *Shipping/Receiving Clerk*
Linda Heberling, *Billing Clerk*
CUEDS Division
Dean Carpenter, *Supervisor*
Frank Snavely, *Data Processing Representative*
Pearl Hoffman, *DCC Operator*
Tami Schmick, *DCC Operator*
Paul Butler, *DCC Operator (Upper Darby)*
Mary Ann Size, *DCC Operator (Scranton)*
Jean Smith, *DCC Operator (Trafford)*
General Services Division
Elizabeth C. Weimer, *Advertising/Marketing Specialist*
Karin Guerrini, *Auditor*
Cathy Miller, *Accounting Clerk*
Eryl Pettit, *Secretary*
Sherri Chrisemer, *Machine Operator*

Growth of Pennsylvania
Credit Unions 1933-1983

Year	Number of Credit Unions	Total Members	Total Assets (In Thousands)	Total Shares (In Thousands)	Total Loans (In Thousands)
1933*	7	2,100	$250	$241	$223
1934**	17	4,100	498	456	441
1940	546	201,200	13,321	11,720	9,800
1945	571	213,500	24,034	22,109	6,326
1950	664	317,300	57,389	50,391	33,336
1955	902	461,500	123,589	107,567	75,840
1960	1,195	622,168	238,725	205,241	160,772
1965	1,295	761,626	405,947	351,424	269,146
1966	1,360	802,606	454,910	388,826	311,510
1967	1,400	859,994	500,353	426,950	343,894
1968	1,428	891,959	552,305	469,966	391,339
1969	1,465	941,007	614,898	517,436	457,122
1970	1,503	983,146	678,977	573,792	498,713
1971	1,509	1,013,126	761,201	651,398	550,341
1972	1,473	1,044,743	864,114	746,067	619,973
1973	1,457	1,099,443	974,615	839,431	706,118
1974	1,486	1,164,739	1,091,735	936,425	803,488
1975	1,508	1,227,920	1,255,758	1,089,568	908,529
1976	1,522	1,306,107	1,474,760	1,268,478	1,067,800
1977	1,538	1,411,683	1,729,570	1,499,651	1,302,301
1978	1,559	1,593,145	2,046,247	1,750,104	1,582,450
1979	1,573	1,653,626	2,222,025	1,907,873	1,741,636
1980	1,593	1,740,013	2,445,511	2,178,484	1,743,474
1981	1,592	1,844,507	2,639,104	2,344,554	1,841,030
1982	1,554	1,872,882	3,130,385	2,835,629	1,825,963
1983	1,504	1,845,567	3,688,053	3,381,160	2,046,115

All figures are as of December 31 of the year listed.
*The first credit unions were chartered by the Commonwealth of Pennsylvania in 1933.
**The first credit unions were chartered under the Federal Credit Union Act in 1934.

Index

Italics indicate photographs

426

427

Prince, Leon 114, 116, 118
Progressive Party, American 56
Protestantism and Capitalism 48
Proudhon, Pierre Joseph 26, 35
Public School Employees of
  Philadelphia CU 140

Q
Quigg, Ralph W. 303, 351

R
R.S.R. FCU 362
Rabold, Carl 381
radicalism, 19th Century 47–49
Raiffeisen, Friedrich 26–27, 30–36, 171,
  198, 316, 324
Raymond, Mark 257
Rayneri, Charles 36
Reading Chapter 199, 310
Reading Postal Employees CU 81, 84,
  140, 141
Reading Workers' CU 81
Reagan, Ronald 406, 410
Regulation W 232–233, 238, 245
Reid, Bill 203, 233, 249
Reiter, J. Edward 320
Remrandco FCU 233
Rentfro, Earl 193, 196, 204, 212, 218, 257
Reorganization Plan of 1947, U.S. 262
Report of the American Commission 57
Republican Party, American 56
Rhodes, State Representative 104
Rhye, Milton 179, 181, 185, 187, 201, 211,
  242
Rissell, Theresa 404
Ritter, James *402*
Ritter, Richard *405*
Robb, James 330
Roberts, Maurice 357, 383
Rochdale Principles 24
Roller-Smith CU 259
Roosevelt, Franklin 54, 110, 113, 127,
  129–131, 137, 236
Roosevelt, Theodore 52
Rossell, Alice 400, *405*
Rowland, Paul 391, *405*
Rubber Employees FCU 389
Rural Credits 31
rural electric cooperative movement 78
Russell Sage Foundation 102, 136

S
Saint Augustine's Parish FCU 147
Saint Basil Parish Credit Union of
  Pittsburgh 122, 140, 150, 156
Saint Joseph Parish Mt. Oliver
  Pennsylvania FCU 156
Saint Mary's Cooperative Credit
  Association, The 50

Saint Paul's FCU 373
Sakovics, Josephine 259, 314, 332, 336,
  342, 345, *355*, 356, 358–359, 369
Sander Markets Employees FCU 147
"Save Our Share Drafts" Campaign
  393
Schmidt, Kathryn M. 388, 395
Schminkey, Allen 324
Schueler, Ronald *402*
Schultz, Michael *405*
Schulze-Delitzsch, Hermann 26–30,
  31–32, 35, 410
Schuylkill Valley Chapter 198
Schwartz, Louis 104, 107, 122
Scranton Federal Employees CU 122,
  140, 156
Scranton Postal CU 158
Scranton, William 330
Seanor, William 365, *376*, 387, 391,
  405
Sears, Roebuck Philadelphia
  Employees FCU 122, 156, 170
Second Street CU 141
SEG's (see Select Employee Groups)
Select Employee Groups 394
Sell, Lee 332, 349, 354, *361*, 362, 364, 390
Septer, Donald 324
Servillo, Dom 266, 270, 279, 282, 314, 324
Shanney, Edward 247
Shannon, D.J. 160, 163
Shanosky, Joseph 320, 324, 404
share drafts 392–393
share insurance 316, 317–318, 339
share insurance—litigation 372–377
share insurance—provisional 373–375
share insurance—qualification 370–371,
  374–375
Sheakley, E.R. 229, 238
Sheldon, C.E. 160, 196
Shellhamer, Frank 99
Shellkopf, E.E. 205
Shelly, George 344
Shenango Pottery Employees FCU 150,
  155, 158, 170
Sheppard, Morris 130
Shevenock, George 358, 402
Shipe, Orrin 218, 234, 307
Sigafoo, Lloyd 207, 218–219, 236–237, 238,
  258, 303
Simmons, Carl 237
Sippel, Al 266, 342
Skorstad, Clifford 174, 201, 306
Sleppy, David 395, *405*
Smith, Anthony 101–118
Smith, Coy 395, *405*
Smith, Lucy 259–261, 266, 276, *280*, 300,
  302, 303–304, 314, *321*, 322, 329, 344, 346,
  381, 384
Smith, William 268, 303, 306, 311, 314, 351